The Most Dangerous Man in America

Books by Catherine Drinker Bowen

Friends and Fiddlers

Beloved Friend: The Story of Tchaikowsky
and Nadejda von Meck
(In Collaboration with B. von Meck)

Free Artist: The Story of Anton and Nicholas Rubinstein

Yankee from Olympus: Justice Holmes and His Family

John Adams and the American Revolution

The Lion and the Throne: The Life and Times
of Sir Edward Coke

Adventures of a Biographer

Francis Bacon: The Temper of a Man

Miracle at Philadelphia: The Story of the Constitutional
Convention, May to September 1787

Biography: The Craft and the Calling

Family Portrait

The Most Dangerous Man in America: Scenes from
the Life of Benjamin Franklin

Portrait of Benjamin Franklin 1762 by Mason Chamberlin. (Philadelphia Museum of Art: Given by Mr. and Mrs. Wharton Sinkler '56–88–1)

The Most Dangerous Man in America

SCENES FROM THE LIFE OF BENJAMIN FRANKLIN

Catherine Drinker Bowen

An Atlantic Monthly Press Book
Little, Brown and Company—Boston–Toronto

Second Printing

LIBRARY OF CONGRESS CATALOGING IN PUBLICATION DATA
Bowen, Catherine Drinker, 1897–
  The most dangerous man in America.

  "An Atlantic Monthly Press book."
  Bibliography: p.
  1. Franklin, Benjamin, 1706–1790.   I. Title.
E302.6.F8B79   973.3′2′0924 [B]   74-10658
ISBN 0-316-10396-9
ISBN 0-316-10379-9 (pbk.)

ATLANTIC–LITTLE, BROWN BOOKS
ARE PUBLISHED BY
LITTLE, BROWN AND COMPANY
IN ASSOCIATION WITH
THE ATLANTIC MONTHLY PRESS

RRD-VA

Designed by Susan Windheim

*Published simultaneously in Canada
by Little, Brown & Company (Canada) Limited*

PRINTED IN THE UNITED STATES OF AMERICA

ACKNOWLEDGMENTS

Academic scholars have always been generous to Catherine Drinker Bowen. Whitfield J. Bell, Jr. gave her manuscript careful scrutiny, advised and encouraged her throughout the work. Caroline Robbins discussed the various problems that arose in the manuscript, and also lent valuable advice. Patricia Davis, research editor, was responsible for preparing the lengthy bibliography and also for checking the manuscript. Edward Weeks far exceeded his role as Atlantic Monthly Press editor, not only encouraging Mrs. Bowen throughout the work, but giving particular attention to the preparation of the present volume. Mrs. John Cheswick aided in clarifying Franklin's experiments with electricity. Mary Ellen Morris, expert copy editor, also worked on the manuscript, preparing it for publication. Nancy Wilson gave invaluable aid when Mrs. Bowen was ill, helping with the dictation and arranging material for her use. Mrs. Martha Sellers, Mrs. Bowen's friend and secretary, patiently and skillfully typed these pages. Barbara Rex, friend and longtime consultant, sustained the biography to its sensitive conclusion.

In this final book of Catherine Drinker Bowen's there are a multitude of scholars, friends, librarians, all of whom were equally as determined as she was herself that the "Franklin book," as she called it, would be finished . . . as she wanted.

When Bancroft began work on the ten volumes of his American history he said, "I have formed the design of writing a History of the United States from the discovery of the American Continent to the present time . . . I can find for myself no excuse but in the sincerity with which I have sought to collect the truth from trustworthy documents and testimony."

I have no such glorious, comprehensive plans. I purpose to catch glimpses of Franklin as he streaks, streams, boils by, borne along by a smoking cataract, yet himself cool as an apple in storage.

Catherine Drinker Bowen

PREFACE

I n an era when the fomenting and support of revolution are claimed by youth as their especial attributes, it is significant to recall that two hundred years ago the person feared by the crowned heads of England and many parts of Europe as the most dangerous man in America was Benjamin Franklin — aged sixty-eight to eighty.

I have always wanted to write about Franklin. Indeed, his character and history have long been woven through my books and therefore through my life. Nevertheless, certain events escaped me in all their striking detail: The astonishing *Silence Dogood* letters, written in Boston by a boy of sixteen and printed anonymously in his brother's newspaper . . . Franklin's extraordinary account of his electrical experiments, written from Philadelphia to his scientific friends, fascinating for simplicity of language and a bold invention of terms which we use today: charge, battery, plus, minus, negative, positive, armature, conductor . . . The trip by sailing sloop up the Hudson from

New York to Albany in 1754 to achieve a treaty with the Iroquois — Franklin's first move from the local to the larger scene — and the meeting with Hendrick, the eloquent Indian chief with a tomahawk scar clear across his cheek, the tribal ritual and the great shout of Yo-hah signifying approval . . . "General" Franklin's surprising military career in western Pennsylvania at fifty-odd, his political oversetting by the legislature and his lifelong capacity for ignoring defeat until in its own good time defeat somehow turned to victory . . . The London scenes, with Franklin's host of scientific friends and his relentless, ill-planned quarrel with the family of Penn, and finally his dramatic appearance before the House of Commons in 1766 and his bitter humiliation in Privy Council eight years later.

To describe these scenes became for me a necessity as well as a delight. This book however is not a biography. I made no attempt at full narrative continuity. Rather, the pages are designed so that a reader may open at any chapter or "scene." Not only is narrative continuity superfluous concerning such a well-known — indeed legendary — American, but a complete narration would have defeated my purpose: the wholly selfish, quite arbitrary desire to write only what interested me about this most consistently entertaining biographical subject, not excepting even Sir Francis Bacon. Perhaps my only concession to biographical form is the opening chapter in Boston, when a young printer's apprentice learns his trade and for the first time tries his hand at writing for the public. "I am courteous and affable," Silence Dogood tell us, "(unless I am first provok'd), and handsome, sometimes witty. I have likewise a natural Inclination to observe and reprove the Faults of others, at which I have an excellent Faculty . . . I never intend to wrap my talents in a napkin."

Thus a boy of sixteen created a literary character, a young widow in whose existence one believes from the first sentence, and thus he exercised a talent for satire that would never leave him but increase with the years.

Actually, I did not choose the form of this book; the form, it might be said, chose me and the scenes fell into place. Such a form imposes drawbacks, limitations; what artistic form does not? No space remained for charming letters to young ladies, or pleasant trips from London to Germany and France in the 1760's. I must leave out the legendary near-meeting with Edward Gibbon at a French inn, when Franklin sent to ask if he might wait upon this great man and pay his compliments. Gibbon replied that though he had great regard for Mr. Franklin as a philosopher, he could not in duty to his King hold conversation with a rebel. Franklin sent back a note saying that when in the course of Mr. Gibbon's *History of the Decline and Fall of Empires* he should arrive at the Decline and Fall of the British Empire, as would soon be likely, Franklin "would be happy to furnish him with ample material of which he was possessed."

Wit and wisdom are close allies; one reads and does not forget. More than one of Franklin's diplomatic victories were won by his wit. The scenes I have chosen are not, however, haphazard, but built around a definite plot: the story of Franklin's slow change from an admirer of Great Britain ("Long did I endeavor . . . to preserve from breaking that fine and noble China vase, the British Empire.") to a bitter foe of British administration in all its manifestations. He loathed war: "There never was a good war or a bad peace."

Franklin lived from 1706 to 1790; his life rounds out the revolutionary century. More than with any other American statesman, Franklin's career gives the picture complete: the slow approach of Independence, the war with England, and the final emergence of an American nation. Always, Franklin managed to be on stage for the great events. Though he spent some thirty years in Europe as agent for his country, by happy chance he was in America for the Albany Convention of 1754, the writing of the Declaration of Independence, and the Constitutional Convention of 1787.

This book ends in 1774. Franklin has fifteen years to live. And though in *John Adams and the American Revolution* and *Miracle at Philadelphia,* I had much to say about Franklin, the temptation remains to write the scenes with Franklin center-stage. His old age was magnificent. I cannot bear to have done with this admirable, beguiling character.

CONTENTS

SCENE ONE

THE
DOGOOD PAPERS

CHAPTER ONE

The Franklins of Boston.
Brother James's newspaper. The Mathers
and a bitter quarrel. Benjamin learns
the printer's trade and conceives a
literary character called Silence Dogood.

In the year 1721, Benjamin Franklin, aged fifteen, lived with his parents in Boston, Massachusetts. Here was a thriving factious town of some twelve thousand persons, set in a commonwealth whose legislature quarreled vigorously and continuously with its royal governor, Mr. Samuel Shute, brother of an English earl and by no means sympathetic to his New England constituents. Boston's fleet of seagoing vessels ranked third in the English-speaking world, exceeded only by London and Bristol; no other seaport of North America could compare. Mr. Franklin's house stood on the corner of Union and Hanover streets. He was a candlemaker and soap-boiler; the sign of his trade, a big blue ball, hung out over the door. The family lived in the back of the house, behind the workroom and in the very heart of town, not ten minutes' walk from Long Wharf, where thirty vessels could lie at a time, loading cargoes for Newfoundland or the Azores, Europe, England, Madagascar, Guinea.

3

There were already two newspapers in town when Benjamin's brother James, ten years his senior, undertook to publish a third, the *New England Courant,* designed as something quite different from the *Boston Gazette* and the *News Letter.* In the first place, Governor Shute considered that his commission entitled him to censor everything printed — a prescription which James Franklin had little intention of honoring. Newspapers of the time limited themselves to the printing of ship arrivals and departures, with the names of their captains; also advertisements and bits of local gossip called "Remarkables." Or they quoted from European papers: *"Letters from Moscow advise, that the Danish Envoy Extraordinary, M. Westphalen, having shewn his credentials to the Count Golofskin, Chancellor of the Russian Empire, was receiv'd with all possible Marks of Respect. . . ."*

It is hard to see why such an item, three or four months old, would interest Boston citizens who worked diligently at their trades and kept a cow or two on the Common. James Franklin's editorial ambitions flew higher. He had learned the printer's trade in London, where he spent two years, coming home fluent with phrases picked up in Fleet Street coffeehouses, proud owner of a letterpress and type forms and determined to publish a newspaper that would amuse as well as inform and that would speak out on public issues, as the London papers did. (England was a good fifty years ahead of her colonies in the matter of a free press.) James gathered round him a staff of clever volunteers, soon to be known — and not in complimentary terms — as the *Courant* wits, or the Hell Fire Club, after their counterparts in London. They included John Checkley, bookseller and apothecary, who had lived much abroad; Dr. William Douglass, lately arrived from England and boasting the only medical degree in town; Matthew Adams; Captain Taylor; John Eyre and a "Mr. Gardner" — so inscribed by young Benjamin, who carefully listed the authors with their assumed titles and the dates of their contributions.*

What these young men undertook was hazardous and might well go against the Boston grain, Massachusetts having by no means outgrown its theocracy. The Mathers — the Reverend Increase and his son, the Reverend Cotton — still dominated the town. Moreover, the city fathers, leaders in council and legislature, had been reared in the belief that public morality must be guarded and the authority of magistrates preserved. The Commonwealth, after all, had been founded with the conviction that preserving "pure religious doctrine" and stamping out heresy were spiritual and practical responsibilities of government. Puritan tradition, it is true, had yielded to the extent of permitting (or enduring) King's Chapel for well-born Episcopalians, a Baptist meetinghouse for the lower orders and a small church for French Calvinists. But the old cautions and the old bias remained. Mr. Franklin, who had heard his son James's easy talk and high-flying London notions, pronounced the *Courant* a rash undertaking and advised against it.

The paper consisted of a single sheet, printed on both sides. Its introductory issue informed the "gentle reader" that the publishers, "out of kindness for brother writers" on the other Boston papers, intended now and then "to be VERY, VERY DULL." This little irony, fully developed on the first page, was hardly calculated to soothe. Young Benjamin's part in all this at first had been humble. From the age of twelve he had been an apprentice to his brother, doing such jobs as he was told to do. His father had sworn him for a term of nine years, quite against the boy's will, his ambition being to go to sea; he had a youth's romantic notion of shipping off as cabin boy. And indeed Benjamin truly loved salt water and often so testi-

* Benjamin's file on the *Courant,* in his handwriting, can be seen in the British Museum.

fied in later life. He could swim almost as soon as he could read. His sister Jane said he read at five. He himself, in old age, said he could not remember the time when he could not read.

Mr. Franklin, however, had no intention of sacrificing Benjamin to the deeps. Had not his eldest, Josiah, gone to sea and been lost in some nameless waste of waters? Boston was filled with the widows of sailors; the Reverend Cotton Mather said a fifth part of his communicants were widows either from the old French wars or losses at sea. Before his apprenticeship, Ben had been given two years' schooling — and only two. His father had placed him at eight in the Grammar School * on Boston Common, where the boy rose to the head of his class. But after a year Mr. Franklin took him out and sent him to George Brownell's academy. The Grammar School taught Latin, and what use would Ben have with dead languages? The poor could not afford such refinements. There had indeed been thoughts of making a minister out of Benjamin, his quickness at reading being remarkable, but Harvard College was far beyond the family means. Mr. Franklin had sired seventeen children by two wives. His first wife was English and came with him when he emigrated. When she died, Josiah married Abiah Folger with whom he lived in Boston. Ben was the fifteenth child, youngest of ten sons. All were alive but four, and though by now the older sons were either apprenticed out or launched in various trades, they brought in very little money, and there were Ben's two younger sisters, his mother and his father's older brother, Uncle Benjamin. The house on Union Street remained crowded; sometimes they sat down thirteen at table.

Mr. Brownell took girls as well as boys for scholars, and taught everything from dancing to cyphering, spelling and spinet playing, advertising the same in the *Gazette*. Benjamin proved slow at doing sums, and failed

---

* Later the famous Boston Latin School.

in arithmetic. At ten his father gave over his son's schooling forever and brought him home to help with the soap-
boiling and candlemaking business. For two years the
boy shaped wicks and stirred the smoking vats in his father's shop. Benjamin hated what he had to do; the
stench of the hot tallow seemed to follow wherever he
went. A brother, Ebenezer, had been drowned in the
vat at sixteen months — before Ben was born, but he
knew about it. Yet Benjamin was aware, as were his
brothers, that Mr. Franklin was a just man, and kind. In
the town he commanded respect; neighbors came in the
evening, seeking advice. Mr. Franklin owned his house
and was a communicant in the Old South Church, a
status attained after nine years' initiation.

In choosing a trade for his youngest son, Mr. Franklin
showed patience, to say the least. It became plain the
boy would never make a tallow chandler; he was forever
slipping away, down to the docks or out to the salt
marshes for fishing or trapping. This Benjamin of the
flock, this youngest son of a youngest son for five generations, was sturdy, physically very active, and though bid-
dable at home, could be willful; he had an unpredictable
streak. His father feared that some fine morning he
might be missing, hidden aboard a ship outward bound.
Mr. Franklin began taking Ben for walks about Boston.
In so large a town, many trades were to be found. The
narrow streets were crowded with carts, horsemen, sled-
loads of wood coming from the Neck, wheelbarrows,
coaches, stray animals; a man had to dodge his way across.
Since the fire of 1711, the new houses were of brick, many
of them with three stories. On High Street, the Province
House, where Governor Shute lived, was splendid with
the royal arms emblazoned on a front balcony; above the
cupola rose a weather vane of gilded bronze — an Indian
archer with three feathers in his headdress, and big glass
eyes.

But it was not these splendors that Mr. Franklin took

his son to see; their walks were all business. Together they observed different artisans at work: joiners, bricklayers, turners, braziers, carpenters, roofers. Benjamin watched. He liked the feel of a tool in his hand and often said so in later life — the cold slap and smell of mortar along bricks, the wood curling out fresh under a carpenter's awl. Perhaps printing would appeal to a boy who had so marked a taste for book-reading. Already Benjamin had gone through his father's small library of polemical treatises, also such books as *Pilgrim's Progress* and *Plutarch's Lives.* Yet the lad had caviled at signing the articles. He would be twenty-one before he was free; the years stretched ahead like a prison term.

Once at the press, however, Benjamin learned fast. The smell of printer's ink was surely more pleasing than the stink of tallow. The thump of the wooden press as the bar was driven home . . . the crackle of paper as it was laid on the bed . . . muted sound of the printer's bully inking type . . . sucking of the sheets as they came off the press — all this Ben lived with day by day for five highly impressionable years. Certain things a man does in his youth, certain scenes, sounds, smells — daily, ordinary matters — can remain with him all his life, basic, inescapable, part almost of his blood and musculature. At fourteen, Ben's hands and wrists were strong and he was developing the chest of a swimmer; before long he would pride himself that he could carry a large form of type in each hand, running up and downstairs with them when other apprentices managed only half the load. Benjamin as printer's apprentice was rebellious; he has testified that he longed for escape. Yet to his life's end Franklin remained a printer and took pride in it. Wherever he lived in Europe or America and no matter how exalted his reputation, he managed to have a press at his disposal. It is no accident that his last will and testament, written at eighty-three (the year before he died), begins, *"I Benjamin Franklin of Philadelphia, printer . . ."*

During these apprentice years, Ben moved from home and lived with his brother James and other apprentices in Queen Street near the printing house. Here he had access to much wider reading. Friends among booksellers' apprentices lent volumes overnight, to be returned in early morning before the master's shop opened. The town boasted six other printing presses and a surprising number of bookshops; volumes were sold at auction in the coffeehouses. Such money as came his way, Benjamin saved to buy books. His brother's friend, Matthew Adams, noticed the boy, gave him the run of his library, and was generous with the loan of volumes.

During the first three years of Benjamin's apprenticeship his brother printed almanacs, tracts, sermons, broadsides, ballads, even designs on silk and linen — a skill he had learned in London. At some time during this period, James prevailed on Benjamin to try ballad writing; it might bring in a few pennies. Ben promptly produced a sailor's chantey, about the capture of Teach, the pirate; also a ballad called "The Lighthouse Tragedy," recounting the dismal drowning of a certain Captain Worthilake with his two daughters. Captain Worthilake, Franklin said later, "sold wonderfully, the Event being recent, and having made a great Noise." This, he confessed, flattered his vanity, "but my Father discourag'd me by ridiculing my Performances, and telling me Verse-makers were generally Beggars."

Benjamin's father was practical to the bone — as he had need to be. His influence upon his son was strong — both for what it taught and for the rebellion it engendered; the youth's escape from the parental roof was to be quite as significant as what he learned at home. Benjamin's sketch of his father, written many years later, shows a simplicity of style, an easy, convincing clarity of phrase which marked the author throughout his life:

My Father [wrote Franklin] was of middle Stature, but well set and very strong. He was ingenious, could draw prettily, was skill'd a little in Music, and had a clear pleasing Voice, so that when he play'd Psalm Tunes on his violin and sung withal as he sometimes did in an Evening after the Business of the Day was over, it was extreamly agreable to hear. He had a mechanical Genius too, and on occasion was very handy in the Use of other Tradesmen's Tools.

The *New England Courant* brought out its first issue on August 7, 1721. With the paper's appearance Benjamin's life at once took on excitement, a new dimension. James and his friends kept the "Foreign News" to a minimum. Not only was it inevitably very stale, but there was at the moment little that had pertinence for Massachusetts. France and England were enjoying an uneasy, temporary peace. There were no raids along the frontier, no towns burned or settlers scalped by the Canadian French with their Indian allies. The *New England Courant* flourished in a period known as "the interlude between the wars" (1713–1739). Even so, a zealous Jesuit missionary, Father Rasle, inflamed with anti-Protestant zeal, managed to stir up sporadic raids by the Abnaki tribe in Maine. "The Indians to the Eastward," the *Courant* called them, reporting that militia had been dispatched to deal with the situation.

What the *New England Courant* stressed, what indeed its editors reveled in, were domestic conflicts; quarrels and factions in Boston and surrounding counties. The immediate issue was inoculation as a preventive for smallpox. James Franklin and his friends were violently anti-clerical, which at the moment meant anti-strict-Congregational, anti-strict-Puritan morality, and more succinctly, anti-Mather. Because the Mathers encouraged inoculation was reason enough for the *Courant* to be against it. Dr. Douglass, moreover, was genuinely convinced that inoculation spread the disease — "propagated the infection," he wrote. And had Douglass not studied at Edin-

burgh, Leyden, and Paris? Nobody in the Commonwealth possessed equal credentials.

Boston, that summer of 1721, was suffering the worst
epidemic the town had ever experienced. Nearly half
the inhabitants were down with smallpox, and among
these mortality was high. Bells tolled for the dead, and,
with ten churches, this meant considerable tolling, at
considerable expense to the community. In town meeting, the selectmen passed a motion to limit every tolling
to one bell, "not longer than six minutes; for Indians
and Mulattoes, but once for each." Inoculation of course
was new; Cotton Mather called it transplantation. The
treatment had originated in Turkey; Mather heard of
it from his black servant, Onesimus (presented to Mather
by his parishioners), who had been inoculated in Africa.
At Mather's instance, Dr. Zabdiel Boylston took up the
practice, and on June 26, inoculated his young son,
Thomas, and two Negro slaves. According to Dr. Douglass, this was done without giving other physicians time
to consult. Moreover — said Douglass in the *Courant* —
Boylston was no licensed physician (which was true) but
"a certain cutter for the stone."

Actually, Mather had addressed a letter to the local
physicians, including Douglass. Zabdiel Boylston, moreover, was a man of ability and intelligence, skilled in his
profession (with or without a degree). Boston split in
two over the subject; feeling ran high and hot. When
Judge Samuel Sewall had himself and family inoculated,
the selectmen, fearing the spread of infection, forced
them to move to the Province Hospital on Spectacle
Island in the harbor. A Dr. Dalhonde declared in the
Courant that inoculation was no better than murder;
he had seen it, he said, when serving as a soldier in Italy.
At the height of the controversy a "grenado" was thrown
into Cotton Mather's house with a note tied to it: "Cotton Mather, you Dog. Dam you! I'll inoculate you with

this, with a Pox to you." Fortunately the "grenado" did not go off; the General Court offered fifty pounds to find the man who threw it.

In the *Courant*'s opening issue, Dr. Douglass roared off on the front page, speaking, he said, "at the request of several gentlemen in Town," and aiming his shaft directly at Mather and Boylston. Inoculation was "a practice of the Greek old women, its practitioners no better than quacks; the whole invention an epidemic Distemper of the Mind."

In broadside and pamphlet the Mathers fired back. Perhaps the most surprising part of the entire controversy is the fact that the clergy, in loyal support of the Mathers, father and son, declared inoculation to be God's will. It was the physician and lay citizens who bolstered their cause by calling the practice irreligious, interfering with God's providence — an argument which since the beginning of time, antagonists have bent to their advantage. Yet citizens feared greatly for other children, pondered whether or not to inoculate them. Cotton Mather, with his immense prestige, could easily have disregarded the *Courant*'s gibes and gone his way. But the man was by nature contentious and could not brook interference. Meeting James Franklin on the street, Mather demanded why the *Courant* persisted in vilifying and abusing Boston ministers of the Gospel. "Curses," cried Dr. Mather, "await those that do so! The Lord will smite through the loins of them that rise up against the Levites! I would have you consider of it."

Gleefully, James reported this conversation in his paper, published also the fact that "Dr. M———" had declared the *Courant* a libel sheet, its editors detestable as Turks or pagans, deserving indeed, their soubriquet of Hell Fire Club. Something about Cotton Mather invited impudence from the young or the rebellious. To rouse his anger was tempting, fair game indeed for the deistical spirits on the *New England Courant*. Under the full-bottomed wig, Mather's long face and dark brows were mobile, easily distorted by passion. Mather existed as a very symbol of the Puritan New Englander, and times were changing. Night and day beset by the devils of an Old Testament conscience, Mather confessed himself in terror of God's awful vengeance, thereby — says his diary — suffering "inexpressible agony." Also he lived under the shadow of a distinguished father; Increase Mather had been president of Harvard College, and since 1664, pastor of the North End Church. Until Cotton turned sixty he remained "Mather the younger."

Such a man, passionately religious, tormented by the indecisions induced by conscience, intelligent and sensitive, truly invited the blows of fate. Actually Mather was one of the most public-spirited men of his time. Possessed of a library of three thousand volumes and deeply interested in science, he corresponded with scholars abroad and would soon be elected a Fellow of the Royal Society of London. On the other hand, there is no doubt that Dr. Douglass was sincere in his opposition to inoculation and his conviction that the practice spread the infection; if James Franklin followed his lead it was less from principle than from a desire to sell papers. It is Mather who emerges as hero of the affair, not only because he would be proven right in his medical judgment, but because of his courage as champion of the new treatment. By it he exposed himself to public abuse, physical danger, and the very real possibility of losing his position as pastor. "The Town is become almost an Hell upon Earth," he wrote in his diary. "The People rave, they rail, they blaspheme; they talk not only like Ideots but like Franticks. And not only the Physician [Boylston] who began the Experiment, but I also am an Object of their Fury, their furious Obloquies and Invectives. . . . The Cursed Clamour . . . will probably prevent my saving the

Lives of my two Children from the Smallpox by way of Transplantation. . . . My *Sammy* begs to have his life saved by receiving the Small-pox in the way of *Inoculation.* . . . My God, I know Not what to do, but my Eyes are upon Thee!"

The epidemic eased, then ended. And as suddenly as James Franklin had begun his crusade against inoculation, he cut it off — though he by no means dropped his public ridicule of the Mathers and the clergy in general. Governor Shute remained a convenient target. Governor Shute persisted in claiming his right to censor the press; James Franklin's crony on the paper, John Checkley, had already engaged in a protracted public battle over this. There was also the matter of the governor's salary, which Shute said had been decided in London as one thousand pounds, but which the Massachusetts legislature voted down to three hundred and sixty pounds — owing, they said, to depreciation in the currency. The governor, in fact, had but to recommend a measure for the legislature to oppose it. Most royal governors of necessity led unhappy lives in the colonies. They crossed the ocean ignorant of the people and problems they were to meet; when Shute had arrived in 1716 the welcoming parade was said to be "demonstrative but inexpensive." His Excellency compounded his offenses by sporting a scarlet coat, gold lace, a side sword and powdered wig. Just to see him descend from his coach on Sundays at church was enough to irritate. He had been advertised as a dissenter but soon announced himself an Episcopalian. A "court" had developed around him.

The *Courant* did not do battle at once with governor or legislature, but shifted direction for a time, advertising for short pieces from contributors, "serious, sarcastic, ludicrous, or otherways amusing." Straightway the paper was favored by letters from Abigail Afterwit and Timothy Turnstone (written by James Franklin). Matthew Adams wrote Harry Meanwell; "Mr. Gardner" was Fanny

Mournful. Benjamin, now sixteen, observed these contributions closely, drawing up his careful record of the
authors' names.

Humorous pieces written for old newspapers inevitably
seem heavy-handed to another generation, let alone another century. Yet the *Courant* articles were lively, spir-
ited, sometimes really funny. Provincial societies are apt
to exhibit a sort of soul-cracking solemnity. Travelers
from Europe remarked upon it even late in the century
and found it notably dispiriting, especially in New England. Evening parties could be nightmares of stiffness
and decorum. Citizens had not had time to acquire the
poise, the easy badinage of Old World drawing rooms.
Rigidity, clannishness, suspicion of the stranger; these
were the hallmarks of a raw New World. James Franklin,
endeavoring to pierce the shell and introduce a measure
of the sophistication he had admired in London publi-
cations, took on a challenging though not impossible
campaign.

For James's brother Benjamin, however, this new editorial policy was a delight and an invitation. After setting
type for half a dozen of these satirical pieces, Benjamin
decided to write one himself. Of course there would be
difficulties; James was not likely to accept anything from
his young brother's pen. Already the two had fallen out
with each other, and on numerous occasions. It cannot
have been entirely James's fault. A lad of sixteen, extraordinarily bright, bounding with energy and ambition,
is no easy person to have at close quarters. The world-
famous Franklin philosophy of self-discipline had not as
yet been undertaken, let alone achieved. The immediate
cause of their quarrels is not known. But James (wrote
Franklin later),

. . . was passionate and had often beaten me, which I took
extreamly amiss. . . . Tho' a Brother, he considered himself
as my Master, and me as his Apprentice, and accordingly ex-

pected the same Services from me as he would from another; while I thought he demean'd me too much in some he requir'd of me, who from a Brother expected more Indulgence. . . . I fancy his harsh and tyrannical Treatment of me, might be a means of impressing me with that Aversion to arbitrary Power that has stuck to me thro' my whole Life.

Whatever Benjamin wrote to the *Courant* would have to be done cautiously, even clandestinely. For his imaginary contributor Benjamin fixed upon a woman in her twenties, pert, handsome, signing herself "Silence Dogood." Had not Dr. Mather himself, among his voluminous writings, published a well-known little book called *Essays to Do Good?* The name itself, Mistress Dogood, would indicate satire. Mather's essays had appeared in the form of queries from a lawyer, a constable, a church deacon, and a military man, all of whom inquired, "What is there I may do for the service of God and the welfare of man?" Benjamin knew the book; long afterward he confessed that he had been influenced by Cotton Mather.

Benjamin did not approach his venture unprepared. He had long been aware of his lack of learning and was at pains to remedy it. A meager two years of schooling had been enough only to initiate an appetite for books, a curiosity to learn that would remain with Franklin until his dying day. He had found himself humiliated by his ignorance of mathematics.

I took Cocker's Book of Arithmetick [he tells us], and went thro' the whole by myself with great Ease. I also read Seller's and Sturmy's Books of Navigation, and became acquainted with the little Geometry they contain, but never proceeded far in that Science. And I read about this Time Locke on Human Understanding, and the Art of Thinking by Messrs. du Port Royal.

After the ballad-making experiment and his father's ridicule, Ben had set to in earnest, teaching himself to write by whatever method he could devise, being "extreamly ambitious," he later confessed, to be in time "a tolerable English Writer." The process of learning, the struggle and experiments, Franklin had described in some detail:

While I was intent on improving my Language, I met with an English Grammar (I think it was Greenwood's) at the End of which there were two little Sketches of the Arts of Rhetoric and Logic, the latter finishing with a Specimen of a Dispute in the Socratic Method. And soon after I procur'd Xenophon's Memorable Things of Socrates, wherein there are many instances of the same Method. I was charm'd with it, adopted it, dropt my abrupt Contradiction, and positive Argumentation, and put on the humble Enquirer and Doubter. And being then, from reading Shaftesbury and Collins, become a real Doubter in many Points of our Religious Doctrine, I found this Method safest for my self and very embarrassing to those against whom I us'd it. . . . I continu'd this Method for some few Years, but gradually left it, retaining only the Habit of expressing my self in terms of modest Diffidence, never using when I advance any thing that may possibly be disputed, the Words, *Certainly, undoubtedly* . . . but rather say, I conceive, or I apprehend a Thing to be so or so, It appears to me . . . or it is so, if I am not mistaken. This Habit I believe has been of great Advantage to me, when I have had occasion to inculcate my Opinions, and persuade Men into Measures that I have been from time to time engag'd in promoting.

The modest diffidence, the attitude of humble inquiry so painstakingly acquired, were one day to checkmate skilled diplomats on the European continent and rouse Franklin's own countrymen to emotions ranging from angry suspicion to delighted agreement. The Continental Congress of 1775 . . . the Paris peace table of '83 . . . the Constitutional Convention of '87; these would bear witness to Franklin's success with his "habit," as he called it. The wonder is that he began the practice so early. Having observed Dr. Mather, all thunder and command, inviting ridicule; and having experienced at the end of a stick his brother James's temper — Benjamin discovered a method of disarming an adversary (as old as Socrates) with what must have been close to joy. The program suited his nature.

At about this time, Ben came across an old volume of Addison's *Spectator* (it was the third). The easy bantering way of writing seemed indeed the very embodiment of a style for which Ben was seeking. Taking the *Spectator* as a model, he reproduced pages from memory, or turned them into verse and back again to prose. He made notes of what he read, jumbled the notes like a pack of cards, and after some weeks reduced them to the best order he could before forming full sentences and completing the paper — anything to gain flexibility and enlarge his vocabulary. It was laborious work.

My Time for these Exercises [he wrote] . . . was at Night, after Work or before Work began in the Morning; or on Sundays, when I contrived to be in the Printing House alone, evading as much as I could the common Attendance on publick Worship, which my Father used to exact of me . . . And which indeed I still thought a Duty, tho' I could not, as it seemed to me, afford the Time to practise it.

Like other ambitious youths of the century (John Adams among them), Benjamin deliberately engaged in letter writing as an exercise. With a friend of his own age, John Collins, he embarked on a correspondence, wherein the two set out queries and argued them through. Mr. Franklin happened upon the letters and read them. He told his son flatly that Collins was by far the more skillful writer, though Ben, he said, spelled better and pointed his letters more stylishly, owing no doubt to his work at the press. The only encouragement Ben received came from his father's brother, Uncle Benjamin, who had arrived from England in 1715 and lived with the family on Union Street, and who himself had filled several quarto volumes with his own poetry — some of it addressed to young Ben.

Benjamin has said that he liked to do his writing in the printing house on Sunday, when the workmen were absent. We see him sitting alone among piles of rag paper, the heavy wooden press standing idle and waiting. He was at pains, of course, to disguise his hand. Silence Dogood was his own signature:

To the Author of the *New-England Courant*
Sir,
It may not be improper in the first place to inform your Readers, that I intend once a Fortnight to present them, by the Help of this Paper, with a short Epistle, which I presume will add somewhat to their Entertainment.

And since it is observed, that the Generality of People, now a days, are unwilling either to commend or dispraise what they read, until they are in some measure informed who or what the Author of it is, whether he be *poor* or *rich, old* or *young,* a *Schollar* or a *Leather Apron Man,* &c, and give their Opinion of the Performance, according to the Knowledge which they have of the Author's Circumstances, it may not be amiss to begin with a short Account of my past Life and present Condition, that The Reader may not be at a Loss to judge whether or no my Lucubrations are worth his reading.

At the time of my Birth, my Parents were on Ship-board in their Way from London to N. England. My Entrance into this troublesome World was attended with the Death of my Father. . . . For as he, poor Man, stood upon the Deck rejoycing at my Birth, a merciless Wave entred the Ship, and in one Moment carry'd him beyond Reprieve. Thus, was the *first Day* which I saw, the *last* that was seen by my Father; and thus was my disconsolate Mother at once made both a *Parent* and a *Widow.*

When we arrived at Boston (which was not long after) I was put to nurse in a Country Place, at a small Distance from the Town, where I went to School, and past my Infancy and Childhood in Vanity and Idleness, until I was bound out Apprentice, that I might no longer be a Charge to my indigent Mother, who was put to hard Shifts for a Living.

My Master was a Country Minister, a pious good-natur'd young Man, and a Batchelor. . . . He endeavour'd that I might be instructed in all that Knowledge and Learning which is necessary for our Sex . . . and observing that I took more than ordinary Delight in reading ingenious Books, he gave me the free Use of his Library, which tho' it was but small, yet it was well chose, to inform the Understanding rightly, and enable the Mind to frame great and noble Ideas.

In this situation, Silence declared that she lived "a chearful Country life," spending her leisure time with the neighboring females, "or in some shady Retirement, with the best of Company, *Books*." The rest of her story she would save, she added, for the next letter. Trusting throughout to please and not offend, she signed herself finally as, "Your Humble Servant, SILENCE DOGOOD."

CHAPTER TWO

Young Benjamin sees himself in print.
And says an abrupt farewell to Boston.

Whenever or wherever Benjamin composed his Do-good letters, he slipped them, properly folded, under the printing house door by night, that it might seem the letters were brought by the hand of some citizen. The *Courant* appeared on Mondays; Benjamin had the satisfaction of seeing his first composition very soon in print — every word, apparently — not in the first column, to be sure, but in the second, following a solemn communication on the nature of honor, signed "Philanthropus." James Franklin's friends had the habit of congregating at publication time, to look over the *Courant* and see their own pieces in print. Benjamin watched as they took up the paper, heard laughter and exclamations, speculation as to the possible author of *Silence*. More than fifty years later, Franklin remembered it.

I had the exquisite Pleasure of finding [my piece] met with their Approbation. and that in their different Guesses at the

Author none were named but Men of some Character among us for Learning and Ingenuity. I suppose now that I was rather lucky in my Judges: And that perhaps they were not really so very good ones as I then esteem'd them.

This last, however, was modesty after the event. There is small doubt that Benjamin, on that first Monday afternoon, felt anything but purest triumph. Of course he kept on with Mistress Dogood; James printed, in all, fourteen letters. In the second issue, Silence was advanced to the honored left-hand front page column, under the *Courant*'s masthead, a ship in full sail. No hint of the authorship reached Brother James; Benjamin knew how to be cautious. But what amazes is Mistress Dogood herself. Human, fallible, honest where it suits her to be honest, and possessed of an impregnable vanity, Silence is altogether plausible. Benjamin kept the story moving at a fast clip. In Letter Number 2, Silence receives a marriage proposal:

My Reverend Master who had hitherto remained a Batchelor (after much Meditation on the Eighteenth verse of the Second Chapter of Genesis) took up a Resolution to marry; and having made several unsuccessful fruitless Attempts on the more topping Sort of our Sex, and being tir'd with making troublesome Journeys and Visits to no Purpose, he began unexpectedly to cast a loving Eye upon Me, whom he had brought up cleverly to his Hand.

There is certainly scarce any Part of a Man's Life in which he appears more silly and ridiculous, than when he makes his first Onset in Courtship. The aukward Manner in which my Master first discover'd his Intentions, made me, in spite of my Reverence for his Person, burst out into an unmannerly Laughter: However, having ask'd his Pardon, and with much ado compos'd my Countenance, I promis'd him I would take his Proposal into serious Consideration, and speedily give him an Answer. As he had been a great Benefactor (and in a Manner a Father to me) I could not well deny his Request, when I once perceived he was in earnest. Whether it was Love, or

Gratitude, or Pride, or all three that made me consent, I know not; but it is certain, he found it no hard Matter, by the Help of his Rhetoric, to conquer my Heart, and perswade me to marry him.

Oddly enough, considering Silence Dogood's sex and circumstances, there is in her much of her creator.

My own Character [she writes] . . . I should be best able to give. *Know then,* That I am an Enemy to Vice, and a Friend to Vertue. I am one of an extensive Charity, and a great Forgiver of *private* Injuries . . . and a mortal Enemy to arbitrary Government and unlimited Power. I am naturally very jealous for the Rights and Liberties of my Country; and the least Appearance of an Incroachment on those invaluable Priviledges, is apt to make my Blood boil exceedingly. I have likewise a natural Inclination to observe and reprove the Faults of others, at which I have an excellent Faculty. I speak this by Way of Warning to all such whose Offences shall come under my Cognizance, for I never intend to wrap my Talent in a Napkin. To be brief; I am courteous and affable, good humour'd (unless I am first provok'd), and handsome, and sometimes witty, but always, Sir, Your

> Friend and Humble Servant,
> SILENCE DOGOOD.

Young Benjamin, like Silence, had no intention of wrapping his talent in a napkin. Silence airs her opinion on hypocrisy in religion, on the sin of pride, and on freedom of speech as part of good government (a shot well aimed at Governor Shute and his censorship). This last, Silence confesses she borrowed from the *London Journal,* preferring it to anything of her own contriving:

Without Freedom of Thought, there can be no such Thing as Wisdom; and no such Thing as Publick Liberty, without Freedom of Speech; which is the Right of every Man, as far as by it, he does not hurt or controul the Right of another: And this is the only Check it ought to suffer, and the only Bounds it ought to know.

This sacred Privilege is so essential to free Governments, that the Security of Property, and the Freedom of Speech always go together; and in those wretched Countries where a Man cannot call his Tongue his own, he can scarce call any Thing else his own. Whoever would overthrow the Liberty of a Nation, must begin by subduing the Freeness of Speech; a *Thing* terrible to Publick Traytors.

Silence discusses Night-Walkers — as Jack Tars and their doxies, arm in arm wending their uncertain way toward the Common. She inveighs against drunkenness, listing some twenty current phrases for that condition, all of them useful, Silence says, as disguises. A man never admits he is drunk. Rather, he is "broozey, tipsey, fox'd, mellow, feaverish, almost froze, in his altitudes, sees two moons, &c." Early in the series, Mistress Dogood loses her husband by an untimely death, and forthwith proposes a perfectly feasible scheme for the financial insurance of widows, worked out in careful detail. It being too late for the widow to benefit from the plan, she ends by saying she had nothing to live on, "but Contentment and a few Cows."

A man of sixty might have written it. Much that Franklin printed in later life he got by borrowing, quoting, or "adapting" — always, however, contriving to stamp the writing as unmistakably his own. Whole books have been published, searching out Franklin's literary sources; almost as much ink has been spent thereon as on the sources of Shakespeare's plays or Beethoven's symphonic themes. One writer counted Franklin's vocabulary and found he had 2,168 nouns, 865 adjectives, 760 verbs, 217 adverbs. Little mention had been made however of the Dogood literary style: we can credit young Benjamin with her creation. It is when Franklin is at his homeliest that we recognize the authentic voice. Who else would say, like Poor Richard, "Now I've a sheep and a cow, every body bids me good morrow."

Poor Richard's Almanack is still ten years in the future;

yet Silence Dogood is harbinger of what will come. When Silence lampoons Harvard College, when she vows she is a lover of the clergy and then ridicules them, one sees behind it the influence of James Franklin and his friends, Harvard being a nursery for clergymen. But when Silence takes it on herself to demand education for her sex, Benjamin is surely following his own predilections. Not daring to pass on these bold sentiments as her own, Silence quotes from a man,

> . . . an ingenious Writer * [she says], who . . . has thought of it as one of the most barbarous Customs in the World, considering us as a civiliz'd and Christian Country, that we deny the Advantages of Learning to Women. We Reproach the Sex every Day with Folly and Impertinence, while I am confident, had they the Advantages of Education equal to us, they would be guilty of less than our selves. One would wonder indeed how it should be that Women are conversible at all, since they are only beholding to natural Parts for all their Knowledge. Their Youth is spent to teach them to stitch and sew, or make Baubles: They are taught to read indeed, and perhaps to write their Names, or so; and that is the Heighth of a Womans Education.

It was true. Benjamin liked girls; all his life he was to seek the society of women. Yet the female conversation he heard at home must have been dull indeed. His mother, Abiah Folger of Nantucket Island, was the daughter of an indentured servant whom his grandfather had bought for twenty pounds. Like Silence Dogood's minister, Josiah Franklin married her. A few of Abiah Franklin's letters survive, appallingly written even for a century that indulged in reckless phonetic spelling. During his lifetime, Franklin seldom mentioned his mother, though he was a not undutiful son. But Silence Dogood loved to read and said so, declaring that from her youth she had been "indefatigably studious to gain and treasure up . . . all useful and desireable Knowledge, especially

* Actually it was Defoe, *An Essay on Projects* (London, 1697), with Franklin's alterations.

such as tends to improve the Mind, and enlarge the Understanding."

Thinking perhaps that he had permitted Silence to be a trifle sententious, her creator lets her indulge her notions about poetry. Benjamin had not forgotten the ballads and his father's ridicule; here was a chance to defend local poetizers and heal old sores into the bargain:

June 18, 1722

SIR [writes Silence]

It has been the Complaint of many Ingenious Foreigners, who have travell'd amongst us, *That good Poetry is not to be expected in New-England.* I am apt to Fancy, the Reason is, not because our Countreymen are altogether void of a Poetical Genius, nor yet because we have not those Advantages of Education which other Countries have, but purely because we do not afford that Praise and Encouragement which is merited, when any thing extraordinary of this Kind is produc'd among us: Upon which Consideration I have determined, when I meet with a Good Piece of *New-England* Poetry, to give it a suitable Encomium, and thereby endeavor to discover to the World some of its Beautys, in order to encourage the Author to go on, and bless the World with more and more Excellent Productions.

After this serious beginning, Benjamin has Mistress Dogood soar off into pure farce. Solemnly she quotes a New England elegy which "has lately appear'd among us," on the death of the lamented Mrs. Mehitabel Kitel of Salem. Mrs. Kitel's elegy, says Silence, is a poem "moving and pathetick . . . almost beyond Comparison":

> Come let us mourn, for we have lost a
> Wife, a Daughter and a Sister,
> Who has lately taken Flight, and
>   greatly we have mist her . . .
> She kist her Husband some little Time before
>   she expir'd
> Then lean'd her Head the Pillow on, just out
>   of Breath and tir'd . . .

Benjamin must have been pleased with, "the Pillow on." At any rate, Silence pronounces it a pity that such freely written verse, which scorns the old measures and limits, has no name and cannot justly be called Epic, Sapphic, Lyric, or Pindaric. Therefore it should be called "in Honour of the Dead, Kitelic Poetry." An elaborate receipt follows: *"To make a New-England Funeral Elegy."*

Benjamin's solemn critique on the Kitelic Ode is skillful, and, like the other Dogood effusions, impudent, clever, and, everything considered, a tour de force. *"For the Subject of your Elegy,"* says Silence,

Take one of your Neighbours who has lately departed this Life; it is no great matter at what Age the Party dy'd, but it will be best if he went away suddenly, being *Kill'd, Drown'd,* or *Froze to death.*

Having chose the Person, take all his Virtues, Excellencies, &c. and if he have not enough, you may borrow some to make up a sufficient Quantity: To these add his last Words, dying Expressions, &c. if they are to be had; mix all these together, and be sure you *strain* them well. Then season all with a Handful or two of Melancholly Expressions, such as *Dreadful, Deadly, cruel cold Death, unhappy Fate, weeping Eyes,* &c. Have mixed all these Ingredients well, put them into the empty Scull of some *young Harvard.* . . . There let them ferment. . . . Take out, and having prepared a sufficient Quantity of double Rhimes, such as, Power, Flower; Quiver, Shiver; Grieve us, Leave us; tell you, excel you; Expeditions, Physicians; Fatigue him, Intrigue him; &c, you must spread all upon Paper, and if you can procure a Scrap of Latin to put at the End, it will garnish it mightily. . . .

N.B. This Receipt will serve when a Female is the Subject of your Elegy, provided you borrow a greater Quantity of Virtues, Excellencies, &c. Sir, Your Servant,

SILENCE DOGOOD

After fourteen letters, Benjamin found his stock of invention exhausted, ran out of ideas — and confessed the authorship. The sensation of this disclosure must have been notable. Franklin's *Autobiography* does not give the actual scene. But among his brother's friends there must have been astonishment, laughter, congratulations and boisterous encouragement for the future. Certainly the joke was on James, and certainly he did not relish it. "I began," wrote Franklin, "to be considered a little more by my Brother's Acquaintance, and in a manner that did not quite please him, as he thought, probably with reason, that it tended to make me too vain."

A cocky boy became three shades cockier. Benjamin, having proved himself, could no longer be put down. What he desired above all was to be free of his brother and the terms of his apprenticeship, find some valid reason to cancel the articles and break away. All unexpectedly, the opportunity offered. In the spring of 1722, the *Courant* printed an item — on the face of it seemingly harmless — which enraged the authorities, including the Massachusetts legislature — and brought James Franklin up for censure and even imprisonment. Pirates and ships dealing in contraband had long infested the New England coast, and it was not always easy to distinguish between the two. The legislature, accused of connivance with this traffic, had become a little sensitive. On June 7, James Franklin printed a notice, purporting to come from Newport, Rhode Island, that a pirate brigantine had been sighted off Block Island, armed with swivel guns and carrying forty or fifty men aboard. *"We are advis'd from Boston, that the Government of the Massachusetts are fitting out a Ship to go after the Pirates, to be commanded by Capt. Peter Papillion, and 'tis thought he will sail sometimes this Month, if Wind and Weather permit."*

About this was something altogether too lighthearted, it bore more than a suspicion of irony. "If wind and weather permit"? That was not how government under-

took to pursue a pirate ship! And this Captain Papillion
— was not the word French for a butterfly, and did such
a seaman exist? Actually, James Franklin had made the
whole thing up, including the extra "i" in Papillion.
James was summoned before the General Court, which
declared the paragraph in question to be a "high affront
to the government." The sheriff of Suffolk County was
ordered to "forthwith Committ to the Gaol in Boston
the Body of James Franklyn Printer . . . there to remain during this Session."

The stone prison was damp; his close confinement
made James ill. After a week he petitioned to have the
liberty of the prison house and yard, "humbly shewing,"
he wrote, "that he is Truely Sensible & Heartily Sorry for
the Offence he has Given to this Court, in the late *Courant* . . . and Truly Acknowledges his Indiscretion and
Indecency when before the court, for all which he En-
treats the Court's forgiveness." It would be edifying to
hear what James had said that day in the legislature. We
know he refused to name the author of the offending
paragraph; we know too that Benjamin was taken up
along with his brother and examined before the council.
"They contented themselves with admonishing me," Benjamin afterward wrote, "and dismiss'd me, considering
me, perhaps as an apprentice who was bound to keep
his Master's Secrets." At any rate, a certificate from Dr.
Zabdiel Boylston accompanied James's petition, attesting
to the prisoner's illness — surely a bighearted gesture on
Boylston's part, considering the treatment he had received from the *Courant* during the inoculation controversy. For all James Franklin's brashness, there must have
been something likable about him. The court gave him
the liberty of the jail yard, though they kept him in
prison for another three weeks, until the General Court
adjourned for the summer.

During James's confinement, Benjamin had the management of the paper. He "made bold," Benjamin said later, "to give our Rulers some Rubs in it, which my Brother took very kindly, while others began to consider me in an unfavourable Light, as a young Genius that had a turn for Libelling and Satyr." But no sooner was James back on Queen Street than he resumed his old tricks. Announcing in the paper that he had not meant to offend the government, he promised to proceed henceforth with caution. This nice retraction was followed by a series of satirical verses describing his examination and imprisonment. On July 30, almost the entire issue was taken up in proving by quotations from Magna Carta that the legislature had acted contrary to the British constitution. At some time during court proceedings, the Governor's Council had resolved to put James under bond of one hundred pounds to be of good behavior, but the legislature refused to pass the resolution, apparently because Governor Shute desired it. Shute had become increasingly restive under any flouting of his prerogative concerning censorship of the press.

But on January first, 1723, Governor Shute, disgusted with Massachusetts and all its works and ways, sailed for England to lay his grievances before Privy Council — departing, indeed, with so little ceremony it looked as if he had fled. The *Courant* indicated as much in a quite wildly ironical piece, declaring New England a sinful and self-destroying people for thus "sinning away" one of "their most extensive blessings." This might have mollified a legislature that hated the governor if James, in the same issue, had not printed a long front-page article (entitled, in Benjamin's list, "Essay against Hypocrites"), the subject of which was easily identifiable as the Reverend Cotton Mather. James printed also a mock letter, addressed palpably to himself, declaring that no man should cast reflections on the civil government, or "abuse and vilify rulers, magistrates and grandees."

This time, James really overstepped himself. How he had the courage — or the effrontery — to do it, one will never know, nor what Brother Benjamin thought of the proceedings. Certainly the entire episode — satirical pieces, censure, imprisonment, mock retraction and all — gave young Benjamin a harshly practical lesson concerning the interaction of magistrates, newspapers, gospel ministers and libel. Following the offensive issues of January, 1723, the Massachusetts legislature appointed a committee, which for a second time censured the *Courant* for its mockery of religion and government.

The fight for freedom of the press in America was to be a long one, and there can be no doubt that James Franklin and his *New England Courant* may be counted as a step forward, even though James's personality somehow precludes the name of martyr. Surely, martyrdom is not undertaken in such a lighthearted spirit; from first to last James — except when he fell sick in jail — was enjoying himself.

But after the offensive issues of January, 1723, James Franklin was forbidden by the legislature to publish the *Courant,* "or any Pamphlet or paper of the like Nature, except it first be supervized by the Secretary of this Province." This, of course, meant the kiss of death for the *New England Courant;* the spirit would be squeezed out of it at once. James and his friends met and decided to try printing the paper under the name of Benjamin Franklin; the court's charge, after all, had not discontinued the *Courant,* but only James's editorship. To avoid possible censure for letting the paper be printed by his apprentice, James returned the old indentures to his brother, with a full discharge of his apprenticeship written on the back, to be shown if challenged.

Here, all at once, was Benjamin's independence, the key to freedom. Fifty years later he noted it: *"Whereby I became free,"* he wrote. He signed new — but secret —

indentures for the remaining five years of his term, well aware that his brother would never dare to show them. The *Courant's* issue of February 11 bore the colophon: "Printed and sold by BENJAMIN FRANKLIN in Queen Street where ADVERTISEMENTS are taken in." So far as the authorities were concerned, it was a flimsy scheme; Benjamin later confessed as much. The new arrangement, it seems, did not enhance Benjamin's standing with his brother; perhaps James resented it. At any rate, quarrels flared up anew; Benjamin's father began to take James's side.

At length [wrote Benjamin] a fresh Difference arising . . . I took upon me to assert my Freedom, presuming that [my brother] would not venture to produce the new Indentures. It was not fair in me to take this Advantage, and this I therefore reckon one of the first Errata of my Life: But the Unfairness of it weigh'd little with me, when under the Impressions of Resentment, for the Blows his Passion too often urg'd him to bestow upon me. Tho' he was otherwise not an ill-natur'd Man: Perhaps I was too saucy and provoking.

When he found I would leave him, he took care to prevent my getting Employment in any other Printing-House of the Town, by going round and speaking to every Master, who accordingly refus'd to give me Work. I then thought of going to New York as the nearest Place where there was a Printer: and I was the rather inclin'd to leave Boston, when I reflected that I had already made myself a little obnoxious to the governing Party; and from the arbitrary Proceedings of the Assembly in my Brother's Case it was likely I might if I stay'd soon bring myself into Scrapes; and farther that my indiscrete Disputations about Religion began to make me pointed at with Horror by good People, as an Infidel or Atheist.

Benjamin now enlisted the help of young John Collins, who persuaded the captain of a New York sloop to take Ben as passenger. This friend of his, said Collins, had got a girl with child and would be compelled to marry her —

an argument which plainly melted the seaman's masculine heart. Benjamin sold some books to raise passage money and slipped on board privately. The wind was fair. In three days Benjamin found himself at New York, "near 300 Miles from home," says the *Autobiography*, "a Boy of but 17, without the least Recommendation to or Knowledge of any Person in the Place, and with very little Money in my Pocket."

Not long afterward, on August 17, 1723, the *New England Courant* — still published under Benjamin's name — carried a most significant advertisement: *"James Franklin, printer. in Queen Street, wants a likely lad for an Apprentice."*

SCENE TWO

FRANKLIN
AND ELECTRICITY

CHAPTER THREE

Science in the eighteenth century.
Franklin and electricity, with some
account of his life from 1723 to 1743.

And new philosophy calls all in doubt;
The element of fire is quite put out;
The sun is lost, and th'earth, and no man's wit
Can well direct him where to look for it.

John Donne

Men of great soul, what astonishing things have
they arrived unto!" So said Cotton Mather in his
book *The Christian Philosopher*, published in 1721.
Mather's name . . . his books . . . his ideas . . . were
to enter often into Franklin's life; the early enmity would
soon be forgotten. In himself Mather typifies the beginnings of science in America — the cautious reaching outward from Puritan dogma, the letting in of new and
dangerous notions concerning earth, air, the flesh and the
firmament. In Mather's time and in Franklin's time, the
study of physics was called *natural philosophy;* the study
of plants, *natural history.* By the "Christian Philosopher,"
its author meant the scientist as Christian, a daring contradiction in terms. How could the two be reconciled,
God's authority and man's new revelations?

Born only twenty years after Galileo's death, older than Franklin by nearly half a century, Mather lived through times of soul-shaking discoveries. Newton, nearly half a century before, had shown that God's universe moved by its own laws: the moon, the planets could be charted in their orbits not by divine revelation but by mathematics, Newton's "method of Fluxions," called calculus. With a prism, a refracting telescope, the nature of light itself was defined. William Gilbert published his work on the magnet, Dr. William Harvey discovered the circulation of the blood. The first thermometer was invented, the first microscope, the first telescope. Men of great soul had indeed made bold guesses, too wide, too bold for Mather's world and even Franklin's world to credit wholly. The seventeenth century had as it were exploded into thought, tearing loose from scholasticism, which said that to learn was merely to repeat the ancient teaching of Greece and Egypt.

What the seventeenth century claimed, the eighteenth century would attempt to demonstrate by experiment . . . classification, nomenclature, technique. An Age of Genius would be followed by an Age of Reason, of Enlightenment and dissemination; the application of the new discoveries to men's daily lives and their condition.

The Christian Philosopher was the first American book of science designed for a popular audience. Mather was not a physicist but a botanist, since youth a serious student of natural history. His purpose, his evangelism, would be to describe in his book all living things he had met upon the earth; then justify his probing by giving glory to God the creator. And when Mather turned from Puritan theology to natural history his prose took wing, took fire. (Franklin's shop in Philadelphia would one day have Mather's books on sale by the dozen.) Like Francis Bacon, Mather desired to study not words but things, believing that a scholar learns not only from books but also by grubbing with his hands in the earth. When a botanist in England suggested to Mather that he send from Boston "such subterraneous curiosities as may have been in these parts of America withal," Mather obliged with no less than eighty-two letters.

The Christian Philosopher stops at nothing. All is grist to his mill: plants, animals, fossils, rocks, worms. "The Flowers," writes Mather, "how charming their proportion and pulchritude! . . . The Anatomy of Plants. . . . The most inimitable structure of the Parts! . . . The Air-Vessels in all their curious coylings!" How wonderful the insects, says Mather, "the great Strength and Spring in the Legs of such as leap!" And man: "The Bones, how admirable in their Circumstances! The Back-Bone is contrived with an Artifice truly astonishing! Had Nature been a blind Architect . . . the Faces of several Men might have been as like as Eggs laid by the same Hen." And how compassionate of the Almighty, to confine the poisonous tarantula to "one little corner of the earth."

Here is science as a hymn, a psalm, a litany. It would almost seem the so-called "practical" eighteenth century came into its scientific heritage through poetry, through the joy of wonder. Francis Bacon had written that "all knowledge and wonder (which is the seed of knowledge) is an impression of pleasure in itself." Three centuries later, Einstein confessed to "a sort of intoxicated amazement at the beauty and grandeur of this world . . . the feeling from which true scientific research draws its spiritual sustenance."

Benjamin Franklin was to be an amateur in science, a part-time philosopher, passionate in his curiosity, and, once the ideas began to flow, persistent as the waterfalls at Cohoe. Franklin had almost reached forty when he began his work on electricity — old, for a scientist. Did not Newton designate twenty-four as the prime of his age of invention? Scarcely ten years of Franklin's life would be devoted to electricity — enough, however, for him to make his extraordinary contribution.

By the 1740's, when Franklin was introduced to electricity, he already occupied a considerable position in the city of Philadelphia. His fortunes had by no means moved in a straight line, or neatly ascending spiral. Yet one does not visualize Franklin standing and meeting events head-on as they arrived. Rather, he intuitively sensed the approach of opportunity, seized it when it came, saw it slip away, and reached out anew. From the start, his ambition had been to become a master printer, nor did he doubt his ability. He returned to Boston after seven months as a journeyman in Philadelphia, confident that his father would forgive his running away and lend him money to go to London and buy a printer's outfit as his brother James had done. Resplendent in a new suit, "genteel from head to foot," he said later, he presented himself (aged eighteen) at James's printing house, showed off his watch and his money to the journeymen, "near five pound sterling in silver," then gave the men something for drink and departed, leaving James in a state of impotent rage.

To his father, Benjamin showed a letter from Governor Keith of Pennsylvania, who, having met Benjamin and taken a liking to him, had promised not only notes of introduction for London but a letter of credit with which to purchase a press and types. Mr. Franklin received his son kindly, read Keith's letter — and remarked that the governor must be a man of small discretion to entrust a mere boy with the management of so much business. Benjamin returned empty-handed to Philadelphia. Relying on the governor's repeated pledges of help, he proceeded to Newcastle and boarded a vessel bound for London. The promised letters were said to be in the captain's mailbag. The ship put to sea — and no letters ever appeared. Governor Keith, notoriously unreliable, had simply abandoned Franklin. Just who paid the passage money we shall never know. But once in London, Benjamin managed to maintain himself for eighteen months under two excellent masters of the trade. One of these, John Watts, employed nearly fifty printers; Benjamin was soon remarked for his strength and speed. He made the acquaintance of Dr. Henry Pemberton, physician and scholar, at the moment superintending publication of the third edition of Sir Isaac Newton's *Principia Mathematica.* Pemberton promised to take Benjamin to see Newton, "of which," wrote Benjamin later, "I was extreamly desirous; but that never happened." On his own initiation, however, Benjamin contrived to meet Sir Hans Sloane, secretary of the Royal Society, and showed him some "curiosities from the northern parts of America," among them a purse made of a newly found fibrous mineral called asbestos. Sloane gave Franklin a guinea for the purse.*

There was about Benjamin surely something beguiling, though certainly he was not handsome. The ability to make friends in high places and low was undoubtedly one of the chief reasons for Franklin's success in life. At nineteen he must already have possessed the pleasant address of his later years, the cheerful, respectful manner with new acquaintances that he had taught himself with such pains, his appearance of attentive inquiry so flattering to all — and a way of telling stories that was nothing short of enchanting. This last is something a man does not learn; he is born with it and never loses it.

In London Franklin made friends at every turn — though all of his adventures by no means turned out well. He lent money to James Ralph, the young American who traveled from Philadelphia with him. Ralph chose to ig-

* The purse can be seen today in the British Museum.

nore the debt. Benjamin never mentions being in love, but he was frank about his sexual appetite, later confessing that the "hard-to-be-governed Passion of Youth hurried me frequently into Intrigues with low Women that fell in my Way, which were attended with some Expence and great Inconvenience, besides a continual Risque to my Health by a Distemper which of all Things I dreaded, tho' by great good luck I escaped it." One is reminded of that very different character and colleague, John Adams, who at seventy-odd confessed that he was "of an amorous disposition, and very early from ten or eleven years of age, was very fond of the society of females . . . all modest and virtuous girls, and maintained their character through life."

Franklin's taste proved less particular. His adventures and entanglements seem to have concerned casual acquaintances among "milleners" and workingwomen. In London Benjamin lived on next to nothing, managing to save a little but dangerously prone to lend money whenever a friend appeared. He wrote, at barely nineteen, what he called "a little metaphysical Piece," entitled, *A Dissertation on Liberty and Necessity, Pleasure and Pain*. The essay was smart, deistical; Franklin printed a hundred copies, distributed them in London and gained some praise and acquaintance thereby. Afterward he regretted the pamphlet (which carried atheistical overtones) and burned all the unsold copies. An *erratum*, Franklin later called it.

There is an enchantment in the things that happened to young Ben; or perhaps the magic lies in his own recollection, the quality of what he remembered. To have a good time was important to Franklin all through life; in one way or another he confessed it often. Fifty years after this London visit, Franklin recalled a boating excursion with his printer friends, when he stripped, leaped into the Thames and swam from Chelsea to Blackfriars, performing every kind of feat, under water and above, that he had practiced in the Schuylkill at home. Sir William Wyndham, friend of Swift and Bolingbroke, heard of it, sent for Franklin, and asked him to teach the two Wyndham boys to swim. A friend from the printing house, named Wygate, educated and intelligent, urged Franklin to tour Europe with him, earning their way as journeyman printers.

There is little doubt that Benjamin could have maintained himself indefinitely at London. But he grew homesick and returned to Philadelphia, arriving in the autumn of 1726. He soon formed a partnership with Hugh Meredith, a journeyman printer, and two years later found himself sole proprietor, including ownership, of the *Pennsylvania Gazette,* founded several years earlier by Samuel Keimer, Franklin's first Philadelphia employer. Slowly but steadily Franklin's business prospered. The Pennsylvania Assembly gave him the contract for printing their second issue of paper money — forty thousand pounds; Delaware ("The Lower Counties") followed suit. Franklin opened a stationer's shop, wrote tracts and pamphlets concerning economics and politics, was elected clerk of the Pennsylvania Assembly and thenceforth had the printing of their laws and other business. He sent his journeymen to far cities — Charleston, South Carolina, New York, Newport, Antigua — helped form presses in New Haven, made partnerships in Newport, New York, Lancaster. He was named postmaster for Philadelphia, which not only brought a salary but helped in circulating his newspaper. Franklin taught himself to read French, Spanish, Latin, Italian. His passion for self-improvement extended to public projects: he organized the first fire company in the colonies, made designs for paving and lighting Philadelphia streets and extending the city watch to a force of police.

Thus Franklin, man of business and civic affairs. At thirty he married — that is, he took as his common-law wife Deborah Read, and set up a household above his shop on Market Street. Deborah had been married before. Her husband, a potter named Rogers, had fled to the West Indies to escape his creditors and never been heard from again. Without sure evidence of his death, a legal marriage of course could not take place. Just why Franklin set up housekeeping with his plain, practical, industrious, high-spirited Debbie has been the subject of endless speculation. Did he know, by then, that he was to father an illegitimate son, William? Was Deborah the mother? It is thought not. Debbie today would be called illiterate, but she wrote better than Franklin's mother and nearly as well as his sister, Jane. William was received into the household, bearing Franklin's name. A second son, Francis Folger, came along a year later.

Thus Franklin joined his life with Deborah, the "Dear Child" of his letters from Europe. The scene is familiar: the house near the Philadelphia market, with the print shop in front where Deborah presided, selling over the counter everything from sealing wax and dictionaries to the famous crown soap made by Franklin's brothers in Boston. Debbie kept the records.

After six years of marriage, Franklin suffered a cruel blow, from which he never fully recovered; at sixty he would speak of it with sorrow. He lost his second son from smallpox. Francis Folger, "Aged 4 Years, 1 Mon. & 1 Day," said the inscription on the small stone: *"The Delight of all that knew him."* Franklin had long ago become a convert to inoculation. Yet he could not have forgotten the stand he had taken against it with his brother James . . . the diatribes in the *New England Courant* . . . Dr. Mather's anger disgust. In Franklin's paper, the *Gazette,* a statement appeared:

December 30, 1736
UNDERSTANDING 'tis a current Report, that my Son Francis, who died lately of the Small Pox, had it by Inocula-

tion; and it being desired to satisfy the Publick in that Particular; inasmuch as some People are, by that Report (join'd
with others of the like kind, and perhaps equally groundless)
deter'd from having that Operation perform'd on their Children, I do sincerely declare, that he was not Inoculated, but
receiv'd the Distemper in the Common Way of Infection: and
I suppose the Report could only arise from its being my
known Opinion, that Inoculation was safe and beneficial Practice; and from my having said among my Acquaintance that I
intended to have my Child inoculated, as soon as he should
have recovered sufficient strength from a Flux with which he
had been long afflicted.

B. Franklin

Cotton Mather, in his *Essays to Do Good,* had recommended the forming of young mens' clubs for discussion, after the manner of the new reforming societies in
England. Mather had himself started twenty such societies
in Boston; every meeting opening with a set of questions,
both pious and practical, with a due pause after each
question, "for anyone to offer what he please upon it."
Franklin's famous Philadelphia society, called the Junto,
followed Mather's program, except that the Junto suggested more genially that queries be read "with a Pause
between each while one might fill and drink a Glass of
Wine."

The Junto, launched by Franklin in 1727, at first was
nicknamed The Leather Apron, to distinguish it from
The Merchants' Every Night, composed of old and richer
citizens, or a certain light-minded society, The Bachelors.
"Do you love truth for truth's sake?" each new member
of the Junto was asked, and must answer with his hand
upon his breast, adding, that he would "endeavor im-
partially to receive and communicate the truth to others."
The questions sound as if Franklin were putting them to
himself: "Whence comes the Dew that stands on the outside of a Tankard that has cold Water in it in the Summer
Time? . . . If the Sovereign Power attempts to deprive a

45

Subject of his Right (or which is the same Thing, of what he thinks is his Right) is it justifiable in him to resist if he is able? . . . Does it not in a general Way require great Study and intense Application for a Poor Man to become rich and Powerful, if he would do it, without the Forfeiture of his Honesty?"

Franklin's Junto was to endure for thirty years; he even thought of making it international. One day Franklin asked the members if they were willing to bring books to the club, making a common library to which all could refer. When the collection proved disappointingly small, Franklin suggested that a circulating library be established for members and any other citizens who might be interested. The Library Company of Philadelphia, as it was called, housed not only books but specimens of natural history and scientific apparatus. There were stuffed snakes, a dead pelican, a collection of fossils — and John Penn's gift of an air pump, described as "costly." Thomas Penn congratulated the Library Company on being the first institution that "encouraged Knowledge and Learning in the Province of Pennsylvania." Later he sent a telescope, geographical globes and an "electric machine."

Franklin's descriptions of the original Junto members are wonderfully indicative of the man himself. Four members, including Franklin, were printers. Hugh Meredith is described as "Honest, sensible, something of a Reader but given to drink . . . Potts, a young Countryman, of great Wit and Humor, but a little idle . . . Webb, an Oxford scholar, lively, witty, good natur'd, but idle, thoughtless, and imprudent to the last Degree . . . Brientnal, a Copyer of Deeds for the Scriveners; a good-natur'd friendly middle-ag'd man, a great lover of Poetry, reading all he could meet with, and writing some that was tolerable; very ingenious at making little nicknackeries and sensible Conversation. Thomas Godfrey, a self-taught Mathematician . . . afterward inventor of what is now

call'd Hadley's Quadrant . . . but, like most Great Mathematicians I have met with, he expected universal Precision
in every thing said, or was forever denying or distinguish-
ing upon Trifles, to the Disturbance of all Conversation.
He soon left us. Nicholas Scull, a Surveyor, afterwards
Surveyor-General, Who lov'd Books, and sometimes made
a few Verses . . . Parsons, bred a Shoemaker, but, loving
Reading, had acquir'd a considerable Share of Mathematics . . . Maugridge, a Joiner, a most exquisite Me-
chanic and a solid sensible Man . . . Robert Grace, a
young Gentleman of some Fortune, generous, lively, and
witty, a Lover of Punning and of his Friends. And William
Coleman, then a Merchant's Clerk, about my Age, who had
the coolest clearest Head, the best Heart, and the exactest
Morals, of almost any Man I ever met with. He became
afterward a Merchant of great Note, and one of our
Provincial Judges: Our Friendship continued without
Interruption to his Death upwards of 40 Years. . . ."

"The Club," Franklin added, "was the best School of
Philosophy, Morals and Politics that then existed in the
Province; for our Queries which were read the Week pre-
ceding their Discussion, put us on Reading with Attention
upon the several Subjects, that we might speak more to the
purpose." Here too, said Franklin, better habits of conversation were acquired, the rules being framed so as to avoid
offense one to another.

Franklin now and again went back to Boston, saw his
parents and became reconciled with his brother James.
On one of these visits, in 1743, Franklin happened to see
a Scottish lecturer perform some electrical experiments.
Dr. Archibald Spencer,* educated in Edinburgh, carried
respectable credentials as a physician and male midwife.
Franklin, it seems, watched the experiments at a private

---

* His first name is often given as Adam. Franklin in the *Autobiography* called him Dr. Spence.

showing, Boston having failed to come forward with the requisite number of subscribers (at six pounds each) for the doctor's course in "Experimental Philosophy." Spencer visited Philadelphia soon afterward and delivered two courses of lectures, tickets being sold and a catalogue distributed "at the Post Office," which meant Franklin's house on Market Street.

Spencer talked on "Newton's Theory of Light and Colour"; displayed a machine for measuring the flow of blood from the heart. He rubbed a glass tube and attracted gold and brass leaf; and he repeated Stephen Gray's trick, first done in England, of suspending a boy by silk cords from the ceiling and drawing "sparks of fire" (a spectator wrote) from his face and hands. Dr. Spencer's experiments, Franklin said afterward, "were imperfectly perform'd, as he was not very expert; but being on a Subject quite new to me, they equally surprized and pleas'd me." Before Spencer left America, Franklin purchased his apparatus, including the doctor's device for measuring the flow of blood.

In spite of the initial interest aroused by Spencer, some three years passed before a fortunate occurrence caused Franklin to take up electrical experimenting in earnest. In London there lived a merchant and botanist, a fervent Quaker, Peter Collinson, whose business concerns kept him in close touch with America. He had acted as agent for Franklin's subscription library since its inception. Early in the year 1747, Collinson made the Library Company the present of a glass tube, over three feet long, as big around as a man's wrist, with instructions for its use in obtaining electric sparks. Franklin's letter of thanks is the earliest mention we have of his work in electricity: *

---

* Whenever, in this book, Franklin's letters have not his characteristic spelling and orthography, it is because the originals are lost, and the letters taken from printed copies, where editors altered Franklin's capital letters, etc. This letter to Collinson served as preface to the 1769 edition of Franklin's book, *Experiments and Observations in Electricity*.

Philadelphia, March 28, 1747

Sir,

Your kind present of an electric tube, with directions for using it, has put several of us on making electrical experiments, in which we have observed some particular phaenomena that we look upon to be new. I shall, therefore, communicate them to you in my next, though possibly they may not be new to you, as among the numbers daily employed in these experiments on your side of the water, 'tis probable some one or other has hit on the same observations. For my own part, I never was before engaged in any study that so totally engrossed my attention and my time as this has lately done; for what with making experiments when I can be alone, and repeating them to my Friends and Acquaintances, who, from the novelty of the thing come continually in crowds to see them, I have, during some months past, had little leisure for any thing else. I am &c.

B. Franklin

Franklin's education did not qualify him to make quantative proof by calculus, like Newton; as a schoolboy he had been notably deficient in mathematics. The work that was reported to Collinson over the next five years would all be done by hand, by trial and error, with simple objects as tools. Glass tubes and tubes of resin, a gun barrel, corks, iron shot, wax plates, glass plates: with these, results were to be obtained which would astound Europe and eventually the world. Had the science of electricity not been in such a primitive state — no state at all, actually — this could not have happened. Franklin's opportunity came at a crucial time. Other men had suspected the things he guessed at, but they had not proved them by experiment. The seventeenth century had brought to light the laws of gravity and planetary magnetism; it had seen the invention of many tools. But in the mid-1700's, electricity, like chemistry, remained about where it had been in ancient Greece, when Thales attracted feathers by rubbing his piece of *elektron*, or amber. Chemistry was still ruled by the phlogiston theory and the "vital spirits," and would be until Joseph Priestley in 1772 discovered oxygen and, not recognizing what he had found, called it "dephlogisticated air."

Franklin's achievement seems, on the face of it, hardly more amazing than the fact that the world had taken so incredibly long to find and utilize a force upon whose power our material civilization largely depends. By the 1740's, electricity had come to be considered as a fluid — two fluids, according to the Frenchman, DuFay: one "resinous," residing in amber; one "vitreous," residing in glass.* But Europe looked on electricity as a toy, the newest, latest curiosity. Peter Collinson wrote to Cadwallader Colden in New York that the "phenomena of the Polypus entertained the Curious for a year or two past but now the Vertuosi of Europe are taken up in Electrical experiments." Collinson had his information from the Dutch botanist Gronovius, who had described the polypus as a tiny creature found sticking to duckweed. "But what is most surprising," wrote Gronovius, "cut this Animal in Five or Six Pieces, in a few Hours there will be as many like their Parents." Our "virtuoso's," added Gronovius, did not believe this until the Professors Albinus and Musschenbroek by experiment proved it true.

Apparently the polypus, for all its artistry of reproduction, held less of fascination than the new manifestation of electricity. What can be more astonishing, Collinson asked, "than that the base rubbing of a glass tube should invest a person with electric fire! . . . Let him touch spirits of wine & the sparks from his finger on the touch will sett the spirits in flame. . . . I have seen Oyl of Sevile oranges & camphor sett fire & Gunpowder mixed with Oyl of Lemons will take fire — but what would you say to see fire come out of a piece of thick ice and sett the spirits in flame?"

---

* In two given bodies, two electric fluids exist in equal amount. During the process of charging, said Du Fay, some of one fluid is removed, leaving an excess of the other.

In Europe and England, the *cognoscenti* amused themselves at evening parties with the rubbing of glass tubes, marveling at the phenomena of attraction and repulsion and a variety of quite magical results. At the French court, the Abbé Nollet, a pupil of DuFay, arranged most enjoyable spectacles for his Most Christian Majesty King Louis XV. What could be more entertaining than to see one hundred and eighty grenadiers (linked by wires) leap into the air at one and the same instant, as the abbé released an electric charge. Or to observe no less than seven hundred clerics from the Couvent de Paris, robes, tonsures, and all, spring simultaneously skyward at the abbé's command. . . .

The world has always delighted in marvels, showing itself avid of magic, provided the effect is interesting. Sir Thomas Browne, the learned and witty physician, in the seventeenth century wrote an entire book to refute various common errors concerning nature; he called his treatise *Pseudodoxia Epidemica* ("Contagious Falsities"). The mandrake root, said the doctor, does *not* give a shriek when pulled up. It is not true that storks will live only in "Republicks and free states"; nor is it true that elephants have no joints in their legs. Surprisingly for his day, Browne had a chapter, "Of Bodies Electrical in general"; he referred to electricity as an "effluvium." Not until Galileo's time, William Gilbert's time, had men begun to query openly the workings of God's universe — to query rather than merely to wonder. "This nature knowledge," Gilbert had written, "is almost entirely new and unheard of."

Franklin himself tried the trick with the suspended boy, but set him on a glass stool for insulation instead of hanging him from the ceiling by silk cords. Franklin's very first experiment would later lead to the invention of the lightning rod, though he was by no means conscious of this when he described it to Collinson. Under the date of May 25, 1747, Franklin wrote about "the wonderful effects of Points, both in *drawing* off and *throwing* off the Electrical Fire. For Example, Place an Iron Shot of three or four Inches Diameter on the Mouth of a clean dry Glass Bottle. By a fine silken Thread from the Ceiling, right over the Mouth of the Bottle, suspend a small Cork Ball, about the Bigness of a Marble; the Thread of such a Length, as that the Cork Ball may rest against the Side of the Shot. Electrify the Shot, and the Ball will be repelled to the Distance of 4 to 5 Inches, more or less according to the Quantity of Electricity. . . ."

Schoolchildren do this experiment today and watch with delight the ball bounce away. Nor does the simplicity of the experiment detract from its originality, its essential worth. "When in this State," Franklin's letter continues, "if you present to the Shot the Point of a long, slender, sharp Bodkin at 6 or 8 Inches Distance, the Repellency is instantly destroy'd and the Cork flies to it. A blunt Body must be brought within an Inch, and draw a Spark to produce the same Effect."

In this early experiment, Franklin learned that his rod had to be grounded. "Fix a Needle," he wrote, "to the End of a suspended Gun Barrel, so as to point beyond it like a little Bayonet; and while it remains there, the Gun barrel cannot be electrised (by the Tube applied to the other End) so as to give a Spark; the Fire is continually running out silently at the Point."

There seemed to be nothing intrusive between Franklin's hand and his eye; nothing diverted. Franklin would have fitted a description Thomas Carlyle wrote a century later: "This man is the sort we now call *original men,* men of genius and such like; the first peculiarity of which is that they communicate with the universe at first-hand." One thinks, again, of what Francis Bacon said about himself: "being gifted by nature with desire to seek, patience to doubt, fondness to meditate, slowness to assert, readi-

ness to consider, carefulness to dispose and set in order."
Franklin had read everything pertaining to electricity
that he could lay hands on; he knew well the truth of
Newton's saying, "If I have seen further . . . it is by
standing on the shoulders of giants." A dozen years after
his first experiment when Franklin asked Musschenbroek
in Leyden for guidance on further books to study, the
professor sent a list, but added "in Latin" that he would
wish Franklin to go on making experiments entirely
through his own nature, "and thereby pursue a path en-
entirely different from that of the Europeans, for then
you will certainly find many other things which have been
hidden to natural philosophers throughout the course of
centuries."

From the beginning, Franklin gave credit to others
where credit was due. "This power of points to throw
off the electrical fire," he wrote later, "was first communicated to me by my ingenious friend Mr. Thomas
Hopkinson." Writing to Collinson, Franklin often used
the pronoun *we:* "We electrify upon Wax, in the Dark, a
Book that has a double Line of Gold round upon the
Covers. . . . We rub our Tubes with Buck Skin." Ebenezer Kinnersley, a neighbor, a Baptist minister and early
helper, went on to do significant work by himself. Philip
Syng, a local silversmith, invented a small machine, a
glass globe with a handle by which the globe could be
turned like a grindstone, using the principle of the lathe.
The purpose of this little contrivance — a model of which
is housed today in the Franklin Institute at Philadelphia
— was to do away with the fatigue of rubbing, much
complained of by European experimenters. These early
reports to Collinson were fired off at what would seem
white heat. "In my last I informed you . . ." Franklin
would begin. Yet he had the scientist's care for accuracy
and for repeating an experiment many times before making it known.

In his first letter to Collinson, Franklin revealed his discovery that electricity consists not of two opposing forces but of "a common Element" . . . which he called electrical fire. Franklin showed that the "fluid," in passing out of one body and entering another, is never destroyed but retains its original equality, "the Fire only circulating. Hence have arisen some new Terms among us. We say B (and other Bodies alike circumstanced) are electrised *positively;* A *negatively:* Or rather B is electrised *plus* and A *minus.* And we daily in our Experiments electrise Bodies *plus* or *minus* as we think proper. *These Terms* we may use till your Philosophers give us better. . . . As the Vessel is just sailing, I can not give you so large an Account of American Electricity as I intended. . . ."

It was large enough. Robert A. Millikan, physicist and Nobel Prize winner, has called this experiment "probably the most fundamental thing ever done in the field of electricity." Franklin's single-fluid * theory became the basis on which subsequent advances in electricity were to rest; after 1900, it would be known as the electron theory. Electrons move about conductors much as a fluid might move; Franklin's single-fluid idea led directly to this concept. Out of necessity, Franklin invented words as he went along, terms which today are in such common use it is hard to realize they have not always been part of our language. The business of inventing words to fit a scientific concept is no small matter. "I feel a Want of Terms here," Franklin tells Collinson in one letter, "and doubt much, whether I shall be able to make this intelligible." A new conception must be visualized, and this can only be done in words: vocabulary and conception are one and the

---

* In the single-fluid theory, a given body possessing a normal amount of electric fluid was called *neutral.* During the process of charging, the fluid was transferred from one body to the other; the body with the deficiency being charged *minus* and the body with the excess charged *plus.* But no fluid was lost.

same. A scholar who traced Franklin's vocabulary found at least twenty-five electrical terms which Franklin was the first to use, such as *armature, battery, brush, charged, condense, conductor,* as well as *electrised, plus* and *minus, positively* and *negatively.* Franklin's terminology was wrong when he said the positive charges moved. Not until the electronic era was it determined that the *negative* electrons move — a difference largely academic.

What Franklin revealed in this first letter to Collinson — his one-fluid theory — was not an "invention," but a way of thinking about electricity, a way of looking at the subject that broke through old boundaries and let men proceed to further discovery. This is an achievement possible only to the largest minds. It seems to stem from a quality of imagination that inspired I. Bernard Cohen, historian of science, to call his book *Franklin and Newton,* a title startling in itself. Thomas Jefferson, as Professor Cohen points out, produced various ingenious inventions, such as the moldboard plow; he discovered plants and fossils and had some reputation as a paleontologist. Yet in science or natural history he opened no doors. Would any one think of calling a book *Jefferson and Darwin?*

As Franklin's work expanded, he found artisans in Philadelphia who under his direction made additional "electric tubes: of green glass, about thirty inches long." Franklin began to experiment with the Leyden jar, also sent from England by Collinson, "Mr. Musschenbroek's wonderful bottle," Franklin called it — the glass receptacle now so familiar, lined within and without by tinfoil, and holding a rod or conductor which descends through an insulated stopper. Franklin here confirmed his single-fluid theory, describing the experiments to Collinson — eleven of them, each contained in a single paragraph of his third letter. Together the experiments outlined steps in the adaptation of the condenser (today called a capacitor). As statements of fact, experts claim that Franklin's paragraphs will stand almost without amendment to the present time. Here began the evolution of the electric current, the forging of the link between the Leyden jar and the later voltaic cell. Franklin's "battery" (his own invented term) can be seen today * in the box he made for it; each jar is about fifteen inches high.

Between 1747 and 1750 there were five letters to Collinson on electricity — long, detailed and lively. On April 29, 1749, Franklin called a temporary halt, ending on a typically cheerful note. "Chagrin'd a little," he writes, "that We have hitherto been able to discover Nothing in the Way of Use to Mankind, and the hot Weather coming on, Electrical Experiments are not so agreable; 'tis proposed to put an End to them for this Season somewhat humourously in a Party of Pleasure on the Banks of Schuykill † (where Spirits are at the same Time to be fired by a Spark sent from Side to Side thro' the River.) A Turky is to be killed for our Dinners by the Electrical Shocks; and roasted by the electrical Jack, before a Fire kindled by the Electrified Bottle; when the Healths of all the famous Electricians in England, France and Germany, are to be drank in Electrified Bumpers, under the Discharge of Guns from the Electrical Battery."

* The American Philosophical Society has in its possession thirty-five Leyden jars. Fifteen are in their original condition.

† Printed editions of the letters carry a footnote: "The river that washes one side of Philadelphia, as the Delaware does the other; both are ornamented with the summer habitations, of the citizens, and the agreeable mansions of the principal people of this colony."

CHAPTER FOUR

Thunder gusts and electricity.
The Royal Society. More letters
to Collinson. Franklin's book
on electricity is published.
The kite experiment.

E lectricity possessed no earthly use, and Franklin apologized to Collinson for it, thereby exemplifying the spirit of his century — a new belief in utility. Since ancient times, science — "philosophy" — had distinguished between knowledge and usefulness. Archimedes by mathematical calculation built war machines which terrorized the Roman enemy; afterward, Plutarch chided him for putting geometry to merely practical purposes. It required a Francis Bacon to remove "philosophy" from its ivory tower and place it in the service of mankind, where Bacon said it belonged. By Newton's day the principle had been accepted, though philosophers differed in their definitions. Only once in Isaac Newton's life is it recorded that he laughed; it happened when a friend to whom he lent a copy of Euclid's *Elements* inquired of what use or benefit such a study could be.

In Franklin's time the principle of utility went farther than acceptance. It was the ethos of the era, urgent and flourishing, especially in the New World. Franklin's name has come down to us as the very apostle of this utility. Was he not founder of an American Philosophical Society "for the Promoting of Useful Knowledge"? Inventor of the lightning rod and the open stove that bears his name, Franklin seems, on the face of it, the true example and avatar of the practical man. Moreover, he preached thrift and the care of money: "A penny saved is a penny earned. . . . If a man keep his store his store will keep him." *Poor Richard's Almanack* is rife with such mottoes; Father Abraham's adages went round the world and back for a century and a half. According to Mark Twain, the lives of a million schoolboys were made miserable by such precepts as "Early to bed and early to rise." D. H. Lawrence called the author of *Poor Richard* "stuffy, a sheep in a pen." Carlyle, standing before Franklin's portrait, remarked, "There is the father of all the Yankees." Max Weber in his thesis on the ethic of modern capitalism and its evolution from puritanism gives *Poor Richard* as a prime example.

In truth, if we had no more from Franklin's pen than Father Abraham's advice on the "Way to Wealth," we would have a picture of a shrewd tradesman and nothing else. Common sense is hardly an endearing quality, and Poor Richard says nothing about that wholehearted joy in living which was one of Franklin's most noticeable traits. It seems almost as if, with Father Abraham, Franklin was teaching care and thrift not to the world but to himself, knowing well he needed the lesson. Until the age of twenty-four he had had a truly difficult time making a living, seldom being free of debt. Nor did Franklin admire shrewdness in others: *Poor Richard* remarks that cunning proceeds from want of capacity, remarks also that "avarice and happiness never saw each other, how then should they become acquainted?" Late in life, Franklin confessed that frugality was patently a virtue but one he never could acquire in himself, and that he had been lucky to find the quality in a wife.

Far from profiting him financially, Franklin's work in electricity was, if anything, expensive; it might better be called an indulgence, single-minded and all-absorbing for the moment. Right in the midst of his experiments, when he was proceeding, he said, "with great Alacrity," Franklin retired from his very successful printing business, arranging a partnership with his foreman, David Hall, who was to take entire charge, paying Franklin six hundred and seventy-three pounds outright and agreeing to a substantial amount annually. "I flatter'd myself," Franklin wrote, "that by the subsequent tho' moderate Fortune I had acquir'd, I had secur'd Leisure during the rest of my Life for Philosophical Studies and Amusements." To Cadwallader Colden he confessed that like Colden he was taking the proper measures for obtaining leisure to enjoy life and his friends.

The partnership lasted for eighteen years, after which it expired by agreement. He was forty-two when he retired. The sum of six hundred and seventy-three pounds was no inconsiderable income. Had Franklin stayed in business there is little doubt he could have amassed a fortune — a country place like James Logan's Stenton, with its magnificent library, or the kind of estate built up in America by royal governors. When he retired from business, Franklin moved from Market Street to what he called "a more quiet Part of Town" — the northwest corner of Second and Race streets, nearer the river. Once assured of a competence, he showed no desire for increasing it; Franklin never changed his simple style of living and seemed to have no ambition for outward show. He refused to patent his Pennsylvania Fireplace * and gave the model to his friend Robert Grace, proprietor of

---

* Franklin's sister, Jane Mecom, wrote of it as "your Invention of the Chamber Fireplace."

the iron works where the stoves were cast. Grace, an original member of the Junto, had lent Franklin money to set up independently as a printer, and would not take payment for the loan.

Franklin had a horror of debt, which he looked on as a kind of slavery; a man could thereby sell his freedom. Franklin knew about this at firsthand. Had he not borrowed money to go to England and acquire the tools of his printing trade, borrowed for the journey home and borrowed from the father of his first partner, Hugh Meredith, to set himself up in business? Franklin had seen his friends go down to ruin because of careless business practices. With money a man bought not only independence but he bought *time,* that most precious commodity, to use at his pleasure. For years Franklin spoke quite seriously of founding an international organization to be called the Society of the Free and Easy — meaning free of debt and, it followed, easy in spirit.

It was in the spring of 1749 that Franklin wrote out his first statement concerning thunder gusts and what he succinctly called "the sameness of lightning with electricity." His notes or "minutes," kept as the work proceeded, listed various ways in which the electrical fluid agrees with lightning: "1. Giving light. 2. Colour of the light. 3. Crooked direction. 4. Swift motion. 5. Being conducted by metals. 6. Crack or noise in exploding. 7. Subsisting in water or ice. 8. Rending bodies it passes through. 9. Destroying animals. 10. Melting metals. 11. Firing inflammable substances. 12. Sulphureous smell.

"The electric fluid [the minutes continue] is attracted by points. We do not know whether this property is in lightning. But since they agree in all particulars wherein we can already compare them, is it not probable they agree likewise in this? Let the experiment be made."

Other men before Franklin had noted the similarity

between lightning and the electrical fluid, among them Hauksbee and Freke in England, Winckler in Germany, and the Abbé Nollet in France. Such suggestions were very recent; Euler, the Swiss mathematician, said these men were looked on as dreamers. For centuries, the thunder and the bolt of lightning had been God's weapon . . . Jove's . . . Thor's, loosed in anger against mankind. Certain Greeks had dared to suggest that thunderstorms were caused by "sulphurous inflammable vapors which accumulated in the clouds and broke through in the form of lightning." Descartes, who died in 1650, opined that the upper clouds fell down on the lower ones. But nobody, early or late, had said, as Franklin did, *"Let the experiment be made."*

Under the date of July 29, 1750, Franklin sent off to Collinson his ideas of how the experiment concerning lightning might "be done conveniently." Franklin harbored no grand notions about the value of what he proposed to do. The thought of drawing down the lightning, he said later, "was not so much an 'out-of-the-way' one, but that it might have occurred to any electrician. . . . On the Top of some high Tower or Steeple," he wrote, "place a Kind of Sentry Box big enough to contain a Man and an electrical Stand. From the Middle of the Stand let an Iron Rod rise, and pass bending out the Door, and then upright 20 or 30 feet, pointed very sharp at the End. If the Electrical Stand be kept clean and dry, a Man standing on it when such Clouds are passing low, might be electrified and afford Sparks, the Rod drawing Fire to him from the Cloud. If any Danger to the Man should be apprehended (tho' I think there would be none) let him stand on the Floor of his Box, and now and then bring near to the Rod, the Loop of a Wire, that has one End fastened to the Leads; he holding it by a Wax-Handle. So the Sparks, if the Rod is electrified, will strike from the Rod to the Wire and not affect him."

Franklin was hugely mistaken about the dangers of this experiment. Two years would pass before the idea received enough publicity to be acted on. Oddly enough, in England this particular letter to Collinson, entitled "Experiments and Observations," seems to have been ignored at first by the Royal Society. But early in 1752, the paper was translated into French by a Monsieur Dalibard and published at Paris, where the sentry box suggestion was quickly seized upon. Dalibard himself tried the experiment at Marly; in a few days a Monsieur Delor repeated it. Miraculously, no one was hurt. But in Russia, a Swede, George Wilhelm Richmann, tried to reproduce the experiment and was killed. Musschenbroek received a shock from his Leyden jar which he thought had finished him. He had been trying to gauge the strength of electricity with gun barrel, glass phial and wire. Afterward Musschenbroek wrote a friend in France that not for the whole kingdom would he again undergo such an experience. When his letter appeared in a scientific journal, Joseph Priestley — afterward Franklin's close friend — condemned Musschenbroek as cowardly. "It is not given to every electrician," wrote Priestley censoriously, "to die the death of the justly envied Richmann."

The only reason Franklin himself was not killed was because he never happened to receive a strong enough charge. Twice he was knocked senseless — once when treating a paralytic patient by electric shock, a therapy believed effectual in Europe, but which Franklin later gave up as useless. If such therapy succeeded, he said, it was probably due to the patient's hopeful outlook toward the treatment rather than the effect of the electricity. Another time, preparing to kill a turkey by electric shock, Franklin managed to take the whole charge through his hands and arms. He wrote afterward that, according to his friends, the flash was very great, "and the crack as loud as a pistol shot . . . I felt what I know not well

how to describe, a universal blow throughout my whole
body from head to foot . . . after which the first thing
I took notice of was a violent quick shaking of my body,
which gradually remitting, my senses as gradually returned."

Far from looking on himself a hero, Franklin said he
was ashamed to have made such a blunder; "a match for
the Irishman, whom my sister told me of, who, being
about to steal powder, made a hole in the cask with a hot
iron."

That Franklin's letters to Peter Collinson appeared in
print was due first of all to Collinson and secondly to the
Royal Society of London for Improving Natural Knowledge, its name when founded in 1660; the first historian,
known as "fat Tom Sprat" — actually Bishop of Winchester — said the organization had been founded on
principles laid down by Sir Francis Bacon. Its first secretary was Henry Oldenburg, a natural philosopher, who
for some reason liked to sign his name anagramatically,
as Grubendol; the second secretary was Sir Hans Sloane,
whom Franklin had managed to meet long before, as a
youth in London. In 1703, Sir Isaac Newton was elected
president and ruled the Society according to his liking
until his death in 1727.

The Society's printed *Transactions* make absorbing
reading from the first number. Certain quite definite
rules for style were recommended: "the language of Arti-
zans, Countrymen and Merchants," being preferred to
that of "Wits or Scholars." Furthermore, "a close, naked
natural way of speaking" was urged: "Positive expressions; clear senses; a native easiness: bringing all things as
near the Mathematical plainness as they can."

Nothing could have better suited Benjamin Franklin's
style: the directions pointed to firsthand observation and
experiment as the goal. From all over the world, letters

came to the Royal Society and were printed, setting out
men's observations on what they loved to call "natural
phaenomena" — some freakish, some extremely useful to
mariners and farmers; now and again an intrinsic contribution to science as we know it today. One finds papers
on the "New American Whale-fishing about the Ber-
mudas"; on pendulum watches for calculating the longi-
tude at sea, and ways to ascertain the ocean depth without a plumb line, "contrived by Mr. Hook." We learn
that in Virginia rattlesnakes can be killed by holding
bruised penny-royal to the serpent's nose; in Paris, milk
instead of blood has been found in a man's veins. A correspondent conjectures how much time it would take a
swallow to fly around the world. Interspersed with this
folklore and the truly useful hints to mariners, one comes
suddenly upon a review of "Dr. Sydenham's Book on
Curing Fevers"; also "Mr. Boyle's Experimental History
of Cold."

Hon. Robert Boyle, Thomas Sydenham, Robert Hooke;
these are names to conjure with. Sir Christopher Wren
speculates on the "General Laws of Motion." A correspondent writes "touching the transfusion of blood from
one animal to another"; a physician recommends the
application of musk to the nostrils in convulsive disorders.
The very mistakes are instructive, reminding us that
progress has had a slow and venturesome passage, and
that only fools will laugh at the errors of serious workers.

Among miscellaneous papers in the *Transactions* one
comes without warning upon "A Letter of Mr. Isaac
Newton, Mathematical Professor in the University of
Cambridge; containing his new Theory about Light and
Colours" . . . *"I procured me a triangular glass-Prisme*
[the letter begins], *to try therewith the celebrated Phae-
nomenon of Colours. . . ."*

Plain enough language, surely. As the *Transactions* pass
the century mark and reach toward the 1740's, the names

of Franklin's friends appear: John Mitchell of Virginia; John Lining of Charleston, South Carolina, with his startling work on what today we call metabolism. The polypus makes its entrance; and not long afterward, Franklin's first contribution, concerning the single-fluid theory, which Collinson had turned over to the Society. In the *Autobiography*, Franklin showed chagrin because Letter IV, on thunder gusts, had been, he said, "laught at by the Connoisseurs" — meaning the Royal Society. Franklin was mistaken; from the beginning, the Society had been attentive. All his letters had been read and discussed, and were, a member reported, "deservedly admired not only for the Clear Intelligent Stile, but also for the Novelty of the Subjects." This is not to say that Franklin's discoveries were at once accepted. Conjectures so novel, as yet not exhaustively proven, must bide their time before full credit was given.

The *Gentleman's Magazine* (the first magazine ever printed) was first to publish a résumé of Franklin experiments. The editor, Edward Cave, an extraordinary character, signed himself Sylvanus Urban, Gent.; and owing to a true journalistic thirst for news, often found himself in trouble with the authorities — more than once in jail. But his magazine flourished; it still exists in altered form. Cave bought himself a pair of horses and an old coach, on the door panels of which, in lieu of a crest, he painted a picture of St. John's Gate, the address of his printing office. Cave was extremely partial to Franklin, and put up a lightning rod on the eastern tower of St. John's Gate long before the invention was generally known. In May of 1750, Cave printed Franklin's letter about pointed conductors — from, he said, "a Gentleman in America, whose ingenious Letters on this Subject will soon be published in a separate pamphlet." Collinson had already told Franklin that he had given the first five letters to Cave, and they were now in press "under the

Inspection and Correction of our Learned and Ingenious Friend Dr. Fothergill." Mr. Cave was slow — what publisher is not? A full year passed before the engraving illustrations were ready; meanwhile Franklin had time to make corrections and to send more "Observations" for inclusion.

The letters to Collinson made up a pamphlet of eighty-six pages, selling for two shillings sixpence, entitled, "Experiments and Observations on Electricity, Made at *Philadelphia* in *America*, by Mr. Benjamin Franklin, and Communicated in several Letters to Mr. Collinson of *London*, F.R.S."

The book at once excited comment — more comment, it is said, than if all five letters had appeared separately in the *Philosophical Transactions*. Joseph Priestley, in his *History of Electricity* (1767) said there was hardly any language into which the letters had not been translated, and that it was "not easy to say, whether we are most pleased with the simplicity and perspicuity with which the author proposes every hypothesis of his own, or the noble frankness with which he relates his mistakes, when they were corrected by subsequent experiments."

No philosophical treatise had been composed in such a style. Franklin never hesitated to put himself into his reports, provided it seemed pertinent. Reading them, one is reminded of Sir Edward Coke's famous and lively law reports, a century earlier, of which Francis Bacon said severely that they contained too much *de proprio* — too much of Coke himself. Throughout the letters to Collinson, one feels the drive of Franklin's impatience, holding back, before committing the thing to paper, until he could be sure. "These Explanations of the Power and Operation of POINTS," he writes, "when they first occurred to me, and while they floated in my Mind, appear'd perfectly satisfactory: But now I have wrote them, and considered them more closely in black and white, I must own, I have some Doubts about them. Yet as I have at present Nothing better to offer in their Stead, I do not cross them out: for even a bad Solution read, and it's Faults discovered, has often given Rise to a good one in the Mind of an ingenious Reader."

"Nor is it of much Importance to us," Franklin continued, "to know the Manner in which Nature executes her Laws; 'tis enough, if we know the Laws themselves. 'Tis of real Use to know, that China left in the Air unsupported, will fall and break; but how it comes to fall, and why it breaks, are Matters of Speculation. 'Tis a Pleasure indeed to know them, but we can preserve our China without it." Newton himself had confessed that he had not been able to discover the cause of gravity, but that "to us it is enough that gravity does really exist . . . and abundantly serves to account for all the motions of the celestial bodies, and of our sea."

Like every experimenter, Franklin suffered his moments of disheartenment. To Collinson he remarked that the trouble of copying long letters, which might actually contain nothing new or worth reading — seeing the rapidity of progress being made in England — "half discourages me from writing anymore on that Subject. Yet I can not forebear adding a few Observations on Mr. Muschenbroek's wonderful Bottle, vizt. . . ." One thing about the eighteenth century which amazes is the patient and routine way in which correspondents interminably copied out their letters. "I have sent you the fair copy," they write. It is always assumed that these men had "more time" than we have. Actually they must have had less time — worse light after sunset, fewer contrivances to help them on. The months required for a letter to reach England and a reply to come back — three months or five or six — must surely have discouraged. Very often these correspondents mentioned the name of the captain whose ship carried their letter; probably as a way of tracing them.

"Sir," wrote Franklin to Collinson in August of 1747,

"I have lately written two long letters to you on the Sub-ject of Electricity, one by the Governor's Vessel, the other per [Captain] Mesnard. On some further Experiments since, I have observ'd a Phenomenon or two that I cannot at present account for on the Principles laid down in those Letters, and am therefore become a little diffident of my Hypothesis, and asham'd that I have express'd my-self in so positive a manner. In going on with these Ex-periments, how many pretty Systems do we build, which we soon find ourselves oblig'd to destroy! If there is no other Use discover'd of Electricity, this, however, is some thing considerable, that it may *help to make a vain Man humble*."

A person of genius early knows his worth, knows at least that he is quicker than other men, more persistent, perhaps more reckless in pushing on. By the time Frank-lin was fourteen or fifteen he must have been aware of this difference. At seventeen, escaping from Boston, he had faced the world alone. Surely such an experience leaves its mark; independence has taken root — provided the rebel survives. At twenty, Franklin had commenced a rigorous course of personal discipline, aimed, he wrote, toward "the bold and arduous Project of arriving at moral Perfection." He drew up charts and lists to be checked daily against his performance. Little piety is found in these incredible Franklinian diagrams, with their pen-ciled checks and formidable headings: "Temperance . . . Silence . . . Industry . . . Tranquillity." What one for-gets is the urgent need that must have inspired this dis-cipline. Franklin as a youth had shown hot temper, brash-ness, intractability, also a predilection for wild company of both sexes. In those days he must have been far from easy to live with. Yet in middle life and old age, Frank-lin's good nature was proverbial. Always he preferred to turn away anger by a quip — and usually succeeded. Here was a man of strong, tenacious spirit. Yet had anyone suggested a duel with weapons, Franklin would have laughed till his sides ached. If honesty was the best policy, so was good humor. How much of this may have been native, how much acquired, we shall never know. A strong vein of cynicism ran through Franklin. A person who declares there never was a good war or a bad peace is not apt to act on rash impulse in his personal relationships.

"To make a vain Man humble," Franklin wrote to Collinson. Genius cannot be explained by analysis. Yet now, at the very edge of fame, the faults that Franklin confessed and struggled to conquer reveal what he might have been had he not tried so hard for self-control. One of the "faults" was pride; call it an ineradicable consciousness of superior intelligence. All during his life Franklin would chide himself on what he referred to as the sin of pride. His *Autobiography* declares there is no passion so hard to subdue, and that even if a man should conceive that he had properly overcome pride, he would probably be proud of his humility.

To Collinson, Franklin underlined the phrase about making a vain man humble. And so it can be seen, italicized, in the printed text of his book on electricity. Plainly, the ingenuousness of Franklin's style and its consequent charm helped to make his book so widely read.

Dr. John Fothergill wrote what Collinson called "a pretty preface," informing the reader that the manuscript had not been gone over by its author, who indeed "was only apprized of the step while the first sheets were in the press." Dr. Fothergill was one of the pleasantest Englishmen of his time, a physician, a Quaker and a a person possessing real goodness of heart. Later, in London, he came to know Franklin well. His preface reflects the current innocence concerning electricity, and the personal nature of Franklin's contribution. "The experiments which our author relates," says Fothergill, "are most of them peculiar to himself; they are conducted with judgment, and the inferences from them plain and conclusive; though sometimes proposed under the terms of suppositions and conjectures.

"And indeed the scene he opens, strikes us with a pleasing astonishment, whilst he conducts us by a train of facts and judicious reflections, to a probable cause of those phaenomena, which are at once the most awful, and, hitherto, accounted for with the least versimilitude. . . .

"He exhibits to our consideration, an invisible, subtile matter, disseminated through all nature in various proportions. . . . From the similar effects of lightening and electricity our author has been led to make some probable conjectures on the cause of the former; and at the same time, to propose some rational experiments in order to secure ourselves, and those things on which its force is often directed, from its pernicious effects; a circumstance of no small importance to the publick, and therefore worthy of the utmost attention."

As for the famous, now almost legendary story of the kite, it did not appear in Priestley's *History* until later editions, and then only as directions for erecting lightning rods. Franklin's own account in the *Autobiography* is cryptic and all too brief. He speaks of *Experiments and Observations,* and then remarks, "What gave my Book the more sudden and general Celebrity, was the Success of one of it's propos'd Experiments, made by Messrs. Dalibard and Delor, at Marly, for drawing Lightning from the Clouds. This engag'd the public Attention every where. M. Delor, who had an apparatus for experimental Philosophy, and lectur'd in that Branch of Science, undertook to repeat what he call'd the *Philadelphia Experiments,* and after they were performed before the King and Court, all the Curious of Paris flocked to see them. I will not swell this Narrative with an Account of that capital Experiment, nor of the infinite Pleasure I receiv'd in the Success of a similar one I made soon after with a

Kite at Philadelphia, as both are to be found in the Histories of Electricity."

It is thanks to Joseph Priestley that we possess any account at all of Franklin and the kite. Fifteen years after the experiment, Franklin, in London, encouraged Priestley to write his two-volume *History and Present State of Electricity,* and himself checked the kite story before publication. Priestley told it well; his enthusiasm comes through the words: "To demonstrate, in the completest manner possible, the sameness of the electric fluid with the matter of lightning, Dr. Franklin, astonishing as it must have appeared, contrived actually to bring lightning from the heavens, by means of an electrical kite, which he raised when a storm of thunder was perceived to be coming on. . . .

"The Doctor, after having published his method of verifying his hypothesis concerning the sameness of electricity with the matter of lightning, was waiting for the erection of a spire * in Philadelphia to carry his views into execution; not imagining that a pointed rod, of a moderate height, could answer the purpose; when it occurred to him, that, by means of a common kite, he could have a readier and better access to the regions of thunder than by any spire whatever. Preparing, therefore, a large silk handkerchief, and two cross sticks, of a proper length, on which to extend it, he took the opportunity of the first approaching thunder storm to take a walk into a field, in which there was a shed convenient for his purpose. But dreading the ridicule which too commonly attends unsuccessful attempts in science, he communicated his experiment to no body but his son, who assisted him in raising the kite.

"The kite being raised, a considerable time elapsed before there was any appearance of its being electrified.

* Christ Church spire, not yet erected. Currier and Ives were among those responsible for depicting William Franklin, out in the storm with his father, as a boy of twelve or thirteen. Actually, he was a dapper young man of twenty-one.

One very promising cloud had passed over it without any effect; when, at length, just as he was beginning to despair of his contrivance, he observed some loose threads of the hempen string to stand erect, and to avoid one another, just as if they had been suspended on a common conductor. Struck with this promising appearance, he immediately presented his knuckle to the key, and (let the reader judge of the exquisite pleasure he must have felt at that moment) the discovery was complete. He perceived a very evident electric spark. Others succeeded, even before the string was wet, so as to put the matter past all dispute, and when the rain had wetted the string, he collected electric fire very copiously. This happened in June 1752, a month after the electricians in France had verified the same theory, but before he had heard of any thing that they had done."

In the *Pennsylvania Gazette* for October 19, 1752, Franklin gave directions for carrying out the experiment — about four months after he had tried it himself. There is nothing dramatic about his statement. It is terse, and easy to follow. Franklin has a little foreword: "As frequent Mention is made in the News Papers from Europe, of the Success of the Philadelphia Experiment for drawing the Electric Fire from Clouds by Means of Pointed Rods of Iron erected on high Buildings, &c., it may be agreeable to the Curious to be inform'd, that the same Experiment has succeeded in Philadelphia, tho' made in a different and more easy Manner, which any may try, as follows.

"Make a small Cross of two light Strips of Cedar, the Arms so long as to reach to the four Corners of a large thin Silk Handkerchief. . . ."

CHAPTER FIVE

Franklin is famous. The Gold Medal
and the Abbé Nollet. Franklin's
friends in science. He founds
the American Philosophical Society.

When Priestley said that nothing ever written about electricity was more generally read and admired in all parts of Europe than Franklin's published letters to Collinson, he did not exaggerate. Not only were the lightning rods cheap and easy to erect, but the kite experiment held something of the miraculous. So simple a notion and so daring! Why had no one thought of it before? Franklin, they said, was a modern Prometheus, drawing down lightning from the skies; God grant he suffer not Prometheus's punishment. In every age, people have demanded why it is that an invention, a discovery, occurs at a certain moment of history and is achieved by one man or a small group of extraordinary men. Whence comes this contagion, this sudden urgency in the air?

The times were ripe, people say, centuries later, and men rose to the occasion. This is true on the face of it; true also that Franklin came along at a lucky moment, propitious for his scientific achievements. Yet this is not a total explanation, nor does it help to say that chance favors the prepared mind. We do not even know if Franklin possessed unusual manual dexterity, as sometimes happens with scientists who have made notable discoveries; no fellow worker has left evidence that Franklin was especially deft in handling instruments. When an idea required a machine, a new tool to bring it to birth and make it effective, Franklin knew how to describe the same to skilled artisan friends who worked often at his side.

And while Franklin could not reckon by higher mathematics, he had a masterful way with numbers, as witness his magic squares and circles. He first devised these when sitting as clerk of the Pennsylvania Assembly, bored with proceedings: the ineptness of both political parties — Proprietary on the one hand and Quakers on the other. He began his mathematical doodling with a square of eight, went on to a square of sixteen and then a "Matic Circle of Circles," as he called it. When these devices appeared in later editions of Franklin's "book on electricity" as it was called, the author was again apologetic; the squares and circles were "of no use." * Yet they show a mental concentration and readiness which seems a native gift, something inborn, akin to the ability found now and again in youths of ten who in a few seconds can raise the number 8 to the sixteenth power in their heads. One is reminded, too, of Isaac Newton and the mathematical puzzles that circulated in his time among European philosophers. Newton would let the puzzles lie on his table for weeks; then, coming upon them, would dash off in a few strokes the answers to problems that had required hours of labor on the part of other mathematicians.

---

* Printed by Cave, the actual title was *Experiments and Observations on Electricity, made at Philadelphia, in America, by Mr. Benjamin Franklin, and Communicated in several Letters to Mr. P. Collinson, of London, F.R.S.*

Peter Collinson had written that he expected new things from the New World: "Our Old World is as it were exhausted." Many Europeans, however, found it hard to believe that these great discoveries about the lightning came from across the seas. People were divided in their feelings. Some who admired America wrote poems, using the New World as a symbol of freedom — "where wild in woods the noble savage ran." . . . "O my America, my new-found land!" exclaimed John Donne, apostrophizing his mistress's body. And there were those who scorned North America and all that derived from it. *Experiments Made at Philadelphia* — said the title of Franklin's book. How could the American forests have produced a mind so sophisticated, so *reasonable?* From what library, what university did this knowledge, this mastery derive? America was a place to which convicts were shipped in order to rid England of them. Dr. Samuel Johnson, in his biography of the poet Waller, remarked that Waller's eldest son was disinherited and "sent to New Jersey, as wanting common understanding." Did not the city of Philadelphia stand somewhere in this vicinity?

Yet perhaps it was fitting, as Collinson implied, that seeds sown in virgin soil should produce minds of fresh understanding.

Franklin's renown did not come all at once; he never waked to find himself famous. But fame arrived fast enough, once the lightning rod became common property. Having refused to patent his "chamber fireplace," Franklin refused also to patent the lightning rod. He worked, as every man of genuine talent has worked, for the fulfillment of his own need, his curiosity, the urgent demands of his nature. Then he turned the results over to society. Franklin gave himself no credit for this; philanthropy was not part of the self-pride he deplored. In later life, Franklin became celebrated for wiliness in the world of European diplomacy, and tricks for outwitting the adversary. *Poor Richard,* moreover, early advocated getting the best of one's competitors. Franklin was not a Quaker, but he possessed the Quaker's concern for helping others; when as a youth he had read Mather's *Essays to Do Good,* Franklin took them to heart. His private life never grew remote from family and friends. His older brother, John, in Rhode Island, suffered from the stone. One winter, in the midst and heat of his electrical experiments, Franklin devised a flexible catheter, went to a silversmith and sat by until the instrument was finished, then sent it with a long letter, explaining how, if the catheter did not suffice, it could be adjusted.

In the summer of 1752, the sentry box experiments were repeated in England. That September, Franklin put up a lightning rod on his own Philadelphia house, with two bells attached to give notice when the rod became charged. The lightning flashed, the bells rang vigorously — all too vigorously, it is said, for Deborah's contentment. King Louis of France sent a message to the Royal Society, commending M. Franklin of Pennsylvania for his useful discoveries in electricity. . . . On receipt of the royal message, Franklin confessed to Dr. Jared Eliot (the New England clergyman and scientist) that his crest was "a little elevated." Had Eliot heard of the girl who was observed to grow suddenly proud, and "None could guess the Reason, till it came to be known that she had got on a pair of new silk garters."

In July of 1753, Harvard gave Franklin the degree of Master of Arts, for "his great Improvements in Philosophic Learning, and particularly with Respect to Electricity, Whereby his Repute hath been greatly advanced in the learned World, not only in Great Britain, but ev'n in the Kingdom of France also." Yale followed with a like honor. It was December of the same year before the Royal Society of London had a full report of the kite experiment; ten months later they awarded Franklin the coveted Copley Gold Medal. Peter Collinson sent the medal to Philadelphia by a young friend of Franklin's. Holding it in his hand, Franklin saw on its face Minerva depicted, offering a laurel wreath, at her feet the symbols of science. Collinson forwarded also the speech of the Earl of Macclesfield, president of the Society, announcing the presentation — an elaborate oration, sprinkled with fancy phrases about "the book of nature being a large and comprehensive volume . . . electricity alone the cause of that tremendous appearance, whose effects prove frequently so fatal to many parts of this terraqueous globe."

A very handsome speech, Franklin called it. There was no doubt the medal pleased him. Collinson advised that a short letter of thanks "will be Well taken as you are the First person out of the Nation that has had that Honour confer'd." (Macclesfield had been careful to state that "Benjamin Franklin Esqr. of Pennsilvania, who, though he be not a Fellow of this Society nor an Inhabitant of this Island, is a Subject of the Crown of Great Britain.") Franklin's reply, in beautiful penmanship, with flourishes worthy of the subject, can be seen today at the Royal Society. "Gentlemen," he wrote in part, "I know not whether any of your learned Body have attain'd the ancient boasted Art of multiplying Gold; but you have certainly found the Art of making it infinitely *more valuable. . . .*"

Franklin's ability to raise a smile — indeed, his inability to let such an occasion pass — would throughout life bring him at the same time success and suspicion. Solemn wits (as Francis Bacon called them) are fearful of a man who jests on serious subjects. No one on whom the Royal Society had bestowed its favors, Franklin added, could have a higher sense of the honor than himself.

Franklin needed the support of scientific colleagues abroad. His electrical theories did not lack their detractors. The clergy fulminated, condemning the experiments as impious and presumptuous, a tampering with God's arrangements. Here was no doctor of philosophy, but a common artisan, a printer. "You must remember, Sir," wrote one Frenchman to another, "how much we ridiculed M. *Franklin's* project for emptying clouds of their thunder, and that we could scarce conceive him to be any other than an imaginary Being." French electricians developed into *Franklinists* and *anti-Franklinists.* Chief among the latter was the Abbé Nollet, once DuFay's assistant, now the principal electrician of France, tutor to the Dauphin, and installed in a laboratory at Versailles. When Franklin's book appeared in French, Nollet was beside himself. "He could not at first believe," wrote Franklin afterward, "that such a Work came from America, and said it must have been fabricated by his Enemies at Paris, to decry his System."

Dalibard himself had translated the book into French; his preface did not so much as mention Nollet — an affront not to be borne. "The Abbé is dying of chagrin," wrote Buffon, the naturalist. Nollet did his best to persuade the Académie des Sciences that the "Philadelphia experiments" had never been confirmed. Failing this, he published a series of essays in letter form, six of them addressed to Franklin and couched in a tone highly condescending. Franklin told a friend, Cadwallader Colden, that the abbé "imagines he has taken me all to pieces. In one or two Places, he seems to apply to the superstitious Prejudices of the Populace, which I think unworthy of a Philosopher: He speaks as if he thought it Presumption in Man, to propose guarding himself against the *Thunders of Heaven!* Surely the Thunder of Heaven is no more supernatural than the Rain, Hail, or Sunshine of Heaven, against the Inconveniencies of which we guard by Roofs and Shades without Scruple. But I can now ease the Gentleman of This Apprehension; for by some late

Experiments I find, that it is not Lightning from the Clouds that strikes the Earth, but Lightning from the Earth that Strikes the Clouds. They are electrified negatively and the Earth positively."

Franklin considered answering the abbé, and even began a reply but thought better of it, concluding, he said later, "to let my Papers shift for themselves, believing it was better to spend what time I could spare from public Business in making new Experiments, than in Disputing about those already made." Peter Collinson, more amused than angry, took up the defense. The abbé, he wrote, looked on himself as prince of electricians. "But on a Sudden Springs up a Little Cloud from the West that Eclipses all his brightness." Dalibard and Buffon, Collinson went on, were giving the abbé no quarter. Nollet had gone so far as to erect a machine at Paris to repeat and disqualify Franklin's experiments, and had collected friends to vouch as witnesses. "Undoubtedly," wrote Collinson, "all the City would have rung with it." At this point, a nobleman who had seen the Dalibard experiment with the sentry box suddenly appeared on the scene and exposed Nollet's entire operation as a hoax, "found out the Juggle and Contrivance," wrote Collinson, "gave them their Due in high Language and publish'd the base and Juggling Intention all over Paris."

Even today, physicists are impressed with Franklin's accomplishment, lacking, as he did, all technical training and having only a slight communication with physicists abroad. Robert Millikan, who had declared the single-fluid theory to be the basis on which subsequent advances in electricity were to rest, went so far as to place Franklin among fifteen scientists who, from Copernicus to the twentieth century, have had the most influence. In Millikan's list, Franklin comes fifth, following Copernicus, Galileo, Newton and Huygens.

After considering such encomiums, it is salutary to note

Franklin's letter to his brother John in Rhode Island. John had written that his sufferings from the stone were somewhat abated. Franklin replied that the news gave him much pleasure, then added, after the fashion of younger brothers down the centuries: "You have never mention'd any thing to me of my Electrical Papers nor of that on the Peopling of Countries, nor that on Meteorology, which have passed thro your Hands; So I conclude you have either not had time to read them, or do not like them. . . . I am your Affectionate Brother, B. Franklin."

As Franklin's work in electricity progressed, his friends became more than ever important to his scientific career — the men who encouraged him from abroad as well as everyday associates like his neighbors, Thomas Hopkinson, Ebenezer Kinnersley, and Philip Syng, who worked at Franklin's side and to whom his book on electricity gives full credit. Of these, Kinnersley's name became best known; he gave a course of lectures on "The Newly Discovered Electric Fire." Philip Syng came originally from Ireland, where his father had styled himself "Goldsmith and Gentleman." Syng, a fine craftsman, made the inkpot that sits today on Washington's desk at Independence Hall. He sired twenty-one children, most of them girls, and lived to the ripe age of eighty-five.

Franklin in youth had chosen as companions witty young men, highly undependable, to whom he was forever lending money or books, and who never repaid the debt. John Collins, the youth who had persuaded the ship captain to help Franklin away from Boston in the year 1723, possessed, said Franklin afterward, "a wonderful Genius for Mathematical Learning." But Collins took to the brandy bottle, lost all he had at gambling, and borrowed from Franklin to pay not only his landlady but his ship passage to Philadelphia, "which prov'd," said Frank-

lin, "extreamly inconvenient to me." Of James Ralph,
who accompanied Franklin to England when the two
were not yet twenty, Franklin remarked that he "never
knew a prettier Talker . . . ingenious, genteel in his
Manners, and extreamly eloquent." Yet Ralph as we have
seen, went off to the English countryside, using Franklin's name instead of his own, and Franklin's money.
Hugh Meredith, Franklin's first partner in the printing
business, possessed an incurable propensity to drink; eventually disappeared to North Carolina, reappeared, went
off again with a parcel of Franklin's books valued at
thirty pounds, and never was heard from further. Even
Franklin's early patrons let him down miserably, like Governor Keith of Pennsylvania, who had sent Franklin at
eighteen off to London with fine promises of introduc-
tions to influential people — then reneged on his promises.

By the time he was forty, Franklin had more sense, and
better judgment in choosing those he trusted. His friends
in science proved from first to last of high caliber, not
only reputable but truly fascinating characters. Franklin
reacted strongly to pompous people. A modern mathematician, Jacob Bronowski, says that science as a profession
attracts men whose temperament is "grave, awkward, and
absorbed." Perhaps it was their amateur status which
allowed certain eighteenth-century philosophers to remain at the same time lighthearted and devoted to study.

Of all the goodly company in England and America,
Peter Collinson was the most important to Franklin's
scientific career. It has been truly said that Collinson introduced Franklin to the world. Collinson was the moving spirit in a group whom Franklin would soon know
well in London: William Watson, Dr. Fothergill, Sir
John Pringle, Joseph Priestley, Richard Price, John Mitchell. Peter Collinson had early left the Society of Friends,
but retained always the Quaker simplicity of manner.

The Gainsborough portrait shows a pleasant face with a lofty brow, keen, intelligent eyes and a generous mouth. The artist painted him characteristically, sitting with quill pen in hand, writing a letter. Collinson corresponded with botanists all over the world; his countinghouse in London — he dealt in "mens' mercery" — served as a receiving and forwarding place for seeds and specimens from Linnaeus in Sweden, Gronovius in Leyden, and botanists in New England, Virginia, and the Carolinas. Extremely successful in business, Collinson was in a position to know everybody. Lords as well as scholars came to his house, Mill Hill, near London: Sir Hans Sloane of the Royal Society, Lord Petre, famous for his gardens in Essex, and that fervent and erratic Scotsman and botanical collector, Lord Bute. Collinson's own gardens could show more than fifty American plants, and he introduced a hundred and seventy-one new specimens to England. The Royal Society printed many of his articles in their *Transactions;* the *Gentlemen's Magazine* published some forty-five. One of his papers entered into a debate that had been raging since the thirteenth century: Collinson said that swallows do *not* spend their winters under the mud of ponds, and he went about proving it by their anatomy.

Among Collinson's American correspondents was Cadwallader Colden, whom Franklin first met in 1743. Colden lived up the Hudson River on his vast estate, Coldengham, in Orange County. He belonged to the Governor's Council of the Province, served as surveyor general and would eventually act as lieutenant governor. Colden was extremely knowledgeable about Indians — experience which would soon be of much help to Franklin. But Colden's true interest lay in natural philosophy, where he ranged "with more genius than erudition," one of his enemies said, over all subjects, from mathematics to medicine and botany. Franklin relied greatly on

Colden; their mutual letters are enchanting. "I must own that I am much in the *Dark* about *Light*," Franklin wrote when studying the corpuscular theory. Again, concerning the possibilities inherent in electrical experimentations — "We are got beyond the Skill of Rabelais's Devils of two Year old, who . . . had only learnt to thunder and lighten a little round the Head of a Cabbage."

The letters must have entertained the Royal Society. Who else gave such a turn to abstruse subjects? As for Cadwallader Colden, the great Linnaeus called him *"Summus Perfectus,"* named one of his plants Coldenia, and was so struck by Colden's classification of the specimens near his estate that he spoke in his book of *Plantae Coldenhamiae*. In his sixties, Colden's eyes failed, and he taught his daughter to draw plants; Jane Colden was the first woman in the New World to be distinguished as a botanist. "What is marvelous," wrote Collinson to Linnaeus, "his daughter is perhaps the first lady that has so perfectly studied the system."

There is something moving in the story of these early American scientists, so persistent in the face of ignorance. One of them was Dr. Alexander Garden of South Carolina, who collected and sent to Europe many specimens of plants, fish, and reptiles — very much the gentleman, a Loyalist in the Revolution. In the 1750's, Garden traveled north for his health, met Cadwallader Colden, John Bartram and Franklin. When he got home, Garden wrote despairingly to Linnaeus, saying how happy he would be to pass his time with men "so distinguished by genius, acuteness, and liberality, as well as by eminent botanical learning and experience." And how unfortunate that, instead, he must live in South Carolina, "a horrid country, where is not a living soul who knows the least iota of Natural History."

Charleston contained, however, one other natural philosopher, with whom Franklin corresponded concerning electricity and the matter of bodily heat and loss of weight in perspiration. Dr. John Lining, an amazing man, was a pioneer in the study of metabolism; his work had great value. To contemporaries he was "the celebrated Dr. Lining . . . the ingenious Dr. Lining," and small wonder. For a year, using the new Fahrenheit thermometer, Lining set down the daily rainfall, humidity and force of the wind; at the same time recording his weight morning and evening, his pulse rate, daily intake of food and water, and the weight of his excretions. The Royal Society published his findings in their *Transactions* for January, 1743.

John Bartram, the Philadelphia botanist and collector, was, next to Benjamin Franklin, surely the most interesting among all the mid- and late-eighteenth-century natural philosophers in America. Nobody sent and received so many seeds as Bartram; nobody was so stubborn and assiduous — except perhaps Bartram's son, William, who for two years, during the American Revolution, traveled from Pennsylvania to Florida and the Mississippi River, collecting specimens, and wrote about it without once mentioning the war or the conflict. (The Seminole Indians called William Pric-Puggy, the Flower Hunter.) Father and son lived at Kingsessing on a farm they worked themselves; his father built the stone house which can be seen today, with a misspelled Greek inscription over the lintel.*

John Bartram was self-taught, but he had learned enough Latin to read Linnaeus's classifications. Linnaeus called Bartram the greatest contemporary "natural botanist" in the world. The number of American plants in England doubled largely because of his activity. The most independent man alive, he was read out of the Society of

* Bartram's farm, on the banks of the Schuylkill, in his time three miles from town, is now a botanical garden, charming to visit. Franklin and (later) Washington often drove there to rest and talk.

Friends for denying the divinity of Christ, but kept right on attending Meeting. On the outer wall of his house Bartram carved the words: "It is God alone Almighty Lord the Holy One, by me adored." Bartram was rude to his social superiors, freed the slaves on his place, who stayed on as his paid servants, and always had them sit down with him at table, no matter what guests were present. Peter Collinson looked after Bartram, eventually procuring him a pension from King George; Bartram complained that it was too small. Franklin was very fond of Bartram, addressing him in letters from abroad as "My dear old Friend."

James Logan of Philadelphia had been the first to encourage Bartram, giving him botanical books, explaining Linnaeus's system and urging Bartram to use the microscope. Peter Collinson even referred to Bartram as "Logan's pupil." Logan, a Quaker, had come over with William Penn in 1699 and had waxed rich and important, serving the Province in many capacities, including a term as acting governor. Logan's library at Stenton numbered over three thousand volumes. Natural philosophy, and especially botany, was his chosen field; the Royal Society published various of his treatises. Logan's presence was commanding, his bearing aristocratic. One cannot love him, but neither can his importance be overlooked. Collinson wrote often to him.

The correspondence between scientists in England, Europe and America remained close, enduring and heartening. From Coldengham John Bartram first explored the Catskill Mountains; Linnaeus sent his favorite pupil, Peter Kalm, to Coldengham on his way up the Hudson. It was as a very young man, hungry for discussion and the exchange of ideas, that Franklin had started the Junto. But when he began to know such botanists as Collinson, Colden, Bartram and the rest, Franklin felt the need of something on a higher scale, an association of scholars and philosophers, almost in the nature of an academy. Bartram had been first with the idea. Franklin wrote out a plan, which he printed and sent to friends in America and England. The society, said Franklin, was to consist of "Virtuosi or ingenious Men residing in the several Colonies, to be called *The American Philosophical Society;* who are to maintain a constant Correspondence."

Franklin's Society, after one or two lapses, was to last through the centuries.* Well aware, however, that to all but a few knowledgeable friends in England and Europe, the notion of an American Philosophical Society might seem a contradiction in terms (where in the North American wilderness were philosophers to be found?), Franklin set out a little preface or explanation:

A PROPOSAL [he wrote] for Promoting USEFUL KNOWLEDGE among the British Plantations in America.

The first Drudgery of Settling new Colonies, which confines the Attention of People to mere Necessaries, is now pretty well over; and there are many in every Province in Circumstances that set them at Ease, and afford Leisure to cultivate the Finer Arts, and improve the common Stock of Knowledge. To such of these who are Men of Speculation, many Observations occur, which if well examined, pursued and improved, might produce Discoveries to the Advantage of some or all of the British Plantations, or to the Benefit of Mankind in general.

A correspondence, "already begun by some intended Members," was to be kept up with the Royal Society of London, and with the Dublin Society. James Logan

* The American Philosophical Society for Promoting Useful Knowledge limits its membership, which is honorary, to five hundred residents and one hundred foreign names. In its old building next door to Independence Hall the Society holds meetings twice a year, where scientists, artists, and professors of the humanities, read papers and enjoy discussion and conviviality. Franklin's portrait, painted by David Martin, looks down upon the philosophers, among whom can be numbered more than one hundred and thirty Nobel Prize winners, living or dead.

for some reason refused to take part in the plans, though
he had been glad to sponsor the Junto and the Library
Company. It would have been pleasant, wrote Bartram,
to have Logan's name at the top of the members' list:
"However we resolved that his not favouring the design
should not hinder our attempt, and if he would not go
along with us we would Jog along without him."

Franklin's proposal went into detail as to the annual
collection and printing of experiments, discoveries, improvements — anything that would "let Light into the
Nature of Things, tend to increase the Power of Man
over Matter, and multiply the Conveniences or Pleasures
of Life." Cotton Mather would never have included
pleasure in such a prospectus. But Franklin had moved
very far from puritanism and the New England spiritual
austerities. "Happiness is an idea new in Europe," young
Saint-Just was to tell the French Convention forty years
later. Not quite so new in America, where the weight of
caste, the ancient boundaries of social class did not bear
down. Franklin would never devise a life-plan, for himself or his friends, that did not include the pursuit of
happiness. As with Thomas Jefferson, something in Franklin's nature, the way his blood ran in his veins, demanded
it.

SCENE THREE

THE
ALBANY CONGRESS
OF 1754,
AND FRANKLIN'S
PLAN OF UNION

CHAPTER SIX

Franklin moves from the local to the
Continental scene. The Indians and the
French in North America. Franklin
writes his "Short Hints towards a Scheme
for Uniting the Northern Colonies."

*GEORGE THE SECOND by the Grace of God of
Great Britain France and Ireland, King Defender
of the Faith, and so forth, To Our Trusty and Well beloved John Penn, Richard Peters, Isaac Norris and Benjamin Franklin of the City of Philadelphia, Esqrs. Greet-
ing. . . ."*

The royal instructions that followed were plain, for
all their high-flown language and medieval ring. The
four Philadelphians were to travel to the town of Albany,
as representatives at an intercolonial conference with the
Indians. They were to deliver His Majesty's presents to
"our loving and good Allies the Six United Nations" of
Iroquois, and achieve with them a firm alliance, *"renew-
ing the Covenant Chain,"* for the purpose of defense
against the dangerous and immediate encroachments of
the French king, *"whose Subjects have actually marched
into and Erected Forts and Committed Hostilities within
the known limits of Our Dominions."*

For Pennsylvania as for New York, Indian confer-
ences were no new story. Ever since William Penn's day
they had been held: at Philadelphia, Lancaster, Carlisle.
Lands had been purchased, grievances aired, the covenant
chain renewed, treaties signed, promises given that em-
braced generations yet unborn. But of all such meetings,
the projected conference at Albany was to be the most
important and to boast the most distinguished membership. No previous Indian conference had been ordered
from England, all others being locally inspired by needs
of the moment. This time the need was greater, the
French threat more pressing. That powerful body called
the Board of Trade and Plantations, sitting in London,
had invited to the conference all the colonies north of
the Potomac — nine of them. Governor Hamilton had
chosen the Pennsylvania delegates: two from his Council
(John Penn and Richard Peters), representing the Proprietors of the Province; two from the Assembly (Isaac
Norris and Benjamin Franklin), representing the popular
side of government — and Conrad Weiser, Indian agent
and provincial interpreter.

The choice of Franklin as delegate was natural enough.
Not only had he a hand deep in the political business of
the Province, but he showed a very real interest in Indian affairs, having traveled out to Carlisle, Pennsylvania,
for an Indian conference only the previous year. His
scientific reputation in England and Europe, his honorary
degrees and fame as a philosopher, would be of help at
Albany; the colonists needed prestige in dealing with the
London Board of Trade. That Franklin could turn so
abruptly from electrical experimentation to the problem
of Indians and colonial union shows a singular flexibility
that was part of his nature — the ability to move from
one activity to another without frustration or loss of bal-
ance. A few years previously, Cadwallader Colden had
announced that he was done forever with New York

politics, having retired in favor of botany and natural philosophy. "I wish you all the Satisfaction that Ease and Retirement from Publick Business can possibly give you," Franklin had replied under the date of October, 1750. "But let not your Love of Philosophical Amusements have more than its due weight with you. Had Newton been Pilot but of a single Ship, the finest of his Discoveries would scarce have excus'd, or atton'd for his abandoning the Helm one Hour in Time of Danger; how much less if she had carried the Fate of the Commonwealth."

High-sounding words, that somehow do not carry the authentic Franklin ring. Indeed, it would be hard to credit their sincerity did we not know that Franklin had followed these same precepts himself . . . as in the year 1747 when, in all the climax and excitement of electrical work, he had stopped to write and print two thousand copies of a pamphlet, "Plain Truth," warning against the very real menace of French privateers on the Delaware River. "Plain Truth" had urged an association of voluntary militia for Pennsylvania's defense — and achieved it, thereby angering Thomas Penn, who denounced such actions as too "independent of Government." Franklin was a dangerous man, Penn told Richard Peters at the time, "of a very uneasy spirit and I should be very glad if he inhabited any other Country."

That had been seven years ago. At Albany in this summer of 1754, Franklin would for the first time move far beyond the local Pennsylvania scene. More than half the North American colonies were included in his plans for union, with a possibility of even wider involvement. As for the Six Nations, everyone north of the Carolinas knew that they comprised the powerful Iroquois confederacy of Mohawks, Senecas, Oneidas, Onondagas, Cayugas, and later the Tuscaroras, who lived along the lakes below Canada and whose Indian empire, with its tributary tribes, reached from the St. Lawrence to the James River and from the Hudson almost to the Mississippi.

Between Iroquois and English the covenant chain had indeed become dangerously corroded. Should the French succeed in seducing away the Iroquois — and the French were masters of such seduction — not only the Hudson and St. Lawrence river forts which controlled the fur trade would fall, but the Ohio region with them. France claimed a huge western area by virtue of La Salle's explorations. England's title to the same region rested on the sea-to-sea charters she had granted to Virginia and Connecticut. The Iroquois stood between the English frontier and the French; hence the Iroquois were important out of all proportion to their numbers. According to Conrad Weiser, the Senecas, Cayugas and Onondagas had already "turned French." In the spring of 1753, French soldiers had made their way from Canada down to the Ohio valley, capturing the unfinished English fort and naming it Duquesne, after their governor. Virginia had sent a young Major Washington of the provincial militia to parley with the French or drive them out, but he had been forced to carry home a defiant French answer.

Shall France remain here or shall she not? The most momentous question, it has been said, ever brought to issue on the North American continent. Benjamin Franklin would not have put it in those words, but since boyhood he had been conscious of the threat. This very present danger was part of his heritage, it spoke not only to his mind but to his blood. By 1754 the English outnumbered the French twenty to one in North America, an advantage the enemy offset by incomparable skill in the forests as *voyageurs* and *coureurs de bois;* the frontier called them bush lopers. A Frenchman in the woods, on the rivers, was not a white man aping a Mohawk. He

94

was a Mohawk, smeared his skin with bear grease in summer against the insects, could read the forest signs, endure backbreaking hardships of winter journeyings in the snow. The English, established at Albany, Oswego and points northwest, received the beaver skins collected by Indians. But the Frenchman in savage territory often enough took up his gun and a sack of parched corn and went off alone with one Seneca paddler, leaving at the encampment a Seneca wife whom he treated, all things considered, with surprising respect.

Since 1690, there had been three wars with the French — each conflict bearing a name that echoed the current war in Europe. Franklin's father in Massachusetts had lived through King William's War in the 1690's. Queen Anne's war had lasted from 1702 to 1713; in Europe it was the War of the Spanish Succession. The War of the Austrian Succession, called King George's War in America, took place in the 1740's and was still a live issue in colonial minds. (New York complained that Massachusetts had not yet paid her share of the bounty money.) And if these struggles commenced in Europe between monarchs hungry for empire, in America men fought for their own reasons: for trade and territory, for retaliation or religion or for sport, but above all because the enemy was at hand, a constant threat, an unending harassment. Successive treaties, made in Europe for Europeans — the "Peace" of Ryswick, of Utrecht, of Aix-la-Chapelle — settled nothing and signified little in America. War or no war the fighting continued; blockhouses were besieged and burned, farmers scalped in the fields, women and children brutally murdered. "I gave leave to the Indians at their request," ran the report of a French commander in 1746, "to continue their fighting and ravaging in small parties, towards Albany, Schenectady, Deerfield, or wherever they pleased, and I even gave them a few officers and cadets to lead them."

For a hundred years the country around Albany had been an international battleground. Always the French seemed to seize the initiative. True, a New England army, supported by a British fleet, in 1745 had captured the great French fortress of Louisbourg in Nova Scotia. To avenge it, Admiral d'Anville next year sailed his fleet from Brest — forty ships of war and a hundred transports filled with veteran soldiers — purposing to recapture Louisbourg and ravage the coast as far south as he could. Storm and pestilence destroyed d'Anville's ships and his men. The admiral died with them — it was said by his own hand, in grief and despair. New England saw it as the will of God and gave thanks. From Boston pulpits, preachers reminded joyful congregations of the year 1588 and the like fate of a Spanish Armada. But in the very next peace treaty — 1748 — England returned Louisbourg to France as exchange for Madras in India, thereby undermining New England loyalties, perhaps forever.

Up and down the great rivers stood forts bearing French names: St-Frédéric, La Galette, Pontchartrain, Le Boeuf, linking Canada with the huge territory of French Louisiana — two powerful bastions reaching to the Mississippi. Florida of course belonged to Spain. The French — there was no doubt of it — were trying to coop up the English colonies between the Alleghenies and the sea, "laying a solid foundation," William Clarke wrote to Franklin, "for being, some time or other, Sole Masters of this Continent, notwithstanding our present Superiority to them, in point of numbers."

The trouble was, the colonies persisted in acting separately, while the French moved as a unit, commanded by one supreme authority. Yet ever since their establishment, the colonies had been trying to unite, in groups of three or four at a time. In 1643, a New England confederacy, complete with "XII Articles," was approved by the General Court. William Penn's plan included nine colonies, joined together "for one another's peace and safety with an universall concurrence"; each colony represented by "two persons well qualified for sence sobriety and substance." There was a plan from Virginia, one from New York and another from Carolina. Pennsylvania's governor, alarmed, advised that it would be wiser to keep these colonies separate and jealous, "for while they continue so it is morally impossible that any dangerous Union can be form'd among them." Nevertheless the Board of Trade itself early recommended that New York and Massachusetts Bay combine for mutual security and defense, and in 1721 the Board suggested that the provinces "from Nova Scotia to South Carolina" be put under one captain general whose councillors would come "from each plantation." A certain Earl of Stair had even been fixed on as a fit person. But the Board desired the colonies to pay the charges, which was enough to ruin any plan at the outset. Governor Dinwiddie of Virginia indicated, as late as 1752, that it might be well to have the colonies form two districts, a northern and a southern, in each of which some supervising power be established.

Few of the plans were adopted; none of them lasted. Thirteen colonies not only had different economic interests, but they operated for the most part under different political systems. Rhode Island and Connecticut were the only two chartered governments among thirteen, and proud of it. "Popular governments," Franklin would have called them. Attempts at union they looked on as a hazard to certain civil freedoms not possessed by crown colonies like New York and Virginia, or Proprietary Provinces such as Pennsylvania and Maryland. Rhode Island and Connecticut even elected their own governors — a privilege unheard of anywhere else.

Nevertheless, union was in the air. Men did not like to think about it or dwell upon it, preferring to concentrate on their own particular grievances or ambitions. But the idea was current, familiar; it would not come as a surprise. Franklin had studied every plan; he was primed against every argument. Nor did he forget a certain oration made by an Indian chief at the conference of 1744 in Lancaster, Pennsylvania. That extraordinary Onondaga sachem, Canasatego, in the erect and brawny majesty of his sixty years, had stood before the conference and advised the English to form among themselves some league of unity to make them strong. "Union and amity between the Five Nations," said Canasatego, "have made us formidable. We are a powerful confederacy, and by your observing the same methods our wise forefathers have taken, you will acquire fresh strength and power. Therefore, whatever befalls you, never fall out with one another."

Benjamin Franklin knew about Canasatego and what he said; his press at Philadelphia printed the Lancaster treaty and would print twelve others — beautifully turned out in separate pamphlets. Franklin admired the Indian gift for oratory, the Indian civility and courtesy in conference. To his business partner, James Parker, he wrote in 1751 that he found it, "a very strange thing, if six Nations of ignorant Savages should be capable of forming a Scheme for such an Union, and be able to execute it in such a Manner, as that it has subsisted Ages, and appears indissoluble; and yet that a like Union should be impracticable for ten or a Dozen English Colonies, to whom it is more necessary, and must be more advantageous."

Franklin has been called "friend to the Indians." And indeed, in old age he gave it as his judgment that "almost every war between the Indians and whites had been occasioned by some injustice of the latter toward the former." Franklin of course did not know the Indians as Conrad Weiser knew them, or George Croghan, the western trader, or the remarkable Colonel William Johnson of New York — men who spoke the Indian languages, wore Indian dress and had lived with the savages in their "castles," their longhouses. Fate had set the English colonists among Stone Age savages; in Franklin's eye, all attempts to "convert" these people, make Christians of them, were impertinent as well as useless. Rather, the tribes should be treated with respect, appeased, and won as allies. Franklin would one day write, for the delectation of his French friends, a true tale about Canasatego. How the Virginians, in conference, invited the sachem to send six Indian youths to be educated at their College of William and Mary. How Canasatego with utmost courtesy refused, saying that several of his young people had been brought up at a college in a northern province and had returned ignorant of every means of living in the woods, bad runners, "unable to bear either cold or hunger, build a cabin, take a deer or kill an enemy . . . totally good for nothing." But he would be happy, Canasatego added, to match the offer. "If the gentlemen of Virginia will send us a dozen of their sons, we will take great care of their education, instruct them in all we know, and make *men* of them."

And now Franklin and his fellow delegates set out from Philadelphia toward a city which in terms of French and Indians lay very close to the facts of war. Small wonder the powers in London had selected Albany for this Congress. Called, after the American fashion, a city, Albany contained scarcely more than three thousand inhabitants. But it was the gateway to French Canada and the fur regions of the northwest. From the viewpoint of imperial British policy, no city occupied a position so strategically important. To Albanians it was only by God's mercy their city had not been burned to the ground by the enemy long ago, like Saratoga, Kingston, Hoosick, Schenectady, Deerfield. The Indians spared Albany, where they had often come for conference with the English. To the Iroquois the city was "the place of friendship," due largely to Colonel Peter Schuyler, Albany's first mayor — dead now thirty years but still spoken of by the Mohawks as their friend. "Quidor," they called him affectionately; their version of Peter. Quidor had hunted with the Mohawks in the forest, visited their "castles," and in the year 1710 had taken four Mohawk chiefs to London and introduced them ceremoniously to Queen Anne and the Lords of Trade, hoping thereby to arouse interest in problems of "the northwest frontier" — the Albany region.

It was a Monday morning, June 3, 1754, when the Philadelphia commissioners set off for Albany: John Penn, Richard Peters, Benjamin Franklin, Isaac Norris, and Conrad Weiser. Franklin's natural son, William, almost twenty-three, went along by virtue of his position as clerk of the Pennsylvania Assembly; he had succeeded his father in the post. The role of son to Benjamin Franklin was not easy. Franklin loved his son, whom he called Billy, and enjoyed having him as companion on journeys, here and abroad. Billy had spirit. At fifteen — like his father before him — he ran away, tried to ship on a privateer out of Philadelphia but was found and brought home. Subsequently, Billy enlisted with the troops and spent a winter in camp at Albany, fighting King George's War. Moreover, at nineteen, Billy had traveled with Conrad Weiser and a packtrain out to Logstown on the Ohio River — a hard journey — for the purpose of negotiating with the Iroquois, Delawares, and Shawnees. "A tall proper youth," his father described him at that age, "and much of a beau." In truth, Billy was handsome, open, communicative; people liked him.

The commissioners were to travel overland to New York, thence by sloop up the Hudson River. Counting a stopover in New York City, they would be a good two weeks on the journey. (When people went to Albany they spoke of "embarking," as if they were going to Europe;

it was a three to five days' sail.) Richard Peters had written ahead to a friend in New York, asking him to buy a pipe of the best Madeira and bottle it for the travelers, also a barrel of good cider and two barrels of small beer. "I hope the sloop you hired is a commodious one," added Peters, "with a good-natured steers man. Pray does he find bedding and Tea Furniture?"

At such close quarters it would be well if the delegates found themselves congenial. All but young John Penn were highly experienced in politics, old hands in Assembly and Governor's Council as well as Indian matters. Isaac Norris, at fifty-three, served as Speaker of the House and leader of the Quaker party. Richard Peters was private secretary to the Proprietors — the Penn family — in England. Political climates can shift very rapidly. In a few years (1757) Franklin would throw himself actively against the Penn interests. Yet for the moment, he and Richard Peters were friends, having worked together in the affairs of the Library Company, the English Academy, and the Pennsylvania Hospital. Peters too was older than Franklin. As for young Penn, he had an ax of his own to grind in Albany — a huge commission to achieve, nothing less than to purchase for the Proprietors an enormous tract of Indian land, lying between the Susquehanna River and Lake Erie on the north, and the southwestern frontier of Pennsylvania on the south. As a grandson of William Penn and therefore himself a Proprietor of the Province, John Penn knew this wild region could not be settled until the Indians gave up the land, knew also that Connecticut had well-laid plans to buy and occupy the same territory. This Albany Congress, with the Iroquois already assembled, would be a superb opportunity. Governor Hamilton had officially directed Penn and Richard Peters to "sound out the Indians, when other business will permit, and make a purchase . . . the larger the better."

John Penn himself would have been totally incapable of such a mission; Richard Peters at his side was anything but incapable. Penn had been in America something over a year and a half, and did not like what he had seen. He was a personable man of twenty-four, small of stature with a handsome enough face, hair cropped to his ears and notably well-tailored clothes. The whole Province knew that he was heir to one-fourth of the family holdings — totaling no less than twenty-eight million Pennsylvania acres. With quit-rents at a shilling an acre, the family was reputed to be enormously rich. Franklin himself would publish a quite wild estimate of the Penn fortune, bringing it up to ten million pounds sterling. On paper Franklin may have been right. But who was to collect quit-rents over such a territory? It was impossible. John Penn's Uncle Thomas, in London, an energetic gentleman who ruled the Penn family, said that in fifteen years he had scarcely been able to save a hundred pounds annually.

When young men of good birth in England made "unfortunate alliances," their families were apt to ship them to America. So it had been with John Penn. At eighteen he eloped with the daughter of a London tradesman, whereupon his parents packed him off to school in Geneva, thence to Italy and Philadelphia. Oddly enough, Thomas Penn's agent, Richard Peters, was fugitive for a like reason, having married a servant girl while at Westminster School and been hustled away to the University of Leyden. Eventually, after eight years of Leyden and the Inner Temple law school in London, Peters became an Anglican clergyman and without more ado married a perfectly respectable Miss Stanley, ward of an earl. His first wife's father turned up in the background, and Peters, terrified lest he be arrested for bigamy, fled to Philadelphia.

There is something fascinating about Richard Peters;

no wonder Franklin found him good company. His portrait shows a genial face, with large, dark eyes and dimpled chin. A polished and erudite scholar, Peters not only wrote Greek and Latin, but strangely enough, considering his background, knew about Indians and had been named Indian superintendent of the Province. Even Conrad Weiser, blunt, honest Palatine that he was, respected Peters's way with the savages. "He does not lack affection for them," Weiser had written, early on, "and in time may understand and do their business honestly for them." Peters never succumbed to the temptation to trade with the Indians, remaining thereby in a trusted position; all his business with the tribes was by way of "forest diplomacy," at which he was master — and a tower of strength to the Penn family. At the before-mentioned conference of '44, Peters had met Canasatego; very likely it was from him that Franklin heard about the sachem's refusal of an English education for his brothers. At the Carlisle conference of 1753, the chiefs had urged the English to stay east of the mountains; "their numbers troubled the Indians as much as they troubled the French." When the French came down across Lake Erie and the English crossed the Alleghenies, the Indians were caught, they said, between two edges of a pair of shears, and like a piece of cloth, would be cut to pieces. The usual promises were exchanged, a treaty signed, and presents given. Franklin remembered well the final night of the conference. During official proceedings, liquor had been kept from the savages. "We told them," Franklin wrote afterward, "that if they would continue sober during the treaty, we would give them plenty of rum when business was over." On the fourth night, Franklin and Peters, hearing a great racket out of doors, hurried from their lodging. Around a bonfire on the town square, the Indians, howling drunk, were chasing each other with firebrands, men and women, yelling, said Franklin, like devils in hell. At Carlisle there had been trouble, too, about presents — always a strategic point in dealing with savages. Unsatisfied with the initial offerings, the Indians had refused to begin the talks; commissioners had hurried out to buy more.

Isaac Norris, too, had had much experience with Indians; as early as 1745 he had attended a conference with the Iroquois. Norris, a rich Quaker merchant, actually a Quaker swell, kept his coach and pair, boasted a splendid estate in the northern Liberties — Fair Hill — a fine library and a wife, Sarah, who was daughter to the redoubtable James Logan. Norris wrote fluent Latin and French, but held to his Quaker ways. At the conference of '45, Governor Clinton of New York, son of an English earl, and, like many royal officials, impatient of colonial manners, had been annoyed when Norris kept his hat on indoors, after the Friendly fashion. Norris wore it now, broad-brimmed and black. Brown hair, lined with gray, fell to his shoulders. His eyebrows were dark, his cheeks firm and plump; he looked like a man not troubled with indecision. Strongly anti-Proprietary in politics, Norris would soon be named, with Franklin, agent of the Assembly to fight the Penn interests in England. Norris was a tough, militant pacifist; the Quakers were proud of him.

Four Philadelphians, then, had each his idea to push at Albany: Penn and Peters, a purchase of land for the Proprietors; Franklin, a plan for colonial union with Indians or without them; Norris, a strict adherence to the instructions of his constituents, which urged a treaty with the Iroquois and the delivery of five hundred pounds' worth of Indian presents — together with the avoidance of all further schemes and notions. The Lords of Trade in London had declared for an intercolonial treaty with the Iroquois against the French invaders. And having invited nine colonies to participate, the Lords had been disturbed when only seven accepted. New Jersey, it seems, felt safe and indifferent. When Governor Belcher urged the New Jersey Assembly to send delegates, they said they carried on no trade with the Iroquois and had never been a party to any Indian treaty. Virginia, though she badly needed help in the Ohio region, complained that she had just held an Indian conference of her own out at Winchester, and could not afford another. But Governor Dinwiddie asked Governor De Lancey of New York to act as unofficial representative of Virginia, and was careful to send back to the Iroquois three belts of wampum from Winchester, symbolizing an exchange of goodwill.

The other colonies dispatched their best and finest: justices of the high court and members of the Governor's Council — men whose connections with London, either familial or political, were close. Some of them still lived for the most part in England, such as Peter Wraxall, who was to act as reporter to the Lords of Trade; and Thomas Pownall, the notable Cheshireman whom Franklin had lately met in Philadelphia and who would soon succeed Shirley as governor of Massachusetts. Pownall, like Franklin, favored a union of the colonies. Stephen Hopkins, an immensely capable man, was chief justice of Rhode Island and next year would be governor. From Boston came Judge Thomas Hutchinson, a brilliant figure who would one day be Franklin's implacable enemy. Judge Chandler of Worcester represented the bar and gentry; later, like many Albany delegates, he would be found on the Tory side. Veterans from the famed Louisbourg campaign were looked for, among them Elisha Williams, who in 1745 had acted as chaplain to the New England troops.

Conrad Weiser was in great hopes that Colonel William Johnson of New York would attend the conference and help with translation. Weiser, German-born, had lived with the Iroquois in his youth and been adopted into the Onondaga tribe. But his Indian was rusty, he said, and he felt shy about parading it before such an assembly. Whereas Colonel Johnson, that wild Irishman, did not know the meaning of the word diffidence. Twenty years ago, Johnson had come over from Ireland to manage the vast Mohawk Valley lands of his uncle, Admiral Sir Peter Warren, one of the richest men in England. In no time at all, Johnson himself owned some five hundred thousand acres, gained in a fur trade which he carried on quite independently of the Albanian Dutch *haendlers*. His house, Mount Johnson, was a center and camping place for the Iroquois. Coarse, brave, eloquent, Johnson ate dog flesh with his Mohawk friends, took their daughters to wife and sired a crowd of half-breed children. The Indians called him "Warraghiyagey," and adored him. The French on their upper portages knew and dreaded the sound of Warraghiyagey's jew's harps and hawkbells, of which Johnson had distributed over ten thousand. Albany had not forgotten that day of 1746 when Johnson, stripped and painted, led his whooping Mohawk warriors through the streets. No Englishman ever had such influence with the savages. "I apprehend," Johnson wrote the Lords of Trade, "that the colonies have all along neglected to cultivate a proper understanding with the Indians, and from a mistaken notion have greatly despised them, without considering that it is in their power to lay waste and destroy the frontiers. This opinion has risen from our confidence in our scattered numbers, and the parsimony of our people, who, from an error in politics, would not expend five pounds to save twenty."

Plainly, the delegates at Albany could show a dazzling diversity. Of them all, Franklin proved the best known, a world figure. In person he was erect, sturdy, wore his brown hair to his shoulders and a short wig when formally dressed. His eyes, full-lidded, looked out boldly, his forehead was broad and high, his clothes and linen neat, and worn with style. In the height of manly vigor, Franklin showed as yet nothing of the serene sage of later years whose eccentricities (coonskin hat and lively, ungrammatical French) would charm the Parisians.

Having sailed across the bay from Staten Island Point — it took an hour and a half — the travelers spent the night in a New York coffeehouse and tavern. Next morning, a Thursday, Peters and Conrad Weiser went combing the city for presents to the Indians; they had had enough experience in being caught short. The Pennsylvania Assembly did not enjoy voting that five hundred pounds. Moreover, the Assembly had expected the presents to be bought in Philadelphia, for the benefit of local merchants. Peters, however, balked at having to carry all those wagonloads overland to New York. Also he hoped — he wrote ahead, it would "ingratiate the Pennsylvania delegates with the good people of New York, for laying out our money in their government."

Vermilion by the pound for painting faces and bodies; thousands of flints for guns. . . . Bar lead and shot, knives, brass kettles, strouds (the red and blue English-made cloth that Indians loved). . . . Blankets, gartering, ribbons, bed lacing, beaded shags, powder ("not Hair Powder but Gun Powder," wrote Peters, facetiously). Guns! Above all, guns, "of which," added Peters, "be particular as to their Goodness as well as Price, for a slight Gun is an arrant Frenchman as it will deceive the poor Indian who trusts it."

In New York, Franklin left all this to Peters and Weiser. He needed time by himself to plan his strategy — the most palatable way to present at Albany the idea of intercolonial union. Not a union merely for the purpose of defeating the French, as conceived by the Board

of Trade in London. Franklin saw the chance of a last-
ing confederacy, effective in peace as well as in war — a
better arrangement of all the colonies within the British
Empire. No former attempts at confederacy had had such
opportunity. This Congress numbered highly experienced
politicians on both sides — the government side and the
popular side: royally appointed governors as against assemblymen; judges of the courts versus Speakers of the
House. It is always easier to deal with experienced minds.
"Now, if you were to pick out half a Dozen Men of good
Understanding and Address," Franklin had written to
his former business partner, James Parker, "and furnish
them with a reasonable Scheme and Proper Instructions,
and send them in the Nature of Ambassadors to the other
Colonies . . . I imagine such an Union might thereby
be made and established."

And now, in Albany, there waited not half a dozen men
of good understanding, but a score. As for the "reasonable Scheme," it was in Franklin's head. "Proper Instructions" were unfortunately lacking; the Pennsylvania Assembly had gone so far as to specify that it looked for
no attempts at confederation. But Franklin thought that
with canny planning he could get around this. In the
meantime, here in New York, he would consult certain
friends who had shown persistent interest in federation.
It had been impossible, on this journey, to discuss the
subject with Isaac Norris; his Quaker principles and
politics would have damned the thing at a dozen points.
As to Peters and Penn, their interest was in the Iroquois
tribes and the purchase of territory. But James Alexander
and Archibald Kennedy of New York were not hampered
by local prejudice, their outlook being large. Born and
educated in England, the two had taken a broad part in
public life. Both were members of the Governor's Council — yet both of them hated Governor De Lancey of New
York and all his works and ways. De Lancey was going to

run this Albany Congress, ostensibly at least. It would be well to be briefed at first hand by those who knew him.

James Alexander, a lawyer, had defended Peter Zenger in the notorious case for criminal libel and had thereby been temporarily disbarred from his profession by the governor; he had indeed been accused of working the people up to rebellion. Always, Alexander was on the colonial side when ministerial plans seemed unreasonably oppressive. As an engineer and mathematician, he had corresponded with Franklin on scientific subjects. . . . The second friend, Archibald Kennedy, nearly seventy, was rich, influential, and though a servant of the Crown, being customs collector and receiver general of the Province, remained sympathetic to colonial expansion. Like Franklin, Kennedy saw the colonial position changing, and had already published pamphlets concerning the importance of preserving friendship with the Indians and the proper regulation of the northern colonies. The Americans, said Kennedy, could not be kept dependent by keeping them poor and limiting their manufactures and trade. He had quoted that controversial Whig writer, Trenchard, to the effect that no country would continue its subjection to another "only because their Great Grandmothers were acquainted." Franklin's own pamphlet, *Observations concerning the Increase of Mankind,* pointed out that if America's one million English souls — propagated from eighty thousand immigrants — continued to double in twenty-five years, they would in another century "be more than the People of England, and the greatest Number of Englishmen will be on this side of the Water."

Franklin had written his pamphlet three years ago — in 1751 — and it had circulated widely among his London friends. But he had not as yet consented to its publication, nor would he until 1755, when the Albany Congress was in the past. The Boston edition would be reprinted in London many times. Malthus would quote it in his *Essay on Population* (1798), accepting the author's apparently correct estimate of future population increases in America. Francis Place, the English reformer, studied Franklin's *Observations;* Adam Smith had two copies in his library when he wrote the *Wealth of Nations.* "What an Accession of Power to the British Empire," Franklin had written, "by Sea as well as Land! What Increase of Trade and Navigation! . . . We have been here but little more than 100 years, and yet the Force of our Privateers in the late War [King George's War] united . . . was greater, both in Men and Guns, than that of the whole British Navy in Queen Elizabeth's time."

All of this was in the minds of Franklin, Kennedy, and Alexander when they met in New York that June of 1754 to discuss a possible federation. No matter what plan was eventually proposed, it must have room for colonial expansion. Franklin believed the American birth rate depended upon *land* and its availability. By clearing America of woods, he had written, we were "scouring our Planet, and so making this Side of our Globe reflect a brighter Light to the Inhabitants of Mars and Venus." Westward, across the Alleghenies, was where colonial eyes must turn. Franklin had traveled to the frontier, had worn the fringed jacket of the hunter, and had seen the tree stumps in wilderness clearings. Britain must be careful to secure adequate territory, since on the room — the land — all increase of her people depended. In Pennsylvania alone, many thousands of families were ready to swarm, yet no single colony seemed strong enough to extend itself otherwise than inch by inch. "But if the colonies were united," wrote Franklin, "they might easily, by their joint force, establish one or more new colonies wherever they should judge it necessary or advantageous to the interest of the whole."

The very immediacy of the danger should be a spur to federation. Only three weeks before Franklin left for

Albany, his newspaper, the *Pennsylvania Gazette,* had printed an express from Major Washington in the Ohio region: bad news, with the French and Indians closing in and the inhabitants terrified. Below the article appeared a rough drawing, the now famous woodcut of a snake broken into eight pieces, each piece labeled with initials: "N.E., N.Y., N.J., P., M., V., N.C., S.C." JOIN OR DIE, the caption read. The cartoon had been reprinted in New York, Boston, Williamsburg, and Charleston. Kennedy and Alexander of course had seen it.

The meeting in New York between the three men was fruitful. Franklin returned to his lodgings and wrote out what he entitled "Short Hints towards a Scheme for Uniting the Northern Colonies." The whole covered not more than a few pages, but it was comprehensive and would prove extremely useful at the congress.

"Manner of forming this Union," said a final clause: "The scheme being first well considered corrected and improved by the Commissioners at Albany, to be sent home, and an Act of Parliament obtain'd for establishing it."

CHAPTER SEVEN

Up the Hudson River by sloop.
Politics with the Province of New York.
A notable sale of land
and a treaty with the Iroquois.

At seven o'clock on a Sunday evening, June ninth, the Pennsylvania delegates walked down to a city landing and embarked on the Hudson River for Albany — accompanied, said the *New York Mercury*, by "a great Number of Private Gentlemen." Governor De Lancey and his three councilmen had sailed on Friday. Perhaps the "private gentlemen" came down merely to wish the travelers godspeed; the eighteenth century had a happy way of escorting public characters to the edge of town, "setting them off on their journey." The *Mercury* spoke of more than one sloop; Franklin's was a party of seven, counting the Maryland commissioners who joined them: Benjamin Tasker and Abraham Barnes, landed gentlemen and members of the Governor's Council.

Richard Peters's diary notes that their sloop made four hours by nightfall; they were to be a full week on the water. Franklin loved to travel and often said he required it periodically for his health. And here was a new scene altogether: the wide magnificent river, with cliffs like mountains mile on mile; if a man shouted, his voice came back to him. The Albany sloops had good cabins and often sailed all night. Franklin's friend, Peter Kalm, the Swedish botanist, had made the journey a few years ago at exactly the same season, and spoke of fireflies in the rigging after dark, of porpoises that played and tumbled all the way to Kingston and of sturgeon that leaped from the water.

On the east bank above New York City the great manorial holdings began: Morrisania, Cortlandt, Philipse, Beekman, Rumboldt; now and again their farms were green to the water's edge. Westward stretched the forest, endless, primeval, reaching on and on. No one in the sloop would have ventured to call the forest beautiful. Rather, it was "solemn, interminable, barbaric, harsh"; one meets the adjectives often. Trees were man's enemy and must be felled. Until they were gone there could be neither crops nor fruit; no safety, no ease, no civilization.

When the wind died, the black flies were terrible, as were the mosquitoes at night. Farther north the landscape would show drastic change, very different from the settled environs the Philadelphians were used to. This was frontier country, sparsely populated; the French wars had driven farmers south over the border. The whole Province had not more than one hundred thousand people. But if the land seemed empty the river was astonishingly populous, busy with cargo boats: huge canoes, high-bowed and heavy, made of stout white pine; men stood to paddle them. In whole convoys the boats moved downriver, the oarsmen hallooing as they passed. Clumsy scows, laden deep; flat-bottomed *battoes,* sharp at the ends, rowed with long oars and packed with wheat, peas, lumber, fruit, and above all with the valuable cargo that was the lifeblood of the northwest trade — beaver skins. Not without reason did the official seal of Albany show a beaver, with his broad tail and powerful claws. Thousands upon thousands of skins went yearly down the Hudson. And the "Far Indians" — the Hurons — who came from Oswego and beyond, from the Ohio, the Illinois, the Ottawa and Straits of the Mackinac — paid in skins and traded in skins. Franklin himself was to adopt the beaver for continental bills; he said it represented thrift, persistence, ingenuity: good symbols for republican America.

Rhinebeck came in sight; Kingston, and on the east bank the manor of Livingston. Nine-tenths of New York belonged to the great patroon families; of necessity much of their land lay idle. Said Franklin's friend, Cadwallader Colden, "A Stranger could not believe that some Men in this Province own above two hundred thousand Acres of Land which neither they nor their Great Grand Children can hope to improve." Often enough the land was measured not by acres but casually, in miles: "A tract of seventy miles east and west along Hudson's River." Boundaries were crazily indefinite. A deed between Van Rensselaer and the Indians began, *"at the beaver creek, going on northward to the great fallen plane tree, where our tribe slept last summer; then eastward to the three great cedars on the hillock; then westward, strait to the wild duck swamp; and strait on from the swamp to the turn in the beaver creek where the old dam was."*

Such vagueness made of course for continual lawsuits between claimants; a member of the Beekman family lamented at being "dailey heep't up with Showers of Law Suets." Seven million acres had been given by the Crown in only thirteen grants. Largest of them all was Rensselaerswick, spreading like a whole country on both sides of the river; Albany itself was carved out of Rensselaerswick. The families intermarried: a Cortlandt and a Philipse, a Schuyler and a Van Rensselaer, a Van Rensselaer and a Livingston. Governor James De Lancey, who would direct the Congress, had married a Miss Heathcote, thus adding to his own properties a good part of the enormous manor of Scarsdale.

It was an aristocracy based on wealth, and there was no doubting its greed for power, no doubting also the feuds between the great families, one with another. De Lanceys and Livingstons had long been at swords' points. Royal governors quarreled with the elected Assembly of some twenty-seven members, which sat for two brief sessions each year in New York City, summer and fall. The entire land system of the Province was closely tied to politics; Governor De Lancey, for instance, had five relatives and seven close friends in the House. But a beleaguered Assembly possessed one potent weapon which they owed to the British constitution: the power of the purse. And they had learned to wield it as the House of Commons did, by withholding appropriations until certain concessions were obtained from the governor's party. Rivalry between New York City and the upriver, interior country never ceased; no colony among the thirteen was so factious, so contentious. As late as 1776, John Adams, worn out with arguing for independence against a recalcitrant Province, asked if there was something in the "air or soil of New York unfriendly to the spirit of liberty? Are the people destitute of reason or of virtue? Or what is the cause?"

A knowledge of New York politics was necessary to Franklin's delegation, if they expected to be effective at Albany. James De Lancey held at the moment the two most important positions in the Province: chief justice and governor; his influence was almost incalculable. No other colony was so administered; to the Pennsylvanians it must have seemed disquieting, unnatural. True, the Penns owned more land than any single New York patroon. But the Pennsylvania government felt itself as free as that of Connecticut or Rhode Island, the Quakers being quite as powerful locally as the Penns. What would these autocratic Albanians think of a colonial union, and how best could they be approached? Plainly, nothing could be done without De Lancey's support. Everyone conceded the man's personal attractiveness; he had a most winning presence.

As the travelers neared their destination the forest gave way to fields, strewn with tree stumps and planted with wheat as far as the eye could reach. Wheat flour from Albany was accounted the best in North America. Franklin, himself no farmer, had a passionate interest in agriculture, and exchanged seeds and cuttings with friends abroad and in America. The welfare of the colonies, he would have said, depended on their various soils and the yield therefrom. Was it not therefore a citizen's essential business to know and to care for these matters? Apple and cherry orchards came in sight. There were but few pear or peach trees; Peter Kalm had reported "a worm that ate them." On Becker's Island just below Albany, flax was in flower, blue and thick. Colonel Schuyler owned the island, Albany people liked to go there for picnics. Birds nested above the water: osprey, heron and the bald eagle. On both shores wigwams could be seen. In summer, Indians pitched their tents on the manorial estates, eating from the manorial farms and selling their handiwork of deerskin or birchbark.

For all its reputation as a trading center, Albany had no quay; thrifty Dutch burghers said the ice would carry it away in winter. The harbor was deep; travelers simply stepped ashore somehow at the foot of the steep, long thoroughfare known as Jonker Street. At the top, a good quarter of a mile away, stood a rectangular bastion called The Fort, boasting twenty-one guns, every one of which had roared when Governor De Lancey arrived four days ago. Albanians said that was about all the guns were good for; what the city needed was a stout stockade around it. But the New York Assembly, a safe one hundred and fifty miles south, would not grant the money. De Lancey was captain general of the provincial forces, but not enthusiastic concerning defense, having all along been against wars with France because they ruined the fur trade between Albany and Montreal.

Franklin and his friends heard Dutch spoken on the streets; the houses had stepped gables and half doors; people sat on their front stoops to watch the strangers pass. Everything had been swept spotless for the congress. And a good thing, too, the Dutch turned their cows loose on the streets at night; flies were so thick that people shut up their best rooms in summer to protect the furniture. Roof gutters reached almost to the middle of the street — a crazy way to carry off the rain; in bad weather pedestrians were drenched. Goods remained dear in the shops; as between a Dutchman and a Jew it was said the Dutch came out ahead every time. The *haendlers* or traders were shrewd and overshrewd. "Dutch reptiles," Peter Wraxall called them; to New Englanders they were Frogs, or Van Frogs. The notorious *Albanian spirit* stood for narrow self-interest and close dealing; it was here the phrase "Dutch treat" arose. As Franklin wrote to Peter Collinson,

> . . . the Dutch
> Would fain save all the Money that they Touch.

Delegates to the Congress were slow in arriving. The Pennsylvanians were three days late and so were the four New Hampshiremen, who traveled overland, crossing the ferry at Albany; they said they had got lost in the woods near Kinderhook. They all dined that first night with Governor De Lancey. "Near twenty Gentlemen," wrote Atkinson of New Hampshire, "a Handsome Entertainment, good wine and Arrack Punch." Franklin and his friends were lodged comfortably enough with James Stevenson, Indian agent, merchant, and treasurer of the county. The Mohawks had not arrived, but chiefs of the Cayugas and Oneidas could be seen about the streets, dressed in their best and brightest, their squaws walking behind.

The first meeting of the commissioners took place on June nineteenth, in the city hall — the old Dutch *Stadt Huys*. The Iroquois called it the Covenant House — a plain, square building with a cupola and weathercock, five windows across the front and a low stoop leading to the door. Governor De Lancey presided, his manner at the same time assured and conciliatory. Anyone could see that he was dexterous; in spite of his asthma he spoke well, with none of the Dutch heaviness in his delivery. (The De Lanceys were of Huguenot stock.) The commissions from all the colonial assemblies were read aloud; it was good to hear Governor Shirley's: *"for entering into articles of union and confederation with the aforesaid governments* and for the general defense of his Majesty's subjects and interests in North America as well in time of peace as of war." Among twenty-four delegates, only the five from Massachusetts carried instructions for a union, entirely apart from Indian affairs.

That evening there was a banquet in the city hall, with the mayor and aldermen and a scattering of Indians. Every day the Mohawks were looked for and did not appear. There was official humiliation in this waiting about; the savages knew well the time of meeting. Plainly, they were staying away on purpose. Governor De Lancey had already drafted his welcoming speech to the Iroquois; the Congress went over it in detail. Disagreement about the seating developed; no colony wanted to be upstaged. Finally a north-south order of precedence prevailed, with De Lancey at the head, his New York councillors flanking him; then came Massachusetts, New Hampshire, and Connecticut on the governor's right; and Rhode Island, Pennsylvania and Maryland on his left. Peter Wraxall, recording clerk (he was secretary to the Albany Indian commissioners), occupied a rostrum overlooking the room. Concerning his plans for a colonial union, Franklin bided his time.

On Sunday, Richard Peters preached at the Anglican

church, where delegates saw the set of plate given by Queen Anne to Colonel Schuyler and his sachems in 1710. The whole company rode out to the beautiful Cohoes Falls on the Mohawk River, nine hundred feet across and seventy feet high as measured by Lewis Evans, the indefatigable Pennsylvania engineer; a marvelous sight, with the water rushing down over great black rocks.

Next morning, a Monday, when delegates met as usual at the Albany State House, the Mohawks still had not made their appearance. Governor De Lancey seized the opportunity to present his cherished plan of building two forts in the Indian country to protect the Iroquois from the French and "thereby secure their fidelity to his Majesty." Delegates balked. What colony would pay for the forts? Since the convening of this Albany Congress five days ago, there had been talk, out-of-doors and unofficial, about a possible colonial union. No single Province was willing to build and man defenses, knowing that if they waited, the forts might later go up at the joint charge of everybody. The question was put "that the Commissioners deliver their opinions whether a union of all the colonies is not at present absolutely necessary for their Security and defense."

There is no record of who put the question, but we know that Franklin had a way of engineering his best schemes through other men's voices. That the motion passed unanimously — indeed, that it passed at all — was due no doubt to skillful lobbying, in the past five days, by such powerful persuaders as Franklin, Pownall, Hutchinson, Hopkins, and even the humble but knowledgeable Conrad Weiser, who had long believed in a confederacy. Backward or indifferent delegates had been informed of the immediate mutual peril and of mutual benefits that could ensue. A second motion went through, that a committee be appointed "to prepare and receive Plans or Schemes for the Union of the Colonies and to digest them

into one general Plan for the Inspection of this Board."
Seven members were chosen, representing the seven colonies present, Franklin of course among them. It was what
he had hoped for — a superb chance to become better acquainted with men of the various Provinces and to exchange views in comparative privacy. Hutchinson was
named from Massachusetts, Atkinson from New Hampshire, Pitkin from Connecticut, Stephen Hopkins from
Rhode Island, William Smith from New York. Benjamin
Tasker of Maryland, Franklin already knew; they had
traveled together up the river.

Franklin produced his "Short Hints towards a Scheme
for Uniting the Northern Colonies." The committee had
until Friday to work on their plan. Meanwhile there was
the business of the Susquehannah lands to be bought for the
Pennsylvania Proprietors in the name of the Crown; John
Penn and Richard Peters had been busy from the moment
of arrival. Conrad Weiser reported that Connecticut had by
no means relinquished her ambition to buy into the self-
same territory, "back of the Appalachians." One Lydius,
an Albany merchant, rich, eccentric and secretive, had already made headway. All three Connecticut delegates to
the Congress were members of the newly formed Susquehanna Company, whose purchasing schemes had been ma-
turing for the past year. Into the Stevenson house where
Franklin lodged trooped Cayugas and Oneidas, mocca-
sined, dignified. They would like, they said, to sell their
land to their brother Onas,* but the decision must wait
upon the Mohawks and their honored sachem, Hendrick
Peters. Actually, the Mohawk title to the territory was
questionable. Delawares, Shawnees, Twightwees had first
inhabited this territory; Cayugas and Oneidas had simply
taken over by conquest. William Penn's rule never to permit settlement until the land had been bought from the
aborigines was a practice that fostered goodwill, as Frank-

* Onas had been the Indians' name for William Penn; after his death
it applied to any governor of Pennsylvania.

lin's newspaper, the *Pennsylvania Gazette,* had remarked. (It did not remark that the aborigines, in perfectly logical sequence, sometimes sold the land three times over.)

In the past twenty years a mania for land speculation had swept the colonies. Because manufacture was prohibited by Britain, investing in "wild lands" had become the way to fortune. Everybody tried their hand at it, from Dr. Ezra Stiles of Yale College to George Washington and certain Philadelphia Quakers. Connecticut, which until very recently had acknowledged New York as her western boundary, now reverted to her ancient charter, which said that her border ran to the South Sea, allowing large claims in Pennsylvania. For Penn and Peters, the question therefore was not so much whether the Indians would sell their land but to whom they would sell — to the French, becoming daily more powerful along the Ohio? To Connecticut, whose agent sat at Albany with one thousand Spanish pieces of eight, wrapped and ready for delivery? William Johnson had written Governor Hamilton of Pennsylvania that he preferred Pennsylvania to Connecticut as purchaser; "the poor Indians I am sure have little reason to love or Choose as Neighbors the Crafty Inhabitants of the N. Jerusalem whose Title to that place seems rather derived from the Subtilty of the Serpent, than the meekness of the Dove, to which last your Province is universally allowed to have a better Claim."

In western Pennsylvania the situation had got beyond control, the territory being pestered with squatters, who simply arrived and let their cattle forage through the Indian crops. All along the road to Allegheny the settlers' cabins lay; Germans and Scotch-Irish flowed in from the eastern counties, not by scores but by thousands. Driving them off and burning their cabins did no good; the tide surged on. The Indians knew well that the land would be lost to them sooner or later, no matter what monies changed hands.

At last, on June 27 and 28, the Mohawks came into Al-

bany from their castles of the Upper and Lower Canajoharie — taking their own time, drifting down Jonker
Street according to their pleasure, and led by their re-
nowned sachem. Hendrick Peters — his Indian name was
Tiyanoga — had succeeded Canasatego as spokesman for
the Six Nations. Surely the outstanding Indian of his time,
Hendrick was a close friend of William Johnson, whose
house lay near the Upper Canajoharie Castle. A splendid-
looking man of seventy-odd, Hendrick had a face and
figure, said a contemporary, "singularly impressive and
commanding, with an air of majesty, and appeared as if
born to control other men." His color was dark, his nose
high-bridged and hooked; from the left side of his mouth
a tomahawk scar ran clear across his cheek — a warrior's
badge, eloquent and terrible. Hendrick had traveled to
London in 1710 with Peter Schuyler, and liked to wear the
coat in which he had been painted there, sky blue, richly
laced. His father had been a Mohican, but as a boy the
Mohawks adopted Hendrick and early educated him as a
sachem.

After some days of consultation and high words among
his brethren, Hendrick faced the Iroquois, the Pennsylvanians, and commissioners from other colonies, crowded
into James Stevenson's house. "We are ready to sell you
this large tract of land," he said, "for your people to live
upon. Yet after we have sold our land, we in a little time
have nothing to show for it. But it is not so with you. Your
grandchildren will get something from it as long as the
world stands. Our grandchildren . . . will say we were
fools for selling so much land for so small a matter, and
curse us. Therefore let it be a part of the present agreement that we shall treat one another as brethren to the
latest generation, even after we shall not have left a foot of
land."

It was so agreed, and written into the contract, as it had
been in past deeds of sale with the Indians; these were

traditional words. To read them is terrible — as terrible indeed as the testimony of all treaties, old pacts and promises, forgotten or dishonored by those who made them. A thousand pieces of eight were paid, a thousand more promised when the land should be settled — about four hundred English pounds altogether. The sequel to this sale . . . how Connecticut bought up territory after the Albany Congress dissolved . . . the trouble that ensued until, in 1758, the Penns ceded part of the land back to the Indians — all this is not part of our story. Franklin, however, was much concerned that the Proprietors' purchase should be witnessed and approved by the entire Albany Congress; he had always maintained that public sale, officially witnessed, was the only way to safeguard the savages from exploitation.

In the late June sunshine, some hundred and fifty Indians sat on benches, row by row, in front of Governor De Lancey's house, the full congress grouped before them. The treaty of friendship between the northern colonies and the Iroquois was ready to proceed. This was, after all, the stated reason for the Albany Congress, and would require many days of question and response. To hurry an Indian in conference was as unnatural as to try to domesticate him or convert him to Christianity. Franklin did not believe in such conversion; he had no ambition to make white men of the Indians but wished rather to treat with them fairly and honestly according to their lights. Nor did he look ahead to a time when the Indians might be exterminated or amalgamated with the English. Franklin saw the American forests as limitless, inhabited for generations to come by many times Six Nations — a problem to be met day after day, pragmatically, practically, as the need arose. When Indians attacked, Franklin was ready to do battle and did, with guns and militia. But he said often that he would rather buy the Indians' land than fight them for it.

On the other hand if the Six Nations would accept a friendship pact, so much the better, and so much gained against a French enemy.

Besides Conrad Weiser, two interpreters were ready: Woodbridge of Connecticut, schoolteacher and missionary to the Mohawks; and a Mr. Kellogg for the Massachusetts commissioners. William Johnson, who knew the Mohawks and their language intimately, sat silent; he was in open opposition to Governor De Lancey's Indian policies and everybody knew it. Commissioners recognized also that the Iroquois were the most interesting Indians in North America. The "Romans of the West," they were called. Franklin admired them and had said so. "Brethren of the Six Nations!" began Governor De Lancey, standing before them, "you are welcome. I take this opportunity now you are all together to condole on the loss of your friends and relations, since you last met here, and with this string of wampum I wipe away your tears, and take sorrow from your hearts, that you may open your minds and speak freely."

Delegates knew the Indian ritual, always significant and impressive: the strings and belts of wampum changing hands as condolence or flung down to ratify a clause; the symbols of Chain, Fire, and Tree; the united cry of Yo-hah! sounding in query and response. The Yo-hah has often been described as "musical." Thomas Pownall, reporting from Albany to the Earl of Halifax, wrote (as one fox hunter to another) that the Yo-hah sounded exactly like the call of "Hark Forward!" — shouted by the huntsman to encourage the hounds.

Yet today the omens were not good, especially the presence of only one hundred and fifty Iroquois when five hundred might have been expected. The Scaticook tribe had come along, uninvited, also the River Indians from their village on the Housatonic, "near the Stock Bridge." (Governor De Lancey told Governor Shirley that Massachusetts should feed these tribes, New York being already at great expense to maintain the others.) De Lancey chided the Mohawks for being late. Surely they were aware of the inconvenience to commissioners, detained at so long a distance from home? "The King our common father," went on De Lancey, "as proof of his tender regard," had sent presents for the Iroquois . . . De Lancey described the French threat and begged the Indians not to live dispersed as they had of late, but to collect themselves together in their castles so they might be united and strong. There followed much oratory about brightening the chain of friendship, keeping it inviolable and free from rust. "Open your hearts to us!" finished De Lancey. "Deal with us as Brethren! We are ready to consult with you, how to scatter these clouds that hang over us."

Hendrick strode forward. His reply was blunt. The Mohawks had indeed delayed their coming, he said. And why? Last summer they had traveled to New York City with certain grievances, "and we then thought the Covenant Chain was broken, because we were neglected. And when you neglect business, the French take advantage of it, for they are never quiet. It seemed to us," went on Hendrick, standing tall and easy before the crowd, "that the Governor had turned his back upon the Six Nations, as if they were no more. Whereas the French are doing all in their power to draw us over to them. . . . We remember how it was in former time when we were a strong and powerful people. Colonel Schuyler used frequently to come among us, and by this means we were kept together."

In truth the Iroquois had lost strength; the focus of Indian power lay now in the Ohio region rather than at Onondaga, traditional seat of the Mohawk council fire. After a pause of three days, Hendrick spoke again. In his hands he held a handsome chain belt, which De Lancey had presented in the name of all the colonies. Woven into it were symbols representing King George, the thirteen colonies, and the Six Nations, with a line to draw them all together. Courteously, Hendrick declared he would carry the belt to Onondaga, "where our Council Fire always burns, and keep it so securely that neither thunder nor lightning shall break it."

After this propitious beginning, Hendrick let go and said what he meant. Those who heard him indicated that his manner was at the same time proud and scornful. He spoke again of neglect. In Hendrick's left hand was a stick; with an abrupt motion he threw it over his shoulder. "You have thrown us behind your back and disregarded us!" he said. "The Governors of Virginia and Pennsylvania have made paths through our country to trade and built houses without acquainting us with it. They should first have asked our consent, as was done when Oswego was built. . . . The French are a subtile and vigilant people, ever using their utmost endeavors to seduce us and bring our people over to them. The Governor of Canada is like a wicked deluding spirit. . . ."

It was all true enough. William Johnson, sitting among the commissioners, knew it, though his time to speak was not yet come. If the colonies should lose the Six Nations, it would be nobody's fault but their own. Johnson had often warned of it. Hendrick's tone as he proceeded was contemptuous. "This is the ancient place of treaty where the fire of friendship always used to burn. 'Tis now three years since we have been called to any public treaty here. . . . There are Indian commissioners in Albany, but they have never invited us to smoke with them, but the Canadian Indians come frequently and smoke here, *for the sake of their beaver.*"

Peter Wraxall, at his table, began underlining Hendrick's words, as if the sachem's tone had intensified.

'Tis your fault Brethren that we are not strengthened by conquest, for we would have gone and taken Crown Point, but you hindered us. . . . We were told it was too late, and that the Ice would not bear us. Instead of this you burnt your own Forts at Saratoga and ran away from it, which was a shame

and a scandal to you. Look about your country and see, you have no Fortifications about you, no, not even to this City. 'Tis but one Step from Canada hither, and the French may easily come and turn you out of your doors.

Did William Johnson smile, hearing it? This is what he wanted said. Johnson must have known ahead what Hendrick would say; the sachem had been staying at Mount Johnson before the conference.

"Brethren!" went on the Indian. "You desire us to speak from the bottom of our hearts, and we shall do it. Look about you and see all these houses full of Beaver, and the money is all gone to Canada, likewise powder, lead and guns, which the French now make use of at Ohio."

Once again the words were true. Albanians for years had carried on a secret trade with the Canadian enemy, playing the game two ways for gain. But they had not expected to hear about it from a Mohawk chief, and in congress assembled. "Look at the French!" said Hendrick. "They are men, they are fortifying everywhere. But — we are ashamed to say it — you are all like women, bare and open without any fortifications."

Hendrick turned on his heel, giving place to his fellow sachem, Abraham. "We lay this belt before you!" cried Abraham, ". . . and desire Colonel Johnson be reinstated . . . for we all lived happy whilst he was manager. We love him, and he us, and he has always been our good and trusty Friend. . . . We think our request about Colonel Johnson which the Governor promised to carry to the King our Father is drowned in the sea!"

Turning to the New York agents for Indian affairs — Franklin's host, James Stevenson, among them — Abraham demanded they take notice of what he had said.

"The fire here is burnt out!" the sachem finished, and walked away.

After some days, the commissioners delivered their answer — denying the charge of trade with Canada, defending Johnson's resignation as superintendent for Indian affairs. "If he fails us, we die," the Iroquois replied. Promises were made: certain land transactions would be investigated and satisfaction given; the sale of rum to the Indians would be enforced by law (patently an impossibility; private traders could not be prevented from debauching the red man and cheating him when he was drunk). Franklin had always deplored the practice and urged strict regulation to protect the Indian. Nothing the commissioners said was half so trenchant as what Hendrick had said. Yet in the end the Indians accepted their presents and declared the Covenant Chain to be "solemnly renewed and strengthened." When the great belt was delivered, the Indians, reported Atkinson, sounded out the Yo-hah "seven times over for every tribe."

What else could the Indians do? No doubt Hendrick had planned it so from the beginning. At least grievances had been aired, and that was good. The talks continued for some ten days. Franklin was in and out, busy with committee work. During one session, Hendrick stood up peaceably, holding two wampum belts, which he said represented proposals from the Pennsylvania Proprietaries, concerning the sale of lands. The Six Nations would like to deliver their answer and make their agreement of sale here "in this publick Congress" (wrote the interpreter). Governor De Lancey at once inquired the extent of the purchase. John Penn gave the figures, then said that as the Proprietors had always carried on land purchases with the Indians in the most open manner, he prayed that this particular treaty might also be witnessed here, "to begin a precedent," concerning the public witnessing of such matters, in whatever province consummated.

The congress refused "to begin a precedent" — it was thought at the instance of De Lancey, who strongly disliked sharing Iroquois affairs with Pennsylvanians or with anyone else outside his own province. Franklin, disappointed, would be careful to put into his plan of colonial union an agreement for making all Indian land purchases a public matter — including the regulation and government of settlements in newly bought Indian territory.

On the ninth of July the Iroquois departed, taking with them thirty wagonloads of gifts and asking food for their journey, "to prevent our people from killing the inhabitants' cattle."

"We brighten'd the Chain with them," wrote Franklin afterward, "and parted good Friends. But in my Opinion no Assistance is to be expected from them in any Dispute with the French, 'till by a compleat Union among ourselves we are enabled to support them in case they are attacked."

CHAPTER EIGHT

Franklin's plan.

For Franklin there could be no effectual treaty between colonists and Indians until the colonies achieved a strong confederacy among themselves. During all the negotiations with the Indians and well into July he had labored over it. The committee of seven sat in James Stevenson's house, discussing Franklin's "Short Hints towards a Scheme for Uniting the Northern Colonies." Treating with Indians being at best a slow business, often enough whole days went by while the savages consulted alone.

But why only the "northern colonies"? somebody asked, and the words were changed to "Short Hints towards a Scheme for a General Union of the British Colonies on the Continent." This was not only more comprehensive but more difficult to achieve; previous plans had grouped the colonies in a northern and a southern bloc. Franklin's drafts of even the most complex matters were apt to be surprisingly simple, and so it proved this time. His paper did not so much as mention the French, though it urged a federation which would build forts, "defend the frontiers and annoy the enemy." A governor general, appointed and salaried by the King, would have power of veto over a Grand Council of representatives, chosen by the various provincial legislatures. Franklin's committee changed "Governor General" to "President General." (Thirty-five years and much trial and error would ensue before the United States found the title for their chief executive, discarding Excellency, High Mightiness, Highness — John Adams's choice — and settling for plain Mr. President.)

Here, then, in Franklin's plan, appeared the germ of the federal idea: a President, a large House of Representatives. "One General Government," wrote Franklin, to "be formed in America, including all the said Colonies, within and under which Government, each Colony may retain its present Constitution. . . ." Even after the Revolution, America would find it hard to grasp the federal idea, a government in which there existed "two supremes" — supremacy in each individual state, and supremacy in the "general government" (what today we call "Washington"). The French historian Guizot has remarked that one cannot understand a revolution until one considers its origin, the earliest plans it puts forth. At Albany, prophetic tongues were speaking. No matter if Franklin's Plan of Union should succeed or fail, here in committee and in full congress assembled, there took place a significant rehearsal, years before the play would begin. True, Franklin's Grand Council, or House of Representatives, was a single-chamber affair, no Senate being suggested and no Supreme Court. Representatives would be proportioned not by population but according to "the Sums they yearly contribute to the General Treasury." A characteristic touch was Franklin's notion of funding the common treasury by an excise "on Strong Liquors pretty equally drank in the Colonies or Duty on

Liquor imported," or a tax on public house licenses, or "Superfluities as Tea, &c. &c."

Just how the people in general could be persuaded to such taxes, Franklin did not divulge. All his life, Franklin inveighed against luxury — but he greatly enjoyed drinking with his friends, either in public or in private. His idea, to the last degree impractical, reminds one of John Adams as a young lawyer, valiantly and vainly attempting to close all the public houses in Braintree Township, Massachusetts.

On June twenty-eighth, a Friday afternoon, Franklin reported to the full Albany Congress his *Short Hints,* as enlarged and amended by his committee of seven. Copies were at once taken, no other business being reported. Apparently, delegates simply sat down and made their own copies. On the following Monday, debate opened. Should the Union be established by act of Parliament, as per the final clause of Franklin's *Short Hints?* Connecticut shied away: Parliament might encroach on their charter privileges. On the other hand, union by acts of the separate assemblies would be a slow process. Moreover, there remained the governor's veto and the fact that when bills reached England, they might be repealed by the Crown. Delegates remarked that assemblymen were more fearful of disobliging their constituents than of not holding to the right course. Would it not be more prudent to ascertain beforehand the sentiments of the ministry and Parliament concerning this union? The word "novelty" came up — in the eighteenth century, still a bad word, with connotations of "leveling" or heresy. We must prove, commissioners said, that novelty is not dangerous. Richard Peters's brief notes repeated it: "Novelty not dangerous."

From the ministerial or Crown point of view, novelty would indeed be dangerous. Not only does authority invariably question if the people are ready to govern themselves, but ministers of state are uncomfortable and suspicious when precedent is challenged. It was England, rather than America, that harbored thoughts of colonial rebellion, fearing strong local self-government and what it might lead to. John Evelyn, the diarist, had written of the New Englanders, after a meeting of Privy Council in 1671: "We understood that they were on the very brink of renouncing any dependence on the Crown." When the Lords of Trade from time to time suggested a colonial union, they desired it for a tighter control over these libertarian trends.

The colonists themselves, however, had no notion of separating from the English Crown. English colonists lived under the banner of St. George and took pride in the name of Briton. When they rose against unjust measures they did it in the name of Britons and said so. Was it not part of the British heritage to resist tyranny? Major Washington told his troops in 1756, "Let us show our willing obedience to the best of kings." A correspondent of the *Boston Gazette* urged the colonists to "unite, and rouse up the British lion in each others' breasts." Since earliest days, the world had predicted a grand future for North America — but a future not separate from the British Empire. Even that firebrand Sam Adams, as late as 1774, wrote to Charles Thomson, "Would God all, even our enemies, knew the warm attachment we have for Great Britain."

Certainly, the potential for "liberty" and for "independence" existed from the first; it ran in the colonists' blood. Said Franklin, "Liberty best thrives in the woods." It has been noted that much error has crept into American history by not keeping in view the difference between opposition to measures of an administration, such as the Stamp Act in 1765, and resistance to the supreme power of the Empire or to the sovereignty. At Albany in the summer of 1754, nobody was thinking rebellious thoughts about the mother country. On the contrary, what they desired was protection from the French. They wanted British troops sent over; they wanted the Crown — not the colonies — to pay for the erection of forts along the frontier. Rebellion does not sit well with a yearning for maternal shelter. It would require seven years of war with the French (1756–1763) and total defeat of this traditional enemy in America before British colonists began to think rebellious thoughts. And even then, James Otis would say of the Empire, "What God in his providence has united, let no man dare attempt to pull asunder." Sam Adams's *Independent Advertiser* (which could be crusty) had remarked that "the British constitution is without doubt the perfectest model of government that has ever been in the world." Everything that happened at Albany took place within the context of that pride and that loyalty.

No one set down the debates at Albany, and it is a pity; there would not be such a congregation of brains and ability in America until the Continental Congress of 1774. A member of Franklin's committee of seven — Attorney General William Smith of New York — said the speakers were not many, but of those who stood up, "some delivered themselves with singular energy and eloquence. All were inflamed with a patriot spirit, and the debates were nervous and pathetic. This Assembly might very properly be compared to one of the ancient Greek conventions, for supporting their expiring liberty against the power of the Persian empire." Fear of the enemy can be a potent tonic, and Franklin's committee knew it. Before they presented their plan they had prepared what today would be called a "White Paper," setting out *The Present State of the Colonies.* Though its facts and arguments concerning the French peril had been heard before, they were strongly worded, with an immediacy that brought home the threat when the paper was read aloud in full congress.

Among neighbors and potential allies, jealousy is something to reckon with. At Albany, small colonies showed their envy of large ones, poor colonies of rich ones. Franklin spelled it out. "They were extremely jealous of each other," he wrote. New York held to her full monopoly of Indian trade and lands. Rhode Island, Connecticut, Maryland, were less exposed to Indian threats, being covered by neighboring colonies, and therefore noncooperative. Franklin noted that Pennsylvania, because of the Quakers, had "particular whims and prejudices against warlike measures in general." From the outset, Franklin had believed that an act of Parliament would be necessary to bind these communities, hold them together. Without England's authority behind the union, any colony would be apt to withdraw in disapproval of some measure or expense mutually incurred. The Albany Congress finally resolved "that humble Application be made for an Act of the Parliament of Great Britain, by Virtue of which, one General Government may be formed in America, including all the said Colonies, and under which Government, each Colony may retain its present Constitution."

Considerable care was expended on the number of representatives each colony would be permitted in the Grand Council. At the end, Massachusetts and Virginia were granted seven apiece, Pennsylvania six, and so on down to Rhode Island with two. Philadelphia was to be the first meeting place, "where," wrote Franklin, "the Commissioners would be well and cheaply accommodated." Distance being a great drawback to any intercolonial congress or meeting, Franklin was at pains to describe various routes from north to south. Even the most distant members, he said, could probably arrive from New Hampshire or South Carolina in fifteen or twenty days, the majority in much less time, whether by water or overland. Payment for representatives was fixed at ten shillings a day, with travel allowance. *Some* wages, wrote Franklin, underlining the word, were thought proper, lest suitable persons be deterred from serving; but not *too great wages*, thus tempting "unsuitable persons to cabal for the employment for the sake of gain." (Thirty-five years later, at the Constitutional Convention, Franklin would come out against salaries for all government officers.)

In the gathering of taxes and imports, Franklin said he wished rather to discourage luxury than to load industry with unnecessary burdens. But whatever laws and taxes were imposed, they were not to interfere with the constitutions and governments of particular colonies, "who are to be left to their own laws, and to lay, levy, and apply their taxes as before." This again was a groping toward federalism, toward the "dual sovereignty" that would make workable a United States of America. A shock and a surprise to the world even after the Revolution, it is no wonder the federal idea was greeted at Albany with suspicion. Wary as foxes, delegates skirted round the issues, sniffing out local loss or advantage. Concerning the raising of troops, caution in the wording was especially necessary. Suppose, said Franklin, that a thousand men were needed in New Hampshire on some emergency? To fetch them by fifties and hundreds out of every colony, as far away as South Carolina, would be hardly feasible, and the occasion perhaps passed before they could be assembled. Therefore it would be best to have no general impressment, but to raise soldiers near the place where they were needed, pay them bounty money and discharge them when the service should be over. *Officers were to be nominated by the president general and approved by the Grand Council.*

Colonial soldiers had always grumbled at being forced to serve under British regulars, even though they did not hesitate to ask England to send troops. Franklin at Albany mentioned the Louisburg expedition, "in the last war," when substantial farmers and tradesmen enlisted as common soldiers under officers of their own country [New England], "for whom they had an esteem and affection, who would not have engaged . . . under officers from England." In the summer of 1755, Washington himself, fighting under General Braddock in Pennsylvania, balked at taking orders from British colonels who were ignorant of the wilderness and of wilderness fighting.

Of special interest to Franklin were the clauses marked "Indian Purchases" and "New Settlements." The president general of the union, "with the advice of the Grand Council" (prophetic of a later phrase, *advice and consent of the Senate*) was empowered to direct all Indian treaties that concerned the general interest, make peace or war with the Indians, create laws for regulating the Indian trade, and be in charge of any purchases from Indians for the Crown, or lands not within known boundaries. New settlements, rather than being made by particular colonies or by land companies, would be under the direction of the united government "till the Crown shall think fit to form them into Particular Governments."

Here, actually, was one of Franklin's chief reasons for coming to Albany; here also a foreshadowing of the great Northwest Ordinance of 1787. Had the colonies been willing to subscribe to it at Albany, this clause alone might have averted much serious conflict.

The Indians were gone. On July ninth, delegates directed Franklin to "make a draught of the Plan of Union as now concluded upon." Franklin did it, and next day his fresh draft was gone over, clause by clause. The final vote came late that afternoon. Oddly enough, nobody kept strict count. Thomas Pownall wrote that opinion was unanimous, "except N. York and in some points Mr. Norris of Philadelphia and he only so far differ'd as the principles of the Party he is at the head of [the Quakers] lead him to appear." Connecticut balked altogether — surprising nobody; of the two "popular governments," Connecticut's retraction had been expected. Thomas Hutchinson's *History of Massachusetts* said the plan was "unanimously voted" at Albany. It looks as if Franklin came nearest the truth when he wrote Cadwallader Colden on the way home that there had been "a great deal of Disputation about the Plan, but at length we agreed on it pretty unanimously."

The Congress resolved that commissioners take the plan home and lay it before their constituents, also that copies be delivered to the governors of those colonies that had sent no delegates. On Friday, July 11, the Albany Congress met for the last time. Governor De Lancey made a final plea that forts be built on the shore of Lake Ontario; it was rejected on grounds that a general union might render them unnecessary. William Johnson and Thomas Pownall came forward with schemes for military defense, spelled out in some detail — factual, knowledgeable, feasible. Franklin asked that they be given the consideration of all thirteen governments.

The congress dissolved. By horseback and sloop the delegates departed. In these three weeks, what had been accomplished? The Indian treaty had carried more form than substance; it would hold or break according to the fortunes of war along the frontier. The Pennsylvania Proprietors had made their purchase of lands. Yet when all was said and done it was the plan for colonial union that held significance. Those who were for the plan could tell themselves much had been achieved in the way of education and persuasion. They had arrived in June, aware that few colonies approved; they left knowing they had swung most of the commissioners to their way of thinking, and that the union showed a chance of success. Nineteen delegates out of twenty-four in the end had gone beyond the instructions of their home assemblies. (The five Massachusetts commissioners brought instructions favorable to union.) The new phrase, "the General Government," had finally been received without gagging. One thinks of the Constitutional Convention of 1787 in Philadelphia, and John Randolph of Virginia opening with his daring phrase, "a *national* government," whereby he cleared two fences and took the lead.

Perhaps, in 1754, Benjamin Franklin and his friends were oversanguine; they went home with spirits high. Franklin ordered his sloop to stop off at Cadwallader Colden's landing on the Hudson. Coldengham was about nine miles from Newburgh. Franklin hoped to find horses to take his party there, but failing, he returned on board and left a note for his friend: "I put a transcript of our whole Treaty and Transactions in my Pocket to show you . . . I heartily wish the Union may be approv'd of by the Assemblies of the several Colonies, and confirm'd by the King and Parliament, with some Improvements that I think necessary, but could not get inserted in the Plan. When one has so many different People with different Opinions to deal with in a new Affair, one is oblig'd sometimes to give up some smaller Points in order to obtain greater." Six months later, writing to Peter Collinson in England, Franklin used much the same words: "Tho' I projected the Plan and drew it, I was oblig'd to alter some Things contrary to my Judgment, or I should never have been able to carry it through." *

Franklin, with his son Billy and the others, went home to Philadelphia. On August seventh the Pennsylvania Assembly received the Plan of Union from Governor James Hamilton, who told the legislature he saw in it great strength and clearness of judgment; he recommended it as well worthy of the closest and most serious attention. But on August seventeenth, their last day of meeting, the Assembly voted down the plan, not even

* See bibliographical note.

referring it to the next session for deliberation. Franklin had been shabbily treated. "By the management of a certain member," he wrote, "the House took it up when I happen'd to be absent, which I thought not very fair, and reprobated it without paying any attention to it at all, to my no small mortification."

It was an old political trick; very likely the "certain member" was Isaac Norris, whose antiwar and antidefense principles had already been noted as an obstacle. It has been suggested also that the Assembly was irked at Franklin's willingness to send the plan directly to England, over the heads of colonial assemblies. The Pennsylvania government was notoriously difficult, forever quarreling with its governor; the Quaker party, beginning to lose its long political control, balked at every measure. "The Assembly ride restive," wrote Franklin, a little later; "and the Governor, tho' he spurs with both Heels, at the same time reins-in with both hands, so that the Publick Business can never move forward; and he remains like St. George in the Sign, always aHorseback, and never going on."

As for New York, its Assembly simply let the plan slide away, though the Governor's Council approved, and legislators agreed that such a union of the colonies would be "salutary for their own defense." But commercial ambitions can be powerful. A confederation would cancel New York's monopoly over the fur trade — something no De Lancey supporter dared risk, and the provincial Assembly was honeycombed with De Lancey supporters. Virginia had sent no representatives to Albany, but the plan ran directly counter to that colony's vast claims as implied in its sea-to-sea charter, and consequent ambitions in the Ohio Valley. Even Massachusetts rejected the plan, though not without struggle and serious debate, influenced apparently by its agent in London, William Bollan, who in September wrote that he feared members of Parliament had "a design for gaining power over the Colonies" by way of a union. Even so it was not until January, 1755, that the General Court of Massachusetts made its final decision.

Everywhere, local interests and local "liberties" remained paramount, though General Braddock's troops had arrived and a full-scale French and Indian war was ready to be launched. "From Georgia to New Hampshire," said Thomas Hutchinson's *History,* "not one of the Assemblies inclined to part with so great a share of power as was to be given to the general government." Plainly, the inspiration that had swung the Albany Congress evaporated when the brilliant men who had headed it were dispersed. The plan was too new, too radical; people were not ready for it. Abiel Holmes (grandfather of the justice), in his *American Annals,* has a nice touch: "The same day (4 July)," he writes, "on which Franklin signed the Plan of Union in Convention at Albany, Washington capitulated with the French at Fort Necessity. Exactly twenty-two years afterward (4 July, 1776) Franklin signed the Declaration of Independence, while Washington was successfully commanding the armies of America."

Franklin confided his disgust to Peter Collinson. "Every Body cries, a Union is absolutely necessary; but when they come to the Manner and Form of the Union, their weak Noddles are presently distracted. So if ever there be an Union, it must be form'd at home by the Ministry and Parliament." In London the Lords of Trade turned down the plan. Not only had the colonial assemblies rejected it, but the Lords expressed astonishment at this notion of a general government "complete in itself" — in short, a government that displayed so little dependence on the Crown. William Johnson's suggestions about defense measures the Lords considered seriously, recommending that Johnson be put immediately in charge over the Iroquois. Nevertheless the Board of Trade did indeed form a plan of its own, and very quickly. Dated August 9, 1754, it is an emergency measure of military defense against the French, concerned with forts, garrisons, the raising of troops and the management of Indian affairs, rather than the internal government of the colonies.

To the overwhelming defeat of his plan, Franklin showed a characteristic reaction. Although confessing personal mortification, he at once commenced to develop the scheme further, on a broader basis. In this man's nature as he progressed through life, surely a most noticeable trait is his response to personal failure. Again and again we see Franklin project some public plan: in Philadelphia, in London, in Paris. Again and again the plan is defeated and the news of it noised abroad. Franklin does not wilt, nor does he snarl and strike back. He simply waits, writes out his ideas in letters to friends — invariably made public — and begins the charge from another position.

Such an attitude, displayed through more than half a century of active life, implies an immense self-confidence, or at least an extraordinary belief in one's self. John Adams, for instance, when defeated, yelled his agony, sent indiscreet letters to enemies (as did Sir Francis Bacon). Adams confided angrily in his diary, or wrote despairingly to his wife, Abigail. Franklin's *Autobiography* is famous the world over for its candor. Yet in it he never agonizes. Following some tight situation, Franklin sets down a feasible, daily plan for recovery. Or he says something ironical and funny, then proceeds to the next matter at hand. Franklin has often been accused of being "practical," to the exclusion of loftier feelings. Yet his practicality seems not an evasion but a short cut, as of one who, having already thought the business through, decides the time has come to state a conclusion.

The fate of his Albany Plan was "singular," wrote Franklin, much later. "The Assemblies did not adopt it, as they all thought there was too much *prerogative* in it, and in England it was judged to have too much of the *democratic.*" Franklin admitted that some things in the union might appear of "too popular a turn." But he did not cease to think about it, write of it, talk about it. During the autumn and winter after the Albany Congress, in his character as postmaster general,* Franklin made a long journey of inspection. In Boston he met with Governor William Shirley, whose ideas for a union leaned strongly to the prerogative side, more so than had seemed evident at Albany. To Shirley the plan too much resembled the old charter governments of Rhode Island and Connecticut — unfit, he said, even for a particular colony, let alone for "establishing a General Government and *Imperium* over all. . . ."

Franklin set out his ideas in a series of letters to Shirley, written while he was in Boston — plain, vigorous, and strikingly prophetic of the stand he was to take when Revolution began. The "Shirley Letters" would later appear in colonial newspapers, and over the years be reprinted in the *London Chronicle,* the *London Magazine,* the *Gentleman's Magazine,* the *Gazette.* English political writers would take them up, for paraphrase or quotation. "I apprehend," Franklin wrote to Shirley under date of December 3 and 4, 1754, "that excluding the *People* of the Colonies from all share in the choice of the Grand Council, will give extreme dissatisfaction, as well as the taxing them by Act of Parliament, where they have no Representative. . . . In Matters of General Concern to the People and especially where Burthens are to be laid upon them, it is of Use to consider as well what they will be *apt* to think and say, as what they ought to think." . . . And concerning taxation, was it not supposed to be the undoubted right of Englishmen never to

---

* This was one of the few offices held by Franklin that he had himself solicited. He worked hard at it and greatly increased the efficiency of the service.

be taxed but by their own consent, given by their representatives? The colonies having no representatives in Parliament, a refusal to permit them the right of their own
representatives in the Grand Council, "shows a Suspicion
of their Loyalty to the Crown, or Regard for their
Country, or of their Common Sense and Understanding,
which they have not deserv'd . . . rather like . . . treating them as a conquer'd People, and not as true British
subjects."

The British Iron Act of 1751 had prohibited colonists
from building rolling mills and steel furnaces. Franklin
at the time had objected strongly. Now he reminded
Governor Shirley that as things were regulated, "our
whole Wealth centers finally among the Merchants and
Inhabitants of Britain." It must seem hard measure to
colonial Englishmen, that by hazarding their lives and
fortunes in settling and subduing new countries, "extending the Dominion and increasing the Commerce of their
Mother Nation, they have forfeited the native Rights of
Britons, which they think ought rather to have been given
them, as due to such Merit. . . ."

Franklin sent a copy of this letter to Peter Collinson,
endorsed, *"On the Proposal of excluding the American
Assemblies from the Choice of the Grand Council, and
taxing the People in America by Parliament."* Shirley, in
conversation, apparently had yielded to the notion of
allowing colonial representatives in Parliament; he said
it would "unite them more intimately with Britain." He
would hope, Franklin replied, that by such a union, "the
people of Great Britain and the people of the Colonies
would learn to consider themselves, not as belonging to
different Communities with different Interests, but to
one Community with one Interest, which I imagine
would contribute to strengthen the whole, and greatly
lessen the danger of future separation."

One thinks of Thomas Jefferson, writing his rough

draft of the Declaration of Independence: *"We might have been a free and great people together."* One thinks of Increase Mather the Puritan, agent from a factious Massachusetts, in 1691 declaring to King William in London: "Your Majesty may, by the assistance of New England, become the Emperor of America. I durst engage, that your subjects there will readily venture their lives in your service. All that is humbly desired on their behalf is only that they may enjoy their ancient rights and privileges." The Revolutionary War was to be a civil war, the most agonizing of conflicts. No one can read American history thoughtfully without wondering if his country could somehow have been spared that conflict, and whether separation — indeed, domestic revolution — could have been achieved without bloodshed.

Seven years after the Battle of Yorktown, and five years after peace was signed — in the year 1788, as the new government under the United States Constitution was going into effect, the publisher of the *American Museum* (Mathew Carey) received a letter from a subscriber, enclosing an old article of Franklin's. "Reasons and Motives for the Albany Plan of Union," it was entitled. Carey asked Franklin if he wished, before publication, to make any changes. Franklin said no, but asked for the proof sheets. To these he appended what he called a "Remark," requesting that it be included without his signature:

Remark, Feb. 9, 1789

On Reflection it now seems probable that if the foregoing Plan or some thing like it, had been adopted and carried into Execution, the subsequent Separation of the Colonies from the Mother Country might not so soon have happened, nor the Mischiefs suffered on both sides have occurred, perhaps during another Century. For the Colonies, if so united, would have really been, as they then thought themselves, sufficient to make their own Defence, and being trusted with it, as by the Plan, an Army from Britain, for that Purpose would have been unnecessary: the Pretences for framing the Stamp-Act would then not have existed, nor the other Projects for drawing a Revenue from America to Britain by Acts of Parliament, which were the Cause of the Breach, and attended with such terrible Expence of Blood and Treasure: so that the different Parts of the Empire might still have remained in Peace and Union.

INTERLUDE

FRANKLIN IS FIFTY

CHAPTER NINE

A military excursion.
Franklin is named agent for Pennsylvania.
His enemies. He embarks for London.

Life, like a dramatic Piece, should not only
be conducted with Regularity, but methinks it
should finish handsomely. Being now in the last
Act, I begin to cast about for something fit to end
with.
— Franklin to George Whitefield, July 2, 1756

W HEN a man is fifty, he pauses to take stock. Has he
proved himself, and will the gods grant him yet
time for fulfillment? Franklin considered himself, he
said, "in the declining years of middle age." And he
spent his fiftieth birthday — January 17, 1756 — not handsomely at all, but crowded into a hut at Gnadenhutten,
near the town of Bethlehem, with the Pennsylvania militia,
cold and soaked to the skin.

Franklin was not without military experience. There
had been his association for defense in 1747, when the
French came up the Delaware and Franklin raised ten
thousand militia — scaring Thomas Penn into remarks
about the "Oliverian spirit" and a possible Cromwellian
commonwealth rising in the Province. There had also

been Franklin's famous procurement of wagons and horses to carry General Braddock's army across Pennsylvania to Duquesne on the frontier. Braddock, down in Maryland, had been in despair, ready to abandon his campaign. Franklin scoured the country around Lancaster, York and Cumberland, setting out posters to inform the preponderantly German inhabitants that they would be well paid for their contributions. If they did not provide horses and wagons, "Sir John St. Clair, the Hussar, with a body of soldiers," would march in and requisition what was needed — "which I shall be sorry to hear, because I am very sincerely and truly, your Friend and Well-wisher, B. Franklin."

These new settlers had known hussars only too well in Germany; the very title was a bogey. Actually, St. Clair, deputy quartermaster to Braddock, was no more a hussar than was Franklin. But in two weeks' time, 150 wagons and 259 horses were forthcoming. Franklin advanced more than a thousand pounds of his own money to pay for them and pledged his entire fortune in case Braddock (whom the farmers said they did not know and could not trust) defaulted on payments.

A year later, Indians crossed the mountains from the west. Up around Conestoga Indians were attacking settlers, massacring and murdering. Franklin drafted for the Assembly a militia act — the first in the Province; military requisitions were supposed to originate with the Crown. Pacifist Quaker politicians held back, but the Assembly, after much wrangling, passed the act. Governor Denny promptly vetoed it, disliking its provisions for officers appointed by the people rather than by the Crown.

Franklin, furious, published in the *Pennsylvania Gazette* a bitter piece, entitled, "Dialogue with X, Y, and Z, concerning the Present State of Pennsylvania." Says Z, *"For my Part, I am no Coward. But hang me if I'll fight to save the Quakers."* Says X, *"That is to say, you won't pump ship, because 'twill save the Rats, as well as your-self."*

Frontiersmen from Northampton County, enraged by the Province's failure to act, rode into Philadelphia with a wagonload of scalped corpses and dumped them on the State House steps. The Assembly at once passed an act issuing sixty thousand pounds for defense. Franklin, with his son as aide-de-camp, went up to Bethlehem and supervised the building of three forts across the mountains. Indian raids continued at Gnadenhutten, and Franklin was commissioned to take the field. For a month he remained with his troops in the freezing winter weather, sleeping on board floors, wet through, and somehow taking it all for granted as part of a citizen's duty. The Moravians addressed him as "General." What uniform Franklin wore we do not know; very likely the fringed leather jacket and trousers of the frontier. William, however, had his captain's green tunic, faced with red, an epaulet on one shoulder — acquired at Albany when he served against the French in '49. Father and son commanded fifty cavalrymen and some three hundred rangers. Franklin, "friend of the Indians," was ready to fight savages when fighting was in order; he offered a bounty for every scalp taken from an attacker. No detail escaped his interest. While the blockades were being built he stood, watch in hand, timing the axmen as they felled the trees: two men could take down a tall pine in six minutes. True, his managing of the soldiers was sometimes more Franklinesque than military. The troop chaplain, Mr. Beatty, complained because the men would not attend prayers in the fort. Franklin remembered that each man was issued every day a gill of rum, served half in the morning and half in the evening. "Mr. Beatty," said Franklin; "what if you were to act as steward of the rum, and deal it out only just after prayers. Would this be below the dignity of your profession?" Beatty liked the thought, said Franklin; "and never were prayers more generally and more punctually attended."

In February, Franklin came home, no worse for his weeks in the field — and was promptly commissioned colonel of the Philadelphia City Regiment of Militia, numbering about twelve hundred men. The first time their colonel reviewed them, the troop escorted him afterward to his house in Race Street, and standing before the door, fired their six brass cannon in salute, "which shook down and broke several Glasses of my Electrical Apparatus," Franklin reported, adding that his new honor "prov'd not less brittle; for all our Commissions were soon after broke by a Repeal of the Law in England."

The Penns in London were vastly annoyed by Franklin's military reputation. What right had these provincials to name their own officers? In a few months the Proprietors had news which exacerbated them further. The frontier being once again peaceful, Franklin prepared for a journey into Maryland and Virginia to oversee the post office. The officers of his regiment decided to escort their colonel as far as the lower ferry, and accomplished it in much style, some thirty or forty uniformed men on horseback, with swords drawn all the way. Thomas Penn wrote indignantly that *he* had never received such honors in Philadelphia, nor had any of his appointed governors of the Province: it was proper only to members of the blood royal. Penn even reported the incident to the ministry, as proof that Franklin was planning a military coup d'etat. "He is a dangerous Man," Penn had told Richard Peters, his secretary in the Province, "and I should be very Glad if he inhabited any other Country, as I believe him of a very uneasy Spirit. However as he is a sort of Tribune of the People, he must be treated with Regard."

In February of 1757, this Tribune of the People was named by the Assembly as their agent, "to solicit and transact the affairs of the Province in England." Not all the colonies sent special agents to London. Massachusetts employed the very experienced William Bollan; Connecticut was about to send a lawyer, Jared Ingersoll. Pennsylvania already retained Robert Charles, an Englishman who had lived in America; also Richard Partridge, a London merchant and Quaker who too had experienced colonial life. Sometimes the agents were Englishmen who had never seen America; Edmund Burke was to be one of these. Some, like Robert Charles, belonged to the species currently known as "placemen"; today they would be called career men.

The position of colonial agent was not easy. Actually he served as lobbyist, his chief business being to present legislative bills or petitions to the proper parties — the Board of Trade, Privy Council or some department of Parliament. Except for one or two rich merchants like Barlow Trecothick — later lord mayor of London — colonial agents had little or no status in government circles. Official England looked on them with a sour eye; peers and cabinet ministers dealt with them through lowly intermediaries.

Benjamin Franklin, with his scientific reputation, might expect to be in a higher category. Also he knew exactly why he was being sent and the present bounds of his mission: to meet with the Board of Trade and with the brothers, Thomas and Richard Penn, and effect some improvement in Pennsylvania affairs. Isaac Norris, Speaker of the House, was also named, but excused himself on a plea of ill health. Until Thomas Penn became principal Proprietor in 1746, things had gone well enough. But Thomas could not agree to the Assembly's control over the public revenue: its claim to vote taxes and supply. He said the Assembly usurped his lawful prerogative. Penn's deputies — the successive governors of the Province — obeyed his secret instructions, vetoed bill after bill in the Assembly, whether for limiting public houses (whose license fees went into the Penns' pocket), or for emitting paper money on loan, or for raising troops in defense against the Indians.

To the Proprietors' peremptory messages the Assembly framed long, querulous replies — and nothing ensued but quarrels, dissatisfaction and chaos. At Albany nearly four years earlier, Franklin had seemed friendly to John Penn, the Proprietor's nephew, and had agreed to a purchase of land from the Indians, largely as a means toward Franklin's cherished plans for settlement in the west. But landlordism and government in the same hands were showing themselves incompatible — to Franklin's mind, disastrous. Everywhere, plans for public improvement seemed blocked by the Proprietary party: the foundation of charity schools, the progress of the English Academy, relations with the Indians (always a delicate matter).

What the Assembly really wanted was freedom from external control, the management of its own business throughout the Province. Pennsylvania had outgrown its leading strings. Moreover, the Proprietors were eternally scheming for avoidance of taxation on their estates. "Instructions" to the governor demanded, in effect, that the Penns' best lands be assessed at the same rate as the inhabitants' poorest lands. To Thomas Penn's "Propositions" the Assembly drafted indignant replies, also a "Report on Grievances," which Franklin was to carry to London: *We the unhappy People of Pennsylvania are to be pitied who must perish by the Hand of the Enemy, or comply with Instructions, or rather Laws, made for us by ill-informed Proprietaries, at a Thousand Leagues in Distance: Laws unsuitable for our Circumstances, impracticable in their Nature, or if practicable, ineffectual.*

Richard Peters reported to his master concerning the petition: "These keen strokes of the Assembly against the Proprietaries are the performance of B.F. and were still more bitter before they underwent correction. . . . I am afraid," went on Peters, "that B.F., whose face at Times turns white as the driven Snow with the extremes of Wrath may assert Facts not true. . . ." Peters added, "I have a very high Opinion of B.F.'s virtue and uncorrupted honesty but party Zeal throws down all the pales of Truth and Candour and lays all the Soul waste to Temptation without knowing or suspecting it."

Richard Peters had known Franklin for years, and at close quarters. If Peters said that B.F.'s face turned white with anger it was true, despite the stereotype of benign philosopher that has come down the centuries. Before he died, Franklin left many portraits. In them we see him bland, full-cheeked, with brow unruffled, mouth an even line, and eyes that confront the world in the stillness of perfect self-possession. Or the face is bent to a book in his hand, the spectacles slip a little down the nose. Here indeed is *paterfamilias,* the Founding Father. Here sits a blameless and self-contained scholar in his study. And if, beyond the window the painter makes lightning flash against the storm, it is only to announce that this man has conquered Jove's thunderbolts. Somehow the portraits are a travesty, belying Franklin's life and actions, what he did and what he overcame. If with a kite string he "tamed the lightning," it is no more remarkable than his taming of his own nature. The bright, arrogant boy who antagonized his father and Brother James, the shrewd man of business who outwitted competitors and early amassed a comfortable fortune, the man of deep resolve and driving persistence — this is the Franklin who at fifty-odd could turn "white as the driven Snow with the extremes of wrath."

People feared Franklin. His ability to contain his words, to keep silence when provoked — this trick, acquired through years of self-discipline, only confounded Franklin's enemies the more. An opponent who turns pale and stifles his anger is an opponent who will act later on, when he is ready. Furthermore, it has been said that men dislike genius. And indeed, the presence of genius makes people uneasy; they have the instinct to reduce genius to ordinary capacity, and as fast as possible. The stories and the vicious talk followed Franklin all his life . . . *This man of many parts, did you know his reputation as a womanizer? How many illegitimate children has he sired? He chose a woman beneath him and made her his common-law wife. Did you know he could down two bottles of port at a sitting and liked to tell off-color stories?* *

"They talk of sending the Electrician home [England]," a Philadelphian wrote sourly to London. "He jumps at going. . . . He is artfully insinuating that he goes on his Countrys Service . . . he is wicked enough to Blind the People." Thus Dr. John Kearsley, later to be mobbed and imprisoned for his Tory views. Foremost among the Proprietary party — and therefore inimical to Franklin — were men who had once been his friends: William Allen, chief justice of Pennsylvania, who had materially helped Franklin's campaign for the postmastership; also the Reverend William Smith, an Anglican clergyman who had worked with Franklin in the founding of the charity schools and the English Academy (later to become the University of Pennsylvania). Former governor James Hamilton a few years before had named Franklin a justice of the peace; now he turned against his protégé. Another former governor, Robert Hunter Morris, advised the Penns that "Mr. Franklin is a sensible Artfull man, very knowing in American affairs, and was his heart as sound as his head, few men would be fitter for Publick trust; But that is far from being the Case, He has nothing in view but to serve himself. . . ."

---

* No one can write about Benjamin Franklin without being treated to an infinity of gossipy bits, told with relish. "Old Ben was a great man," said a Boston taxi driver to this writer. "But he had one weakness — women. Did you know he left twelve bastards and died of syphilis?"

All of these gentlemen discussed among themselves — and reported to London — the possible and probable reasons for Franklin's desire to go to England. Surely the man must be ambitious for place and power under the Crown? Already he held one Crown office, the postmastership. It was even rumored that by turning the Province into a royal government, Franklin looked one day to be governor himself. Wrote William Peters (brother of Richard) to Thomas Penn: "Many People think their mighty Favorite Mr. Franklin has a Design to Dupe them as well as you, by working his Scheme so as that the King shall be oblig'd for saving the Province to take it into his own hands." For himself, Penn replied, he did not believe the ministry would advise the King to give Franklin such an appointment.

Richard Peters was even more specific. "Certain it is," he wrote Penn, "that B.F's view is to effect a change of Government, and considering the popularity of his character and the reputation gained by his Electrical Discoveries which will introduce him to all sorts of Company he may prove a Dangerous Enemy. Dr. Fothergill and Mr. Collinson can introduce him to the Men of most influence at Court and he may underhand give impressions to your prejudice. In short Heaven and Earth will be moved against the Proprietors."

Thomas Penn seemed indifferent to this news: "I think I wrote you before that Mr. Franklin's popularity is nothing here, and that he will be looked upon very coldly by great People, there are very few of any consequence that have heard of his Electrical Experiments, those matters being attended to by a particular Sett of People . . . but it is quite another sort of People, who are to determine the Dispute between us."

Penn was right. The courtiers and placemen who surrounded George II, the fox-hunting squires and landholders who ruled Parliament, for the most part had interests far removed from science and natural philosophy —

matters which after all were better suited to Cambridge dons. This was something that Benjamin Franklin, as provincial agent in London, had yet to find out for himself. In America, however, he was well aware of his position. Preparing for his departure — "I leave some Enemies . . . ," he wrote his young political supporter, Joseph Galloway, "who will take every Opportunity of injuring me in my Absence. However, as they are my Enemies, not on my own private Account but on that of the Publick, I seem to have some Right to ask the Care of my Friends. . . . I chearfully leave my dearest Concerns under that Care."

A nation is not built on benignity, nor a revolution staged by easygoing men. Franklin in 1757 was not acting for the American nation — that did not exist — but for his Province and for himself. Of course he wanted to go to London. *Home,* he called it: "I am to go home immediately." From every period of history, there remain words and phrases that cannot be comprehended by later generations, or felt in all their poignancy and immediate meaning. One is the word "home" as used by colonial Americans — used proudly, fondly. Franklin was about to cross three thousand miles of ocean, dangerously infested by enemy ships. He would of course be no stranger in London; many friends awaited him. To one of these, William Strahan the printer and publisher, Franklin wrote in terms suggesting that he was merely crossing the county line for a visit. "Look out sharp, and if a fat old Fellow should come to your Printing House and request a little Smouting * depend upon it, 'tis your affectionate Friend and humble Servant, B. Franklin."

The packet for London was due to sail at the end of March — or so Franklin was told by Lord Loudoun, Braddock's successor as commander in chief for North Amer-

* Printers' slang for part-time work.

ica. Loudoun came to Philadelphia and talked with Governor Denny and Franklin about the Assembly's dispute with the Proprietors. "Neither of them agreed in the Facts which the other pledged," the Earl reported to England; "but Mr. Frankland was much more acquainted with the affair than the Governor." Early in April, Franklin set off for New York to take ship, together with his son William, their two Negro servants, and an escort of some dozen friends riding alongside Franklin's chaise.

It was a pleasant journey of four days, with a stopover at Elizabeth Town to dine with Jonathan Belcher, governor of the Province, and young William writing to his "dearest Betsy," while the horses were waiting, "to let my Charmer know of my Welfare." His charmer was Miss Graeme, daughter of a Philadelphia physician. William expatiated on "the Morning of our Love," which unfortunately was destined never to reach its noonday; William in England would become otherwise interested and end the affair.

Franklin's packet, the *General Wall,* planned to start off in convoy with Lord Loudoun's ships, which were to sail north for some kind of action against the French at Louisburg. But the noble earl proved incredibly dilatory. Days went by, and weeks. The general sat at his desk, preparing reports while his transports gathered barnacles on their bottoms until they were fit to founder. Deborah came from Philadelphia, bringing their daughter Sally, now a pretty girl of thirteen. There were family excursions in the Jerseys, with William expressing amazement that America had anything to show so beautiful as the falls at Passaic.

And still the Pennsylvania agent waited, idle, sending letters to his friends: The Drs. Lining and Garden in Charleston; Isaac Norris and Galloway in Philadelphia. "I have been very low-spirited all Day," Franklin wrote his wife in May. "This tedious State of Uncertainty and long Waiting, has almost worn out my Patience. . . . I know not when I have spent Time so uselessly. . . . I left my best Spectacles on the Table. Please send them to me."

Long ago, at Newcastle, a Pennsylvania governor had delayed and promised, promised and delayed until a boy of eighteen set sail for London with none of this world's goods beyond the clothes on his back and a few pounds in his pocket. . . .

Lord Loudoun invited Franklin to dine. French frigates, the general said, had been seen off Egg Harbor. There could be no setting sail until a convoy was arranged. In a few days the report proved groundless — and still the commander in chief delayed. "After waiting here above Seven Weeks for the Sailing of the Pacquet," Franklin wrote to Isaac Norris, "the Time of her Departure is no more ascertain'd now than it was the Day of our Arrival." At a loss for action, plainly depressed, Franklin made his will — a remarkable document, providing for his friends and no less than twenty-two relatives, and opening with the now celebrated words, *I Benjamin Franklin of the City of Philadelphia, Printer.* A cheerful peroration confesses in eighteenth-century deistical style an honest gratitude to "that BEING OF BEINGS" for granting a long life "in a Land of Liberty, with a People that I love." Thanks also, Franklin continued, "for conducting me thro' Life so happily, so free from Sickness, Pain and Trouble, and with such a Competency of this World's Goods as might make a reasonable Mind easy; that he was pleased to give me such a Mind, with moderate Passions, or so much of his Assistance in governing them. . . ."

Did any man before or since address his God in more practical terms — thanking Him for enough money to make a reasonable mind easy, and for teaching him how to govern that mind?

Franklin's parents were dead, and of his brothers, only Peter was left, aged fifty-five. Of Franklin's remaining sisters, his closest tie was with Jane Mecom, the youngest,

now forty-five and the mother of nine. Franklin cared
deeply for Jane, had taken her son Benjamin to train as
printer, sent him to Antigua and set him up there. A half-
sister, Elizabeth Douse, at seventy-nine had become a
family problem. Jane wrote that she would be removed
from her house, where she lived alone, and placed where
she could be conveniently cared for. Franklin answered
Jane in words which he never dreamed would follow him
down the years — words that are indeed the very image of
Franklin himself; worldly yet kind, shrewd yet benevolent.
In the lives of heroes it is well when fate forces them to
inactivity, and they perforce turn inward and tell us what
they think about plain things, family matters and the
vexations common to all mankind:

As *having their own Way,* is one of the greatest Comforts of
Life, to old People, I think their Friends should endeavor
to accommodate them in that, as well as in any thing else.
When they have long liv'd in a House, it becomes natural to
them, they are almost as closely connected with it as the
Tortoise with his Shell, they die if you tear them out of it.
Old Folks and old Trees, if you remove them, 'tis ten to one
that you kill them. So let our good old Sister be no more
importun'd on that head. We are growing old fast ourselves,
and shall expect the same kind of Indulgencies. If we give
them, we shall have a Right to receive them in our Turn.

As to her few fine Things, I think she is in the Right not
to sell them, and for the Reason she gives, that they will
fetch but little. When that little is spent; they would be of
no farther use to her; but perhaps the Expectation of Possessing them at her Death, may make that Person tender
and careful of her, and helpful to her, to the amount of
ten times their Value.

Finally, on June twentieth, Franklin's packet sailed from
New York, commanded by a Captain Lutwidge. Twice
they were chased by enemy ships, but outran them. Franklin showed avid interest in the packet's design, her sails,
the way she was laden and the reason for her swiftness. On

the twenty-sixth day they neared Falmouth, in Cornwall, set all the sail they could carry, bounded on before a fair wind — and that night barely missed foundering off the Scilly Isles. Only an accidental yaw of the ship revealed a lighthouse, so close that it looked, wrote Franklin, like a cartwheel over their bows. Just in time the ship bore round, all sails standing — "An Operation dangerous to the masts," Franklin wrote, "but it carried us clear, and we escap'd Shipwreck, for we were running right upon the Rocks on which the Lighthouse was erected."

They landed at Falmouth on a Sunday morning in July and heard the bells ring for church. "We went thither immediately," Franklin wrote his wife, "and with hearts full of gratitude returned sincere thanks to God for the mercies we had received: were I a Roman Catholic, perhaps I should on this occasion vow to build a chapel to some saint; but as I am not, if I were to vow at all, it should be to build a *light-house*."

SCENE FOUR

FRANKLIN
IN LONDON
1757–1766

CHAPTER TEN

London and the Penns. A visit
to Scotland. The French are beaten
in America. Franklin returns briefly
to Philadelphia, suffers political defeat,
and embarks once more for London.

Lodgings had been provided for the Franklins near
Charing Cross. Robert Charles, Franklin's fellow
agent — his "Assistant" — had seen to it; 7 Craven Street,
the address was. The house, a pleasant, small dwelling of
three stories, belonged to their landlady, a widow named
Mrs. Margaret Stevenson. The street, once called Spur Al-
ley, ran down from the Strand to the Thames, almost under the shadow of Northumberland House. The Franklins
had four furnished rooms on the second floor, with "every
thing about us pretty genteel," Franklin reported. From
Franklin's bedroom a bay window fronted the street; in
the room behind he was to keep his electrical apparatus.

It was an address respectable enough, almost fashion-
able, within walking distance of official London, Whitehall,
Westminster and the Houses of Parliament. Westminster
Bridge was new, and the city was very proud of it. The
tide rushed through pale stone arches; swans sailed near
shore, and in midstream the wherries plied from St. James's

Palace down to the Tower of London, east of Paul's Church standing on Ludgate hill. Here was a city of seven hundred thousand souls, boasting green parks, ducal mansions, streets rife with poverty, dirt, disease, and a populace which from time to time exploded into terrifying riots of protest and fury.

William, who had been entered years before as student of law at the Middle Temple, began attendance at once; he had not far to go. As soon as Franklin was settled, he went round to call on Peter Collinson in his shop near Westminster Bridge. Collinson had been looking for his friend since early June. Full of plans, he said that Hanbury, the great tobacco merchant, had asked to be notified of Franklin's arrival, that he might introduce him to Lord Granville, president of Privy Council. Accordingly, Hanbury called for Franklin in his carriage and took him to Granville. Franklin could hardly have expected a cordial reception; not only was his lordship known as a high prerogative man, but he happened to be married to Thomas Penn's wife's sister. Granville received Franklin civilly enough, then read him a patronizing lecture concerning Pennsylvania's mistaken ideas about their constitution. "You Americans," said Granville, "contend that the King's Instructions to his governors are not laws, and think your selves at liberty to regard or disregard them at your own discretion. But those Instructions . . . are first drawn up by Judges learned in the Laws; they are then considered, debated and perhaps amended in Privy Council, after which they are signed by the King. They are then, so far as relates to you, the *Law of the Land;* for THE KING IS THE LEGISLATOR OF THE COLONIES."

Setting down the words afterward, Franklin put them in capital letters. It was the first of many such shocks he was to experience. Were the colonial assemblies and their wishes then to be overlooked altogether? "The King's Instructions," in Pennsylvania's case, went direct from London to Thomas Penn's minion — the governor; if the Assembly must slavishly follow such instruction, they were lost. Franklin did not let Granville's remarks go unchallenged. In his understanding, said Franklin, the colonies were to make their own laws; when once the King had assented he could not repeal or alter them. Franklin left the minister's house alarmed, he said, as to what the sentiments of the court might be concerning Pennsylvania.

His next move was to call on the Penns, whose house stood not far from Craven Street. Dr. Fothergill, very knowledgeable, had advised against presenting the Assembly's complaints formally, in writing. Better to try, first, what conversation and tactful approach would do. Franklin got nowhere with tactful conversation. The brothers, Thomas and Richard Penn, met him with their lawyer at hand, Ferdinand John Paris, shrewd and hard. "A proud angry man, who had conceived a mortal enmity to me," Franklin said. After several inconclusive meetings — always monitored by their lawyer — the Penns requested something in writing, and Franklin drew up what he called "Heads of Complaint," brief and to the point, giving the Assembly's grievances and ending with a matter the Penns could not bear to hear mentioned: the present exemption of their estates from taxation, which, declared Franklin, "to the Assembly and People of America, appears both unjust and cruel."

Ferdinand Paris placed this paper in the hands of England's attorney general, where it lay unanswered, according to Franklin, for "a Year wanting eight Days." Plainly, matters were going to move very slowly indeed. Just before Christmas, Franklin appeared, on Pennsylvania's behalf, before the all-powerful Board of Trade, Lord Halifax presiding — a peer with little sympathy for Americans. Franklin seems to have said little or nothing. But he was compelled to hear a bitter reprimand delivered to his fellow agent, Robert Charles, whose requests on behalf of the Assembly (of the same tenor as Franklin's) were termed "arrogant and insolent, groundless and injurious." Robert Charles happened to be a notably tactless man, with a carriage said to be "haughty." He had long served as colonial agent — perhaps he needed toning down by the new Pennsylvania agent. Nevertheless the encounter proved that the Proprietors did indeed possess strong political backing. What Franklin had not realized was that the Penns were skilled politicians, in a position to cultivate the right people. Moreover, they had laid their plans a long time since.

From now on, matters with the Penns moved from bad to worse. January of 1758 saw a terrible confrontation, where Thomas Penn declared that the Province was only a kind of corporation acting by charter from the Crown, and could have no privileges or rights but what was granted by that charter, in which such privileges as that now claimed were nowhere mentioned.

"Your father's charter," Franklin retorted, "expressly says that the Assembly of Pennsylvania shall have all the power and privilege of an Assembly according to the rights of the freeborn subjects of England." To this Penn replied that the royal charter granted to his father had never been any secret; if inhabitants were deceived it was their own fault. Franklin could hardly believe his ears. Were the Penns, like Granville, denying rights of Britons in America, simply shrugging them away? Reporting the scene to Isaac Norris, Franklin wrote that Penn had spoken "with a kind of triumphing Laughing Insolence, such as a low Jockey might do when a Purchaser complained that he had cheated him in a Horse. I was astonished . . . and conceived that Moment a more cordial and thorough contempt for him that I ever before felt for any Man living. A Contempt that I cannot express in Words, but I believe my Countenance expressed it strongly . . . his Brother [Richard] was looking at me and must have observed it; however finding myself grow warm I made no other Answer to this than that the poor People were no Lawyers themselves and confiding in his Father did not think it necessary to consult any."

The Penns had indeed noted Franklin's anger. He looked, they wrote to Peters, "like a malicious V[illain] as he always does." Somehow, Peters managed to see Franklin's letter about the meeting and quoted it copiously to the Penns, including the reference to a low jockey. After this the Proprietors refused to treat with Franklin on any pretense; he could approach only through their lawyer. Dr. Fothergill, distressed, chided Franklin for the language he had used to Isaac Norris, and reported to a friend in Philadelphia that "B. Franklin's reputation as a man, a philosopher and a statesman, only seem to render his station more difficult and perplexing: Such is the unhappy turn of mind, of most of those, who constitute the world of influence in this country."

Influence, connections: these were the key words. To accomplish anything in government circles a man should be intimate, not with the friends that Franklin had chosen but with the King's ministers, the Lords of Trade and leaders of policy. Franklin must be allowed time, Fothergill continued, "and without repining. Great pains had been taken, and very successfully, to render him odious and his integrity suspected, to those very persons to whom he must first apply. These suspicions can only be worn off by time and prudence." Franklin still had much to learn; the ways of governmental bureaucracy are not fathomed in a month or a year. He reported to Isaac Norris that Privy Council ought to have brought the Proprietary issue to the House of Commons, "but they are afraid the Parliament would establish more Liberty in the Colonies than is proper or necessary, and therefore do not care the Parliament should meddle at all with the Government of the Colonies." Franklin clung to an optimistic — and mistaken — conviction that members of the English Commons were independent-minded public servants who possessed real sympathy for British citizens in America. Actually, the Commons followed the ministerial lead. Most members would have agreed with Charles Townshend when he declared "the colonies should be governed like Ireland, keeping a body of standing forces, with a military chest and the abridgment of their legislative powers." It was a viewpoint derived from ignorance rather than bad feeling. Lord Halifax in the Board of Trade held to it firmly.

Dr. Fothergill had been right; the American agent needed time, and he needed prudence.

Meanwhile, in Pennsylvania, crazy rumors circulated concerning Franklin's reputed "success" in England: He had been made a baronet . . . he was to be governor of the Province. Franklin's sister, Jane Mecom, sent off a note to Deborah: "If I dont Express my self proper you must Excuse it seeing I have not been acostomed to Pay my Complements to Governor & Baronets Ladys. I am in the midst of a grate wash & Sarah still sick, & would gladly been Excused writing this Post but my husband says I must write & Give you Joy which we [sin]searly Joyn in. . . ."

Neither Jane nor Deborah was ever deterred by such barriers as spelling. Debbie's letters were frequent, lively and — no common virtue with correspondents — answered all her husband's questions and told him just what he wanted to know. Franklin greatly enjoyed these letters; moreover, he believed all spelling should be phonetic and invented a phonetic alphabet in which he corresponded with Mary Stevenson. He never showed himself embarrassed by the plainness of his womenfolk in America, or indeed of his own humble origin.

There was in Franklin an unassailable reserve; if enemy or friend tried to broach it, there is no record that they suceeded. Shortly after his meeting with the Penns, Franklin wrote his wife that he feared he would not be able to return for another twelve months: "I am for doing effectually what I came about, and I find it requires both time and patience. You may think perhaps that I can find many amusements here to pass the time agreeable. 'Tis true, the conversation of ingenious men, give me no small pleasure; but at this time of life, domestic comforts afford the most solid satisfaction, and my uneasiness at being absent from my family, and longing desire to be with them, make me often sigh in the midst of cheerful company."

Franklin, if he wished, could have dined out every night of the week, though he never became the fashion in London he was to be in Paris. His British friends were merchants, botanists, and philosophers of the Royal Society and certain liberal thinkers and dissenting persons who liked to meet at the coffeehouses. London of the time was a place of men's clubs rather than salons. Franklin especially enjoyed the club calling itself Honest Whigs, whose members convened at the George and Vulture, or the London Tavern near St. Paul's, to enjoy conversation, apple puffs, rarebits, wine, and beer. Franklin played chess with John Pringle, later knighted and made president of the Royal Society. James Boswell, who watched the game, reported Dr. Pringle as notably sour and Franklin all jollity and pleasantry: "a prime contrast, acid and alkali."

Nor does Franklin in London mention the society of women, beyond his close friendship with his landlady, Mrs. Stevenson, and her daughter Polly, with whom he was to correspond all his life. Franklin loved the company of young women and they responded. But one would be hard put to find in this converse anything that suggests the flesh and the devil. Franklin's letters to Catherine Greene in Rhode Island and to Polly Stevenson have been published and made much of; actually they are affectionate, avuncular and beyond reproach. As to his landlady, Mrs. Stevenson, the two were on friendliest terms but nowhere can be found a hint of speculation of any closer relationship. All the world knows that Franklin was attractive to women and they to him. William Strahan wrote playfully to Deborah, urging her to brave the ocean voyage and join her husband in London: "Now Madam as I know the ladies here consider him in exactly the light I do (I never saw a man who was so perfectly agreeable to me) — upon my word I think you should come over with all convenient speed to look after your interests; not but that I think him as faithful to his Joan as any man breathing; but who knows what repeated strong temptation may, in time, and while he is at so great a distance from you, accomplish. . . ."

Just where Franklin found his pleasures during these London years we shall never discover. No record exists, and no bastard offspring beyond William. This was a lusty man, and discreet as he was lusty; if he had amours he did not talk about them. Strahan tried to lay a bet that his letters would fetch Deborah by the next ship. But Franklin refused, well aware that nothing could induce his wife to cross the ocean. During that first autumn in London, Franklin had been confined to his room for nine weeks with a severe cold or influenza, somehow surviving the good Dr. Fothergill's bleedings, purges and clysters. Franklin wrote his wife that Mrs. Stevenson had been obliging and took great care of his health: "But yet I have a thousand times wished you with me, and my little Sally with her ready Hands and Feet to do, and go, and come, and get what I wanted. There is a great difference in sickness between being nurs'd with that tender Affection which proceeds from sincere Love."

As soon as he was up and about, Franklin shipped off a handsome list of presents to his family: English china and silver, cut glass, breakfast cloths for the table ("No body breakfasts here on the naked Table," Franklin wrote.) . . . Carpeting for the best room, damask table covers, gowns for Deborah and Sally, a pair of silk blankets just taken in a French prize ship, "such as were never seen in England before — very neat to cover a Summer bed instead of a Quilt or Counterpain." There were books, music — and finally a large beer jug to stand in the cooler. "I fell in love with it at first Sight," Franklin wrote, "for I thought it look'd like a fat jolly Dame, clean and tidy, with a neat blue and white Calico Gown on, good natur'd and lovely, and put me in mind of — Somebody."

Franklin lived well in London, hired a coach for twelve guineas a month and entertained his friends elegantly at dinner in his rooms. Living was expensive, yet there was small choice; the American agent could not present a grubby front. Not the least of his expenses were certain highly necessary fees and gratuities handed out to underlings at Whitehall, or in the Commons lobby and the antechambers of the great. Franklin never abandoned his electrical interests. Housed in the room behind his bedchamber he set up what he called his "Philadelphia Machine," which produced a spark "nine inches long" — causing scientific colleagues to marvel. Lord Charles Cavendish said so powerful a machine had never been seen in England before. Franklin operated it, he said, "from a buckskin cushion with a long flap"; a wire ran through his window down to Mrs. Stevenson's yard. Franklin also played for his friends on his musical glasses; he invented a three-wheeled clock and persuaded James Ferguson, the astronomer, to improve it. Next door to the Craven Street lodging was a printing house; Franklin liked to drop in and talk shop with the pressmen, sometimes sending out for beer to drink a toast: "Success to printing!" The grate in Franklin's room burned cannel coal. "Sea-coal," Franklin called it, annoyed at the thick, oily smoke it sent up the chimney. "The whole Town," he wrote, "is one great Smoaky House, and every Street a Chimney, the Air full of floating Sea Coal Soot, and you never get a sweet Breath of what is pure, without riding some Miles for it into the Country." It was one of the few complaints Franklin ever made about London. To English architecture he seemed oblivious, expressing neither interest nor admiration unless to note some device he could borrow for American use.

In November of 1758, William was called to the bar, a barrister. The Franklins celebrated by having their wigs refurbished at four pounds each, and ordering new suits from the tailor. Later the two went off to Scotland, where they stayed six weeks and Franklin had the time of his life. Edinburgh gave him the freedom of the city; the universities entertained him, and he met and conversed with the best minds of Scotland — which in fact meant the best minds of the kingdom. Edinburgh houses were built very high, sheltering seven or eight families and possessing no yards, cellars, or outhouses. A city ordinance commanded every family to collect its night pots at ten P.M. and throw the contents into the streets, to be gathered up by carts.

Sydney Smith, the witty canon of St. Paul's, was later to say that Scotland meant "odious smells, barbarous sounds, bad suppers, excellent hearts and most enlightened understandings." At dinner one confronted such horrors as solan-goose, cock-a-leaky, or tups-head. But the air was always cool, there were no flies as in Philadelphia, and Franklin was not one to notice what he ate, or if he did he never mentioned it. He stayed in the country houses of Sir Alexander Dick, who presided over the College of Physicians, and of Lord Kames the advocate, with his sensitive, strong face and quick mind. He met Adam Smith, who had lately published his *Theory of the Moral Sentiments* — a book much more widely read than his later *Wealth of Nations*. David Hume, already accused of "heresy, deism, scepticism, atheism," was of this goodly company. The third edition of *Hume's Philosophical*

Essays had been kept back by his publishers because recent earthquakes had frightened readers into superstition. Then as now, no publisher tempts the gods too far.

One evening at the house of Robertson, the historian, Dr. Alexander Carlyle was present. A handsome, formidable divine known as Jupiter Carlyle, he remarked much later that Franklin's son had been "open and communicative," better company than his father, and that several of the company had observed "indications of that decided difference of opinion between father and son which in the American war alienated them altogether." British friends often showed interest in Franklin's relationship with his son. Strahan, a far more intimate observer than Carlyle, had written Deborah that he considered William one of the prettiest young gentlemen he ever knew from America — adding that his father was at the same time "his son's friend, his brother, his intimate, and easy companion." The words were destined to be sadly ironic. An easy companionship from father to son seldom succeeds in the long run, and the "pretty young gentleman" would cause Franklin the deepest sorrow of his life, next perhaps to the death of his son Francis.

The Scottish visit passed all too quickly; Franklin later referred to it as "six weeks of the *densest* happiness" he had met with in any part of his life. "Did not strong Connections draw me elsewhere," he wrote Lord Kames, "I believe Scotland would be the Country I should chuse to spend the Remainder of my Days in." Before the Franklins returned to London they had covered fifteen hundred miles, visiting Ireland, inspecting the salt mines of Norwich, the pottery kilns of Staffordshire, the weavers of Yorkshire. Franklin's eye was bright to observe such skills as might be brought home to the infant industries of his country.

In November of 1760, Montreal surrendered to the British; Quebec had fallen nine months earlier — events that were to change the face of Europe as well as America. General Jeffrey Amherst had taken Louisbourg, General John Forbes had captured Duquesne. Everywhere, France was beaten. Greatly humiliated, she lost her place as leader in Europe and bided her time for revenge. William Pitt, to all intents and purposes prime minister and re-sponsible for France's defeat, was the universal hero — far too illustrious to give attention, as yet, to a Benjamin Franklin, though Franklin tried to see him. "He was then too great a Man," wrote Franklin later, "or too much occupy'd in Affairs of great Moment." Victory followed victory for England's arms: Canada reduced, India con-quered, no less than twenty-five islands important to world trade seized, and ten million sterling in plunder taken.* "The park guns will never have time to cool," wrote Horace Walpole. "We ruin ourselves with gun-powder and skyrockets. Victories come tumbling so over one another from distant parts of the globe, that it looks just like the handiwork of a lady romance-writer." Frank-lin told Lord Kames that no one could rejoice more than he on the reduction of Canada — "not merely as I am a Colonist, but as I am a Briton. I have long been of Opinion, that the Foundations of the future Grandeur and Stability of the British Empire, lie in America; and tho', like other Foundations, they are low and little seen, they are nevertheless, broad and Strong enough to sup-port the greatest Political Structure Human Wisdom ever yet erected."

England had a new king, twenty-two years old, grand-son of George II; in October of 1761 the Franklins were

---

* By the Treaty of Paris concluded in February of 1763, Great Britain returned to France the captured sugar islands of Guadeloupe and Martinique in the West Indies in exchange for all of Canada. France also won fishing rights on the Newfoundland banks and two small islands off that coast. Pitt, who had been dismissed by George III, pro-tested this decision, which was unpopular at the time as the sugar islands were considered an important source of revenue and Canada was considered negligible commercially.

in London for his coronation. George III, wrote Franklin, was a generous and virtuous young ruler, "the very best in the World and the most amiable." What reason was there to think otherwise? Charles Pratt, attorney general (afterward Lord Camden) remarked to Franklin that the Americans, notwithstanding their boasted affection, would one day set up for independence. "No such idea," returned Franklin, "is entertained by the Americans, or ever will be, unless you grossly abuse them."

"Very true," Pratt replied. "That I see will happen, and will produce the event."

Both men were right. Few Americans would come out for Independence until blood had been shed at Lexington and Concord. Yet restlessness had long existed, evinced even in such movements as Pennsylvania's desire to be free of the Proprietors. *External control* was irksome and the Province primed for rescue even by some imagined panacea such as Franklin's notion that royal government would be preferable to a private Proprietor.

Hearings on the Proprietary affairs continued; negotiations with the Board of Trade dragged through the months. "I am obliged to wait," Franklin wrote Galloway, "or take upon myself the blame of Rashness, if I should come to open War with People suppos'd to be so well disposed, who it will be said, might have been brought to very reasonable terms by an Agent of more Temper." The matter was settled after a last difficult hearing before the Board, with lawyers for both sides wrangling persistently. If minutes were taken they have never been found; to this day historians disagree whether the result was a victory for Franklin or a resounding defeat. The Pennsylvania Assembly had submitted for confirmation some nineteen acts: to explain them would require a book-length sortie into the impossibly complicated tangle of Pennsylvania politics and parties. Suffice it to say that of the nineteen acts, eleven were opposed by the Proprietors, who secured Privy Council's veto on six. Franklin won acceptance for the other five. By far the most important of the acts concerned taxation of the Proprietary estates. Franklin himself has described how in the midst of discussion, a Privy Councillor — Lord Mansfield, the great jurist — suddenly rose, and beckoning to Franklin, led him into the clerk's chamber. Provided the Pennsylvania Assembly were permitted to tax the Proprietary estates, said Mansfield, would Franklin and his fellow agent, Robert Charles, give their bond the estates would be equitably assessed? The two agents agreed, and the three returned to the council office, where other adjustments were made, such as a temporary establishment of the provincial credit by means of paper money, and the naming of John Penn as governor. Plainly, the Crown was prepared to support the Proprietors against attack. Provincial defiance must cease; colonial assemblies and their agents could not be permitted to interfere in the imperial system.

Two centuries later, an English historian * would write that Britons, after defeating the French in 1760, were arrogant as Roman-born citizens of the Augustan Age. It is an attitude nicely calculated to crush. Franklin had no intention of giving up the fight. When the Penns' machinations were fully revealed, he wrote angrily, "the Proprietors will be gibbeted up as they deserve, to rot and stink in the Nostrils of Posterity."

Privy Council's decision was made in September of 1760. Franklin remained in England, however, for two more years — a period which until recently has been glossed over by his biographers. During this time Franklin was anxiously occupied in looking after certain monies belonging to Pennsylvania. Parliament had granted a large sum to the colonies for their part in fighting the French; Pennsylvania's share amounted to £26,618, 14s. 6d. The Assembly directed Franklin to receive it and in-

* Harold Nicolson.

vest the money "in the publick funds." To act as broker on such occasions was part of a colonial agent's duties, also he must keep on hand available monies for paying British creditors. Franklin received sixty pounds from the Assembly as his commission; he offered half to Robert Charles, who refused, saying he preferred payment direct from the Assembly. (He never received it.) Franklin invested the entire Parliamentary grant in government annuities; which, considering the glorious news from Europe, could be considered both safe and advantageous. Everyone looked for the stock to rise a beneficent twenty percent when peace should be formally signed with France. Agreement seemed imminent. People talked of a conference at Augsburg; horses had even been chosen to draw the British coaches. Franklin's investment of £26,618 rose to £30,000.

Then suddenly the peace movement collapsed. Pitt, aware that a secret treaty — the Family Compact — had been signed by the Bourbon rulers of Spain, Italy and France, proposed to commence hostilities against Spain. Finding no support in the cabinet, Pitt resigned in October of 1761. The market plummeted; Pennsylvania lost £2,492. At this inauspicious moment, Franklin received direction from the Pennsylvania Assembly to pay certain bills outstanding. (Mail from America was so slow in arriving that the time was invariably inauspicious.) Franklin went from banker to banker, vainly begging credit. Finally, in January of 1762, the firm of Sargent and Aufrere agreed to pay all drafts that Franklin could not cover, "without desiring," they said, "any other Security from you, than that which we have in your Character." *

Franklin's mission to England was for the moment ended. "I feel here," he wrote to Strahan, "like a thing out of its place, and useless because it is out of its place. How then can I any longer be happy in England? You have great powers of persuasion, and might easily prevail

* See bibliographical note.

on me to do any thing; but not any longer to do nothing. I must go home. Adieu."

In five years, Franklin's experiences had shifted often and incongruously from bottom to top, from public failure to personal triumph. Officially he had been snubbed and had learned what it was to cool his heels in the anterooms of the great. Nevertheless, he had made friendships that would last a lifetime; indeed, there were moments when Franklin felt himself almost an Englishman. (Richard Jackson offered to propose him for a seat in Parliament.) During the unhappy negotiations over the Proprietorship, Oxford University and Saint Andrews in Scotland gave him honorary degrees; henceforth Franklin would be known as "Doctor." Oxford even included William in the ceremony, naming him Master of Arts. In the autumn of 1762, William, to the intense surprise of nearly everybody, was made governor of New Jersey. It seems that John Pringle, who was Lord Bute's physician, had used his influence with that powerful nobleman to obtain the post.

Just how well Franklin knew Lord Bute is a matter for speculation. The earl, a handsome, prideful man, one of the most powerful in England, friend of George II and George III, was himself a botanist of note, with a famous garden of specimens at his country estate, Luton Hoo, also a superb collection of scientific instruments and electrical machines. It would be odd, indeed, if he and Franklin had not met. Yet Franklin was reticent. Here and there one finds mysterious hints that Franklin's optimism regarding the eventual success of his plans against the Penns stemmed from hope of Bute's influence. John Adams, no friend to Franklin, declared in his *Autobiography* * that the Doctor once "broke out into a Passion and swore, contrary to his usual reserve, that he had an influence with the Ministry and was intimate with Lord Bute."

Concerning William's governorship of New Jersey,

* Written in 1806.

Franklin in later life confessed that he had not been too pleased by this Crown favor. How would it affect his own position? With a son as royal governor of a colony, could a father use every effort to displace the governor of the colony next door? Thomas Penn declared the appointment was bound to make Benjamin Franklin "more tractable; the son must obey royal instructions, and what he is ordered to do the father cannot well oppose in Pennsylvania."

But no word of Franklin's discomfort escaped him at the moment. The *London Chronicle*, announcing William's appointment, revealed at the same time that William had just been married to a Miss Elizabeth Downes, from the West Indies; the wedding was held stylishly at St. George's Church, Hanover Square. John Penn was beside himself, concerning William's appointment. "I am so astonished and enraged at it," he wrote, "that I am hardly able to contain myself at the thought." As soon as the news broke, Franklin's enemies did their best to have the appointment annulled. Later a convenient scandal came to hand: the revelation that William had an illegitimate son, said to be born "of a London oyster woman." (Illegitimate sons of the eighteenth century it seems were invariably fathered upon oysterwomen.) The talk proved vicious and long-lasting. Even John Adams was to propagate it. "Without some kind of backstairs intrigue," wrote Adams much later, "it is difficult to account for that mortification of the pride, affront to the dignity and Insult to the Morals of America, the Elevation to the Government of New Jersey of a base born Brat." By the time Adams wrote the words, William's Tory sentiments had made him generally hated in America. The child, not at first acknowledged, was to be William Temple Franklin, delight of his grandfather's heart.

"Dr. Franklin," arriving at Philadelphia in November of 1762, was much pleased with his warm reception by the

Pennsylvania Assembly; his enemies had let it be known that he would not be welcomed. The Assembly applauded Privy Council's final compromise measures; in the last analysis, taxation of the Penns' estates was what most moved the anti-Proprietary party. They voted formal thanks and gave Franklin a salary of five hundred pounds for each of the years in England, with something added for expenses. Richard Peters wrote in his diary that Franklin "speaks much of Lord Bute"; the earl's portrait hung in his parlor. William sailed home with his bride, and Franklin went to New Jersey to see his son installed as governor, after which he made first payment to a builder for a new house for himself and his wife, to go up on Market Street. Then he drove off to Virginia for the post office, thence to Newport, Boston, and Portsmouth, New Hampshire — managing to fall from his chaise and dislocate his shoulder badly.

Homecoming is glorious but it is also disconcerting; Franklin missed his friends abroad. To Strahan he wrote that if he could prevail on his wife to cross the ocean, he would settle in England forever. "Of all the enviable Things England has," he wrote again, "I envy it most its People. Why should that petty Island, which compar'd to America is but like a Stepping Stone in a Brook, scarce enough of it above Water to keep one's Shoes dry; why, I say, should that little Island enjoy in almost every Neighborhood, more sensible, virtuous and elegant Minds, than we can collect in ranging over 100 Leagues of our vast Forests." And when, in 1763, peace with the French was finally signed, Franklin expressed himself deeply gratified and wrote to London that "the Glory of England was never higher than at present, I think you never had a better Prince."

At home in Pennsylvania, however, Franklin found not peace but trouble. No sooner arrived than he was plunged into public turmoil. Up around Lancaster the Indians

were again on the rampage; Franklin said the late war
had given them a taste for plunder. The celebrated
Paxton Boys — one hundred strong — burst into frontier
settlements and murdered at least twenty innocent Indians, who had been living quietly enough under the protection of the government. Men, women and children
perished alike. Public sympathy was sharply divided;
surely the frontiersmen must have been justified? When
the Paxton Boys let it be known they might storm into
Philadelphia and kill such Indians as had been sheltered
there, certain citizens said openly they would join the
attack.

Franklin, aroused, published an angry, caustic pamphlet, entitled *A Narrative of the Late Massacres*. "Do we
come to America to learn and practice the Manners of
Barbarians?" it demanded. "If an Indian injured me, does
it follow that I may revenge that injury on all Indians?
. . . The only Crime of these poor Wretches seems to
have been, that they had a reddish brown Skin, and black
Hair; and some People of that Sort, it seems, had murdered some of our Relations. If it be right to kill Men for
such a Reason, then, should any man, with a freckled
Face and red Hair, kill a Wife or Child of mine, it would
be right for me to revenge it, by killing all the freckled
red-haired Men, Women and Children, I could afterwards any where meet with. . . ."

The pamphlet alienated all who hated Indians — and
there were many. In February the Paxton Boys carried
out their threat and marched on Philadelphia. Franklin
helped organize a defense; Governor John Penn even
offered him the command, but Franklin chose instead to
carry a musket. There was an extraordinary incident
when Governor Penn fled to Franklin's house at two in
the morning, "for Advice," Franklin wrote, "with his
Counsellors at his Heels, and made it his Head Quarters
for some time." Franklin, with other citizens, went out

and parleyed with the rioters, somehow persuading them to disperse. "And within four and twenty Hours," Franklin wrote to Fothergill, "I was a common Soldier, a Counsellor, a kind of Dictator, an Ambassador to the Country Mob, and on their Returning home, *Nobody* again."

John Penn's arrival as governor had, of course, rekindled the issues for or against Proprietary government. Franklin and Galloway headed such of the Quaker party as wished to get rid of the Penns. On the other side were powerful leaders like Chief Justice Allen and John Dickinson; theirs was called the "Proprietary or Gentlemen's Party." October first was election day for members of the Assembly. Franklin hoped to represent Philadelphia as usual; he had been returned every year during his stay in England. The campaign was bitter, said indeed to be "perhaps the warmest that ever was held in this Province." Young Galloway was Franklin's strongest ally; Dickinson challenged him to a duel. Violent pamphlets against Franklin were published, charging him with every sin in the calendar, including misappropriation of the public funds that had been entrusted to him in England. One of his defenders wrote that "from the tall Knaves of Wealth and Power to the sneaking Underlings of Corruption, they seem to a Man sworn to load him with all the Filth and Virulence that the basest Heads and basest Hearts can suggest." William's bastardy was raked up, thereby impugning his father's morals; also Franklin's obscure beginnings were stressed — he sprang, it was said, "from the meanest circumstances." Franklin was accused of being a leveler who tried to destroy all distinction of birth and position. On the Assembly floor Dickinson declared that "no man in Pennsylvania is at this time so much the object of public dislike"; Judge Allen said that Quakers in the legislature simply did not dare to disoblige Franklin; they worshiped him "as the Indians do the devil, for fear." The Proprietary party, Franklin confessed, ere long would either demolish him or he them.

When the votes were counted, Franklin and Galloway lost their seat by a narrow margin — about twenty-six votes in four thousand. It was Franklin's only such defeat during his entire political career; he said it was due to his pamphlet against the massacre, his anti-Proprietary agitation, and his referring in print to Pennsylvania Germans as "the Palatine Boors herding together." The last had been written twelve years ago, in Franklin's paper on the peopling of countries. But it was skillfully revived, causing the Dutch to complain that Franklin had called them "a herd of hogs." It cost him, said Franklin, a thousand votes. Moreover there were citizens who mistrusted royal government; as Judge Allen said, they feared "the King's little finger we should find heavier than the Proprietor's whole loins."

After the election, an observer wrote that "Mr. Franklin died like a philosopher. But Mr. Galloway agonized in death." Nevertheless, Franklin's party kept a substantial majority in the Assembly, which voted openly for a change to royal government. By a count of nineteen to eleven, the House elected him once more as their agent in England. John Penn said that Franklin and Galloway were like sorcerers, manipulating members at secret conventicles, achieving their ends even though defeated. Their followers were known as the Quaker Party, or the Old Ticket.

Judge Allen wrote at once to the Penns that they might expect Franklin in London, "fully freighted with rancour and Malice." With Dickinson, the judge composed a formal protest against Franklin's appointment, signed by ten names and printed in Bradford's *Pennsylvania Journal.* The protest had six charges, among them the accusation that Franklin was "very unfavorably thought of by several of his Majesty's ministers; it was therefore disrespectful to our most Gracious Sovereign to employ him." Contrary to his usual custom when attacked, Franklin published a reply, signed with his name and written in the first person. For fourteen years, he wrote, he had represented the city of Philadelphia, never once soliciting votes. Now he was reproached with being out of favor both in America and England — and by opponents whose votes had been scarcely a score more than his own. *You, Honourable Sir, my Enemy of seven Years* — so Franklin addressed Judge Allen. The paper was composed four days prior to Franklin's departure for England; a note of sadness can be discerned. At fifty-six, such a journey might well be his last: "I am now about to take Leave (perhaps a last Leave) of the Country I love, and in which I have spent the greatest Part of my Life. ESTO PERPETUA. I wish every kind of Prosperity to my Friends, and I forgive my Enemies. B. Franklin."

On November ninth, Franklin's ship, *King of Prussia,* put to sea from the Delaware capes. Three hundred friends and admirers escorted the traveler to Chester for embarkation; Franklin was rowed to the ship by ten freeholders of the White Oak Company — that stout club of artisans and "mechanicks" based in Philadelphia, and politically opposed to the Proprietary party. Ship cannon, carried down on purpose, roared a salute. An anthem was sung, to the tune of "God Save the King" — three verses of execrable poetry and affectionate sentiments. "It was very endearing," Franklin said:

> O Lord our God arise,
> Scatter our Enemies,
> And make them fall.
> Confound their Politicks,
> Frustrate such Hypocrites,
> Franklin, on thee we fix,
> GOD save us all. . . .

FRANKLIN IN LONDON, 1757–1766

GOD save Great GEORGE our King;
Prosper agent Franklin:
Grant him Success. . . .

It was March before Philadelphia heard of Franklin's safe arrival in England. Governor John Penn wrote to his uncle in London that "the News of Franklin's Arrival in England was received here with great Joy by his Friends. The bells rung almost all night and the whole town seemed to be in motion upon it, especially the Quaker part of it; they ran about like mad men to acquaint such of their crew of the joyfull Tidings as they imagined had not heard it before. People as they met in the street shook hands and wished one another Joy upon this great event. I don't believe these people would have shewn half as much joy at the most signal victory gained in time of war."

Franklin was to be gone ten years; he would never see his wife again. And he would return to an America which was on the very verge of revolution.

CHAPTER ELEVEN

The Stamp Act. The colonies feel
a new power. Victorious Britain
faces a dilemma. Franklin maneuvers
his position, and writes for
the London newspapers.

For Americans the words *Stamp Act* have gathered a
fearsome significance: the very symbol of "British
Tyranny." Yet there is no evidence to show that the stamp
tax would actually have crippled the colonies. Indeed,
Britons in England paid a stamp tax; her citizens bore
heavier burdens than those the Grenville ministry proposed for America in 1764. Before Franklin sailed for
England he had heard of these Parliamentary plans for
raising revenue — including a stamp tax — and was far
from surprised. The wars with France had left the Crown
heavily in debt; the cost of maintaining civil and military
establishments in America had increased fivefold. The
colonies must pay their share. "I am not much alarmed
about your Scheme of raising Money on us," Franklin had
written from Philadelphia to Richard Jackson, member
of Parliament and one of the agents for America. "You will
take care for your own sakes not to lay a greater Burthen
on us than we can bear; for you cannot hurt us without
hurting your selves."

Franklin profoundly believed this. Indeed, he was said to have proposed a stamp tax to General Braddock years before, upon the general's complaint that the colonies would not raise supplies for their own defense — a charge Franklin never actually denied. Much print has been spent in debating whether Benjamin Franklin was a "mercantilist." Certainly he looked on colonial and British interests as bound up one with the other: what benefited the Empire would benefit America. Franklin saw British expansion as eventual British-American expansion, not a threat but a glorious promise; it would be long before he relinquished this dream. The Albany Plan had aimed toward the Empire's further security and development, though in framing it Franklin expressed resentment at the Crown's restriction on colonial trade and manufacture, also at British denial of colonial representation in the union's Grand Council.

The stamp tax had been proposed in the House of Commons by George Grenville in February of 1764. It would not be voted as an act of Parliament until February of '65, nor would it go into effect until the following November. These delays were purposeful; the ministry wished to see how America reacted, allowing time for colonial assemblies to devise other schemes of revenue which might suit them better. The stamp tax was only one of many Parliamentary plans for exacting what Britain looked on as America's responsibility to share an overpowering national debt, incurred largely in defending North American colonies against the French and Indians.

Grenville's proposed measures were for the most part not new, but revivals of trade and navigation laws which had long lain inactive — for America a most salutary neglect. The colonies had simply got round the laws by smuggling. The Sugar Act of 1733 had imposed a duty of sixpence a gallon on molasses from the islands; the law as revived reduced the duty to threepence, at the same time increasing the penalties for infraction. Certain notorious search warrants, called writs of assistance, were given added force in the Courts of Admiralty, where smuggling cases were tried. Contraband trading was immensely profitable on the American coast — it had indeed assumed the proportions of a business, with every kind of device to evade customs duties. The Courts of Admiralty had no juries. American judges had therefore remanded contraband cases to the common law courts, where juries quickly decided in favor of their fellow citizens. Now, however, this practice was blocked, Parliament decreed there should be no appeal from Admiralty court except to England.

Massachusetts had already protested Admiralty procedure, with James Otis eloquent in defense of trial by jury, according to the "ancient English liberties." Contraband sugar — molasses to make rum — paid for slaves to work the cane fields. All during the French wars, New England had traded with the enemy, shifted the flags on her mastheads and thereby profited greatly, insuring a steady flow of that triangular traffic with the islands which was the lifeblood of colonial commerce. And now in the year 1764, James Otis's eloquence was remembered and revived. When a man's pocket is touched the thrust goes through to the heart, lending itself to translation in terms of great principles.

Benjamin Franklin was no romantic; he knew all about the contraband trade. But in England the ministry, seeing plainly that the Sugar Act would not produce the hoped-for revenue, published their plans for wider measures: a currency act, regulating further issues of paper money in America (thus insuring that British merchants would not be paid in depreciated currency), a quartering act, compelling colonists to furnish lodging and supplies for troops sent over for colonial protection; a stamp act, requiring revenue stamps on commercial and legal documents.

Revenue from the stamp tax was not to be carried to England, but remain in the colonies to pay the cost of their defense, which in the year 1765 amounted to three hundred thousand pounds: on the surface a reasonable enough measure. Yet the stamp tax was the first inland duty, as one colony called it, ever imposed by Parliament, with the exception of "the King's post office." The stamp tax touched therefore not only the profits of shipping merchants but the lives of every citizen.

Franklin, so far, had not been persuaded that the stamp tax was "unconstitutional." Surely, Britain had a right to enact laws for her colonies? As long as the Sugar Act, for instance, had not been enforced, the colonies had made no outcry, nor voiced large phrases about the ancient British liberties. Franklin has been called an opportunist. And indeed, if opportunism means that what works is preferable to what does not work, the charge is justified. Having heard from his countrymen enough talk to indicate that the stamp tax was altogether unwelcome and that other plans might be preferable, Franklin left Philadelphia with full intention of suggesting to the ministry some form of revenue that would satisfy British subjects on both sides of the water.

Shortly after reaching London, therefore, he called on George Grenville; with him went two colonial agents who were members of Parliament, Charles Garth and Richard Jackson. Jackson in particular was sympathetic to American affairs, and politically so knowledgeable that he was known as "Omniscient Jackson." To Grenville, Franklin suggested alternate methods of raising revenue. Let the colonies tax themselves in their legislatures or assemblies, exactly as the English taxed themselves in the Commons.

Grenville would agree to none of it. He reminded Franklin that during the French wars, every colony but South Carolina had refused to grant money for defense, even when their borders were menaced. Now that the danger was over, would they be more willing? He brushed Franklin's arguments aside, "being besotted," said Franklin later, "with his Stamp-Scheme, which he chose rather to carry through." Thomas Penn, hearing of this encounter, was unhappy because the agents had chosen Franklin as their spokesman, thereby setting him "in a conspicuous point of Light . . . so that it is impossible to prove him a person of no estimation in America, tho he has acted so bad a part in Pennsylvania."

What Britain did not realize — could not indeed conceive — was the rapid change of heart experienced by the colonies since the French defeat in Canada, an event which altered, for America, the very foundations of the colonial idea. America saw herself as occupying a new place in the imperial system, not yet defined it was true, but deeply felt nonetheless. No longer must inhabitants look to the mother country for protection. Rendered impotent was an enemy not only of a Seven Years' War but of generations. The hereditary foe was vanquished, driven back across the seas. Furthermore, America persuaded herself that she had accomplished this military feat almost single-handed, overlooking the British troops and British money she had so often solicited. Memory in such matters can be short, and victory erases many irksome basic truths. If, in London, Horace Walpole heard the park guns roar their exultation, for America the effect was no less invigorating. True, a royal proclamation reserved for the Indians all territory between the Alleghenies and the Mississippi; colonists were ordered to remain east of a line drawn along the crest of the mountains. The order was temporary, and not disputed by the various assemblies. Yet Britain might as well have attempted to stem the tide at Truro with a string. For the colonies, expansion was the watchword.

Franklin, in London, quite naturally was aware of things the colonies did not know; for instance, that Britons in England paid far higher taxes than even the most highly taxed colonials — twenty-six shillings per capita, as compared with Massachusetts's one shilling. Britons in England complained loudly of their tax burden. Discussion with both friends and enemies convinced Franklin that Parliament would not alter its plans for raising revenue. To his son William, Franklin wrote that all had been "cut and dry'd, and every Resolve framed at the Treasury ready for the House, before I arriv'd in England, or knew any thing of the matter." . . . And to Charles Thomson in Philadelphia, "We might as well have hinder'd the Suns setting. But since 'tis done, my Friend, and it may be long before it rises again, Let us make as good a Night of it as we can. We may still light candles." Accordingly, Franklin went ahead with the primary mission for which he had been sent abroad — to present Pennsylvania's petition for a change from Proprietary to royal government. Maryland also prepared to petition against their Proprietors, the Calvert family — a movement strongly supported by Governor William Franklin of New Jersey.

But when Franklin presented Pennsylvania's formal petition to Privy Council, consideration was postponed *sine die*. Thomas Penn, jubilant, said this meant forever, though in its official report, Privy Council merely said consideration had been postponed "for the present." Franklin determined to keep up the fight. He seemed incapable of accepting defeat on this issue, in which he had misjudged possible ministerial response from the first. The wonder is that continued rebuff did not discourage Franklin in the matter, or that politicians in Philadelphia did not lose faith in his efficacy as agent. He seemed blinded by his own optimism and his virulent dislike of the Penns.

In February of 1765, the Proprietary dispute was overshadowed by a far more urgent matter. George Grenville's revenue bill passed the House of Commons with scarcely a dissenting vote. The stamp tax contained some fifty-five clauses, requiring stamps or stamped paper on a wide variety of objects, such as bills of lading, legal papers, mortgages, bills of sale, playing cards, printed pamphlets, newspaper advertisements, almanacs and calendars, warrants for surveying land, college degrees, licenses for retailing liquor. Payable only in specie, the tax varied from two pounds for a college degree to a halfpenny for a half-sheet pamphlet. A pair of dice cost ten shillings, a license to sell liquor, four pounds, the same for a wine license. The high tax on college degrees assumed that only affluent citizens gave their sons a higher education.

Immense pains had gone into framing this document, every provision having been argued over and discussed. In appointing stamp distributors, Grenville asked for the names of local men; it would be impolitic to send strangers from England. Three Americans were appointed, who happened to be then in London: Jared Ingersoll for Connecticut, George Mercer for Virginia, George Meserve for New Hampshire. All three looked forward to an income from fees, nor had any one of them the least apprehension about returning to execute his commissions in the colonies. Even that well-known patriot firebrand, Richard Henry Lee, applied for the position of collector. As stamp distributor for Pennsylvania, Franklin suggested his friend, John Hughes. (Franklin's enemies would one day say that he had "made application" for this favor. "That pragmatical Fool, Hughes, and that crafty Fellow, Franklin," Judge Allen would write to Thomas Penn.)

The colony of Virginia was first to make formal protest against the Stamp Act. On May 29, 1765, the House of Burgesses passed its famous radical resolves, seven of them declaring that "his Majesty's liege people of this most ancient and loyal colony" enjoyed all the liberties, franchises and immunities that have forever been enjoyed and possessed by the people of Great Britain — among them the liberty to tax themselves. . . . And that "any person who shall . . . assert or maintain otherwise . . . shall be deemed an enemy to His Majesty's Colony."

Franklin read the Virginia resolves and was amazed at their rashness. In June, John Adams, aged twenty-nine, wrote formal instructions for his town of Braintree, Massachusetts, calling the stamp tax "unconstitutional." As protests poured into London from colony after colony, the ministry could only ask, had the Americans gone mad? It was not for colonials to decide what was unconstitutional! Only the Crown could do that — and the Crown meant Parliament and the King. Did the colonies then wish to send representatives to Parliament; was that what they meant by *no taxation without representation*? How many representatives, and in what proportion to Britain's own elected members? "This new and extraordinary doctrine," exclaimed Grenville, "hitherto unheard of in the colonies or any European power!" Alexander Wedderburn, member of Parliament (later to be solicitor general) was correct enough when he said the Americans had cherished no such ideas "until riches gained by the French war introduced the idea of independence." Governor Bernard of Massachusetts wrote home to England that "Great Britain and America had got so widely different notions of their relation to one another, that their connection must be destroyed, if this question is not determined, but only postponed."

As summer wore on, riots took place in town after town on the American coast — stamp masters hanged in effigy, customs houses torn down. Joseph Galloway wrote that it had become actually dangerous to sanction Parliament's conduct; even the judges in court treated Parliament with "the most irreverent abuse." There was contagion in this rebellion. In Boston, Governor Hutchinson's mansion on Beacon Street was ransacked and ruined by a drunken mob; historical manuscripts gathered over many years were burned or thrown into the street. Lieutenant Governor Andrew Oliver's house also was ruined; the two men barely escaped with their lives.

Franklin hated mobbing and violence as he hated war. Plainly, the stamp tax could not be collected; it must be repealed. But was mobbing the way to achieve repeal? It would only inflame the ministry, nor would Parliament capitulate to threats, or even consent to hear petitions that denied its legislative authority. There were now eighteen colonial agents in London, as opposed to the seven that had been there when Franklin came over in 1757. All were at a loss how to proceed. Robert Charles received from New York a petition so incendiary that not a member of the Commons would present it. To do so they said would "incur the censure of Parliament." The Commons was not accustomed to settling colonial problems; hitherto this had been left largely to the ministerial agencies — Privy Council, the Board of Trade and Plantations.

Actually the Stamp Act and its resultant defiance by America had put both Parliament and ministry in an impossible predicament. It was everywhere acknowledged that Englishmen possessed the right to representative government. Why else had Cromwell's rebellion taken place, and after it the Glorious Revolution of 1689 — a king beheaded and a king deposed by Parliament? Yet from the very beginning, Britain's Acts of Trade and Navigation had put colonial Englishmen in second place — more like a conquered people than like equals. The army command in America, for instance, was reserved always for "the King's native born subjects." The matter of taxation pointed up the problem as had nothing else. Ireland, a conquered country, was bound by act of Parliament. Yet Wales was never taxed until represented. Calais, Berwick, Guernsey, Jersey, the Isle of Man — "never taxed," wrote the Duke of Newcastle in his notes.

Richard Jackson had told Franklin that the ministers wished to avoid contests in Parliament. Repeal of the Stamp Act was everywhere talked of but by no means everywhere approved. If repeal was to be debated in the Commons it must be skillfully introduced, and some face-saving device effected before the measure could be seriously considered. Franklin was well aware of all this. Moreover, by now he had won the confidence of his fellow agents, who had seen the Doctor in action. Franklin had his own methods of procedure — a way of talking round a plan, pretending the idea was somebody else's, then easing into it and driving ahead. Concerning colonial riots, his anxiety and indeed his irritation mounted; he wrote to Philadelphia counseling restraint, advising John Hughes that "a firm loyalty to the Crown and faithful Adherence to the Government of this Nation . . . will always be the wisest course for you and I to take, whatever may be the madness of the Populace or their blind Leaders, who can only bring themselves and their Country in Trouble, and draw on greater Burthens by Acts of rebellious Tendency."

The truth was that Pennsylvania's response to the Revenue Act had become deeply embedded in local politics, something which Franklin, as agent for his Province, could not ignore and by inclination did not wish to ignore; he greatly valued his political position in Philadelphia. The Quakers — the Old Ticket, Franklin's party — controlled the Assembly. John Penn said the party was a "Macedonian Phalanx not to be broken by any force that can be brought against them in this Country." And the Quakers desired peace and no tumult on the streets. In Franklin's absence, Galloway ran the party. The Old Ticket greatly desired repeal of the Stamp Act. Yet with equal fervor they still wished to get rid of the Penns and achieve royal government; riot and violence would put them in no position to ask favors of Parliament or King. It was a difficult position. The mechanics and small tradesmen called White Oaks were behind Galloway (and Franklin) to a man.

Yet the angry political battle of the 1764 Assembly election had not been forgotten, nor Franklin's defeat. His enemies now seized the occasion to press an old charge. "I could wish you was on the spot," wrote David Hall, Franklin's partner on the *Pennsylvania Gazette*. "And yet I should be afraid of your Safety, as the Spirit of the People is so violent against every one they think has the least concern with the Stamp Law, and they have imbibed the Notion that you had a Hand in the framing of it, which has occasioned you many Enemies; but I make not the least Doubt, you would be able to clear your Self, if there was a Necessity for it, of all the ill natured Things that have been laid to your charge."

Franklin had never been intimidated by enmity. But these letters were impressive and convincing. "A black Cloud seems to hang over us," wrote James Parker, the newspaperman, from New York. "Poor America is like to bleed, if the Storm blows not over: Nay, it appears to me there will be an end to all Government here, if it does not: for the People are all running Mad; and say it is as good to dye by the Sword as by the Famine; and unless some Stop be put at home [England] dreadful work is like to ensue."

William Franklin in New Jersey was deeply perplexed over what course to follow, having received no instructions from the ministry. He wrote that his father's old friend, Cadwallader Colden, now governor of New York, had got Fort George ready for defense, procured soldiers from General Gage, and lined up ships of war in the harbor to protect the stamps when they should arrive.

The great division had begun between those who would later be Tories and those who would stand for Independence — though no one as yet acknowledged it, and even Sam Adams still professed loyalty to King George. John

Hughes, the stamp master, feared his house would be pulled down, though he was well provided with firearms and determined to defend his possessions even at the risk of his life. "If I live till tomorrow morning I shall give you a further account," he wrote Franklin. Galloway reported later that Hughes's escape from injury was due to seven or eight hundred tradesmen and mechanics, led by the White Oaks and posted at vital points to hold back the mob should it attempt mischief. Actually, it was remarkable how peace was kept in Pennsylvania, compared with Boston, New York and Rhode Island — and this throughout the entire Stamp Act crisis. There were no Liberty Boys in Philadelphia.

Deborah Franklin wrote that for nine days she had been kept in turmoil by neighbors urging her to leave town; she had sent her daughter Sally to Burlington for safety. Cousin Davenport had arrived at her door, declaring that at least twenty people had told him it was his duty to be with Deborah. "I said I was pleased to receive Civility from any body so he stayed with me some time. Towards night I said he should fetch a gun or two as we had none. I sent to my brother to come and bring his gun. . . . We made one room into a magazine. I ordered some sort of defense upstairs such as I could manage myself. I said when I was advised to remove that I was very sure you had done nothing to hurt anybody nor had I given offense to any person at all, nor would I be made uneasy by anybody, nor would I stir or show the least uneasiness, but if anybody came to disturb me I would show a proper resentment and I should be very much affronted. . . . I was told that there was 8 hundred men ready to assist any one that should be molested. . . . I will not stir as I really dont think it would be right in me to stir or show the least uneasiness at all. . . . Mr. John Ross and Brother swore it is Mr. Sam'l Smith that is a-setting the people a-madding by telling them it was you that had planned the Stamp Act.

. . . I shall send this letter by a friend. God bless you and keep you forever is the prayer of yours forever, D. Franklin."

Franklin replied that he honored his wife's courage and the spirit she had shown. As to that pious Presbyterian countryman, it was Chief Justice William Allen, who had set the people a-madding by telling them that Franklin planned the Stamp Act. One could only be thankful not to be charged with planning Adam's fall and the damnation of mankind. "Let us pity and forget him."

Gathering extracts from David Hall's letters, James Parker's, Galloway's and others, Franklin sent them to the ministry. Then he paid a call on Lord Dartmouth, now president of the Board of Trade, and gave it as his opinion that the Stamp Act could not be enforced without totally alienating the affections of the Americans, and thereby lessening commerce. (There was not much doubt which of the two statements affected Dartmouth the most.) Could not three or four "wise and good men," Franklin said, "personages of rank and dignity," be sent to America with a royal commission to inquire into grievances, hear complaints and learn the true state of affairs?

Franklin had always believed in ambassadors, the coming together of "reasonable men" for discussion and enlightenment. Lord Dartmouth ignored the suggestion. In October the colonies took a step serious and unprecedented. Delegates from nine colonies met in New York, calling themselves the Stamp Act Congress, and sat for two weeks, debating measures to be pursued. It was an extraordinary event, the closest approach to union yet achieved by the colonies. Though inspired originally by Samuel Adams, the congress was no riotous meeting of Liberty Boys, its members being sober, highly respected citizens such as Timothy Ruggles of Massachusetts and Christopher Gadsden of South Carolina. The tone of their written resolves was respectful, with much repetition of the words *liege, subjects, sincere devotion to his Majesty's person, inviolable attachment*. . . . Yet what the nine colonies claimed, as "natural born subjects within the kingdom" was anything but humble: representation in the British House of Commons being impracticable, their own assemblies should vote all taxes. "No taxes have ever been or can be constitutionally imposed but by their respective legislatures."

The word *constitutional* again. No wonder that in London, George Grenville found himself bewildered. Nor were these declarations the work of a single colony, but the expression of a majority. This was more than local protest; indeed, the word rebellion hardly covered it. Early in November, the plan for American nonimportation took formal shape. Merchants swore to bring in no more goods or merchandise from Britain until the Stamp Act was repealed. Governor Hutchinson wrote to Franklin that everywhere *Join or Die* had become the motto. "When you and I met at Albany ten years ago," said Hutchinson, "we did not propose an union for such purposes as these."

It was true. The Albany Plan had been no protest against present wrongs but a document of statesmanship, looking to America's future. Nor did the Albany Plan cater to what colonists saw as their immediate interest. Rather, it asked something of them. Men seldom unite for a possible future good, nor is political unity achieved without sacrifice, compromise. A colony, a state, a nation, gives up a measure of autonomy in exchange for other benefits. Men unite for the reason they go to war — in answer to what they recognize as a threat.

Fully convinced that repeal of the Stamp Act was the only hope of reconciliation, Franklin began what amounted to a personal bombardment in the British press. He wrote of course under pseudonyms; forty-two of these have been identified,* used again and again. To begin with, British

* See Verner Crane's valuable book, *Benjamin Franklin's Letters to the Press, 1758–1775.*

ignorance of America was appalling — ignorance of the
American climate, of her terrain, her flora and fauna, let
alone her people. How could Britain understand the
problems when she knew nothing of the country? Somehow she must be made to see. Newspapers carried no
editorials, their place being taken by correspondence.
With the support of his publisher friends — William
Strahan, Caleb Whitefoord, Woodfall, Wilkie, John Al-
mon — Franklin knew he would have no trouble getting into print; his letters went to Strahan's triweekly
London Chronicle, to the *Gazette,* the *Public Advertiser,* and were often reprinted by Edward Cave in his
Gentleman's Magazine. (It had been Cave who printed
Franklin's letters on electricity.)

Franklin opened with his famous parody on news-
writers, perpetrators of those highly inaccurate items
known to the press as *We hears.* Signing himself "A
Traveller," Franklin wrote, apropos of Parliament's
Woolen Act, that superficial readers believed the American sheep gave scarcely any wool at all, not enough for
a pair of stockings a year. Whereas the truth was that the
tails of American sheep were so laden with wool that each
animal trailed behind it a car or little wagon to support
its tail and keep it from dragging on the ground. As to
American fisheries, ignorant people argued that the Upper Lakes of America were fresh, and codfish never came
there. "But let them know, Sir, that Cod, like other Fish,
when attacked by their Enemies, fly into any Water
where they think they can be safest: that Whales, when
they have a Mind to eat Cod, pursue them wherever they
fly; and that the grand Leap of the Whale in the Chace up
the Fall of Niagara is esteemed by all who have seen it,
as one of the finest Spectacles in Nature!"

People actually believed Franklin's hoaxes; he wrote so
reasonably, they said. Long ago, Franklin had learned this
style, half bantering, half serious. As the weeks passed, his

teasing irony became caustic; he employed every weapon his pen had learned, from abuse to friendly appeal. "Give me leave, Master John Bull," he wrote in the *Gazette,* "to remind you, that you are *related to all mankind* and therefore it less becomes you than any body, to affront and abuse other nations. But you have mixed with your many virtues, a pride, a haughtiness, and an insolent contempt for all but yourself, that, I am afraid, will, if not abated, procure you one day or other a handsome drubbing. . . . Pray, when your enemies are uniting in a *Family Compact* against you, can it be discreet in you to kick up in your own house a *Family Quarrel?*"

By this time the Family Compact was no longer secret; the last of three treaties had been signed by the Bourbon dynasties too recently for British comfort. England knew all too well that a possible war with America would bring the continent of Europe into arms against her. Franklin, making the most of this, wrote to the *Public Advertiser* as "Pacificus," referring to a rumor of two hundred and fifty thousand fighting men in North America, many of whom had lately seen service. Yet, "as one Englishman is said to be sure as good as five Americans," he supposed it would not require above fifty thousand men sent over to reduce them. A three or four years' civil war, at perhaps less expense than ten or twelve millions a year, should be sufficient to complete pacification, "notwithstanding any disturbance our restless enemies in Europe might think fit to give us while engaged in this necessary work."

He would have been happy, Pacificus suggested, to furnish any useful hints concerning the controversy between the Mother Country and her rebellious American children. . . . As if the very words had fired him, Franklin followed with the savage suggestion, suavely expressed, that all the capitals of America be burned to the ground, the inhabitants scalped and the shipping destroyed (to prevent smuggling and save the cost of coastal patrols).

Such a plan would of course depopulate the country, but this could be easily remedied by transporting Britain's unemployed, together with the felons from her gaols. . . .

It was like Franklin's piece years ago in the *Pennsylvania Gazette,* where he had angrily suggested, in return for the transporting of British felons to America, that the colonies ship over their rattlesnakes once a year and distribute them in the grounds of nobility and gentry throughout the nation, "but particularly in the Gardens of the Prime Ministers, the Lords of Trade and Members of Parliament, for to them we are most particularly obliged."

Pacificus wrote on January 2, 1766. Within a fortnight, Parliament would convene. Franklin was furiously busy preparing a defense of the American position, seeking a way to introduce this into the House of Commons, and visiting members in order to urge his points. The newspaper pieces were but one weapon in his arsenal — yet one that Franklin, the printer, believed in, and which for him had been, in the past, eminently successful.

Franklin continued to write for British newspapers and would not cease until he left England forever. His publishing friends kept his secret closely. Revolution would be almost under way before London discovered that this American propaganda was not written by a genuine Englishman, but came from "Judas's office in Craven Street."

CHAPTER TWELVE

Franklin testifies
in the House of Commons.

O n January 14, 1766, Parliament resumed after the
Christmas holidays. Grenville's ministry had fallen,
to be replaced by "the Rockingham Whigs" — news which
in America had been celebrated with bonfires and re-
joicing. (The colonies did not need to know the intricacies
of parliamentary government to appreciate who their
friends were.) The young Marquis of Rockingham headed
the new administration. Immensely rich, with inherited
estates in three counties, he was rumored to be more interested in the horse races at Newmarket than in the work
of parliamentary committees. But he showed a liberal
attitude toward the colonies, and had named as his private
secretary a young Irishman, Edmund Burke, shortly to
prove an even warmer friend to America than William
Pitt.

It was common knowledge that Pitt had been for some
time in seclusion at his country estate, afflicted with a
mysterious ailment which the public called gout. He had

been absent from Parliament when the Stamp Act was passed. For America — and for America's agent in London — George Grenville remained the enemy to be reckoned with. A cold, hard man with an unprepossessing face and a marked ability for parliamentary affairs, Grenville still led the very large faction that called for stern measures against America and no repeal of the revenue acts.

Officially, the post of prime minister did not yet exist, though the term was used. "The King's principal minister" led the government. And the King's authority was extensive. Even Pitt, "the great Commoner," addressed His Majesty in terms of utmost servility. At any moment the King could summon "a Cabinet," which meant a meeting of Privy Councillors (the ministers); whoever led them must be able to get along with King as well as with Commons. Under Rockingham the new secretary of state was Henry Seymour Conway, known as General Conway, a military man, singularly handsome in person, nephew to Sir Robert Walpole, principal minister under George II. High government circles were awash with blood relatives — as was the House of Commons. Pitt was brother-in-law to George Grenville; the Duke of Newcastle was Henry Pelham's brother, a member of Pitt's ministry. It was a situation traditional, firmly rooted, and very frustrating for a newcomer who possessed neither birth nor estate. Edmund Burke, for instance, was looked on in certain quarters as an "Irish adventurer."

The American agent in London must take all this into account, nor was it a lesson learned quickly. Franklin by now knew his way fairly well. These intricate cousinships made for "influence" — a word America would fight shy of when later she devised her own national machinery. (George Washington, just before the U.S. Constitutional Convention, wrote in angry italics that *"influence* is no *government."*) Yet the new ministry, Rockingham and his friends, were for the most part strangers to Franklin. With Grenville fell the two Treasury secretaries who had greatly befriended Franklin — Thomas Whately and Charles Jenkinson; also Richard Jackson, fellow agent, who was Grenville's private secretary. Franklin must set out to discover fresh names, connections, meaningful relationships, the political bias of the great and the near-great.

George III in all his panoply of royalty opened Parliament as usual in the House of Lords. He had already written General Conway that he was more and more grieved at accounts from America. "Where this spirit will end is not to be said. It is undoubtedly the most serious question that ever came before Parliament; it requires more deliberation, candor, and temper than I fear it will meet with." Here was a monarch stubborn, self-willed, brave, highly moral in his domestic life and possessing, it has been said, "all the accomplishments which are required for doing business, as business is done by kings — intruding into every department, making everybody's duty his own, and then doing it conscientiously, indefatigably, and as badly as it could possibly be done." * For George III, democracies were an abomination; from first to last he would see the Americans as ungrateful children of England who must be taught a lesson. Now his speech from the throne said little except that all papers concerning "the American disturbances" would be laid before Parliament for its proper action.

The Commons walked through the corridors of Westminster Palace to its chamber in old St. Stephen's Chapel. Debate commenced at once, before a House so crowded that even Strahan for all his experience and connections could not get into the visitors' gallery. Whether Franklin was present we cannot say, but he sent Strahan a report of speeches, written in his own hand. William Pitt carried

* George Otto Trevelyan in *The American Revolution.*

off the honors of the day. He reminded the House that when the resolution for the Stamp Act had been taken, he had been ill in bed. "If I could have endured to be carried . . . I would have solicited a kind hand to have laid me down on this floor, to have borne my testimony against it. . . . *The Americans are the sons, not the bastards of England.* As subjects they are entitled to the common right of representation, and cannot be bound to pay taxes without their consent."

George Grenville, rising to reply, demanded heatedly when the Americans were emancipated? Britain possessed a sovereign power over America; taxation was part of that power. When proposing the Stamp Act he had, he said, asked Parliament if any member would deny this right. Scarcely a voice had been raised. The "disturbances in America" bordered on open rebellion; if not curbed they might well go on to revolution. "When they want the protection of this country they are always ready to ask it. Ungrateful people!"

By the rules, no one is allowed to speak twice in Parliament on the same subject. Pitt rose again, and was immediately confronted with a point of order. The House cried out, "Go on! Go on!" What Pitt said next has become legendary: "The gentleman tells us that America is obstinate; America is almost in open rebellion. I rejoice that America has resisted. The gentleman asks, When were the colonists emancipated? I desire to know when they were made slaves. The Americans have been driven mad by injustice. Would you punish them for madness you have occasioned?" Grandiloquent phrases rolled out: "Would Britain sheathe her sword in the bowels of her brothers, the Americans?" The stamp tax should be repealed "absolutely, totally, and immediately."

It was all very splendid, and the colonies in time would thereby exult — overlooking Pitt's very significant peroration: "Let the Stamp Act be repealed. *At the same time* let the authority of this country over the colonies be asserted in as strong terms as can be devised, and be made to extend to every point of legislation that we may bind their trade, confine their manufactures, and exercise every power whatever, except that of taking their money out of their pockets without their consent."

Next morning, George Grenville, writing to a member of the Commons, said that the fourteenth of January had been the most extraordinary and unfortunate day for this country he had even seen. "I have long been in Parliament but could not have believed what I was a witness to. . . . Oh! what an age!"

On January 28, the House of Commons resolved itself into a Committee of the Whole to consider American affairs. Not only from America but from Britain itself petitions from merchants were pouring in, urging repeal of the Stamp Act. Manufacturers were letting workers go for want of orders, due to the American association for nonimportation. Manchester, Bristol, and Liverpool threatened that an army of one hundred thousand unemployed would march on Parliament and obtain repeal by force. (Members of the Rockingham ministry had traveled from town to town, inspiring these messages.) Yet most of Parliament — particularly the House of Lords — still wished to see the Stamp Act enforced and the American rioters punished, compelled to indemnify the victims of their mobbing.

Franklin's position was critical. Little time remained before repeal would be put to the vote. He redoubled his efforts, stepped up his newspaper campaign, paid continual visits to men whose influence counted, and was to be seen by daylight and by dark buttonholing members of the House of Commons as they went to and from Westminster. "The assiduity of our Friend Dr. Franklin is really astonishing," wrote Strahan. "He is forever with one member of Parliament or another (most of whom by the bye seem to have been deplorably ignorant with regard to the Nature and Consequence of the Colonies) endeavoring to impress them; first, with the Importance of the present Dispute; then to state the Case clearly and fully, stripping it of every thing foreign to the main Point; and lastly, to answer objections arising either from a total ignorance, a partial Knowledge, or a wrong Conception of the matter. To enforce this repeatedly, and with Propriety, in the manner he has done in these last two months, I assure you is no easy Task. By this means, however when the Parlt. reassembles, many members will go into the House properly instructed, and be able to speak in the Debates with Precision and Propriety, which the Well-wishers of the Colonies have hitherto been unable to do. This is the most necessary and essential Service he could perform on this Occasion. . . . All this while, too, he hath been throwing out Hints in the Public Papers, and giving answers to such Letters as have appeared in them, that required or deserved an answer. In this manner he is now employed, with very little Intermission, Night and Day."

In a letter to his wife, Franklin confirmed this, writing that he was "excessively hurried, being every hour that I am awake, either abroad to speak with Members of Parliament or taken up with People coming at home concerning our American Affairs." At some moment — probably the end of January, 1766, Franklin produced a cartoon, shortly to become as celebrated as the *Join or Die* drawing of a dismembered snake that had appeared in 1754. The Stamp Act cartoon shows a female figure, Britannia, sitting on the ground, alive but with severed arms and legs, her eyes cast woefully up to heaven. "Magna Britannia, her Colonies REDUCED," says the caption. Lying near are Britannia's severed limbs, labeled *New York, New England, Pennsylvania, Virginia.*

Franklin had the cartoon printed on cards, and used

them for his messages to Parliament men; he also hired a runner to put the cards in members' hands as they entered the Parliament house. Franklin now bethought himself of his letters to Governor Shirley of Massachusetts, written just after the Albany Congress. There were three of these, strongly urging against taxation without representation, objecting also to Britain's prohibitions against American manufacture, such as the Iron Act of 1751 that forbade the making of steel. In creating new laws, Franklin had written, it is of use to consider as well what the people "will be apt to think and say, as what they *ought* to think."

This of course was what Parliament refused to do. Strahan printed all three letters in his *London Chronicle*. The Shirley letters contained nothing new in the way of argument. Reprinted in America, they were however to be extremely useful in proving that Franklin had come out against parliamentary taxation as early as 1754, and could not possibly be, as his enemies charged, the author of the Stamp Act.

Whenever the House of Commons removed the mace and sat as Committee of the Whole, debates were secret; no one was allowed to enter unless summoned. But the news, as always, leaked out, appearing in newspapers under various fli nsy disguises. A petition from the Stamp Act Congress was presented — and the Commons refused to hear it. The meeting of nine states at New York in October had been clearly an act of rebellion, members said; "a dangerous and federal union." No such congress had been appointed from England, as was the case at Albany. William Pitt, however, advised that the petition be received; next day the Earl of Hardwicke wrote his brothers that Pitt ought to be sent to the Tower.

Debates continued, the House sitting sometimes until three in the morning. (They convened at about three in the afternoon.) Reading the testimony one is astonished at the fairness and moderation of speaking. The rebellion in

America, said a member from Bristol, was an earthquake that would shake His Majesty's dominions. Already, vibration had been felt from Ireland. The attorney general, Charles Yorke, warned that the question was not merely for one session of the House but for posterity.

Considering the emotions aroused, it is to the credit of the Commons that members heard each other through. Less than a hundred years earlier, Britain had effected her own Glorious Revolution, as she called it — dethroning the Stuarts and putting a Dutch prince on the English throne. No one had forgotten that a free country depended upon the Commons speaking its mind freely. The truth was that America's newly proclaimed philosophy of colonial rights was a threat to the mercantile system on which the Empire was built. And however humbly phrased these colonial memorials to the King and these earnest petitions to the Commons, they expressed a new political and economic philosophy; few were ready to accept it. Horace Walpole, member from Lynn, and a most acute observer (later to come out against the war with America), wrote that the insult to Parliament was "unparalleled and struck at the very vitals of the constitution." The colonies, he said, affected to distinguish between the King and Parliament. But the stamp tax had been the act of the whole legislature (King, Lords, and Commons). "Here was disobedience to the law, and rebellion against the principle of all our laws."

Five resolutions were proposed; the first one declared Britain's right to make laws binding the colonies "in all cases whatsoever." If this resolution were not enforced, protested a member, Britain would give up all authority over the Americans and could never possibly recover it without the miseries of a civil war. Had not the colonists already begun, at the Albany Congress, a federal union? "The repeal of the Stamp Act will not content the Americans. A few years, or rather a few months, will turn them away from decent and respectful opposition to [our] whole system of laws or American legislation." William Blackstone, the great lawyer, member from Wiltshire, said the notion of American representation in Parliament did not hold water: "The colonies are dependent upon us, and if they attempt to shake off our dependence, we shall I hope have firmness enough to make them obey."

Colonel Isaac Barré,* who had served in the colonies, observed that America had become a great commonwealth. Someday it would be larger than Europe! Was not such a notion flattering and glorious to Britain and to all humanity? Yet when the Americans should grow more numerous than the British, their representation in Parliament would be dangerous as well as inconvenient. "All colonies," Barré said, "have their date of independence. If we act injudiciously, this point may be reached in the life of many members of this House."

Apart from Edmund Burke, the speakers whose plans and prophecies for the colonies proved valid were those few who had lived in America. Franklin had been right: if Britain would send ambassadors across the ocean to view conditions at first hand, compromise might be reached. George Grenville was of different mind. Hard pressed, he told the Commons he would receive the Americans with open arms — but would receive them penitent. "And if something is not done to support this law," he added, "it will be the last you will pass upon North America."

The secretary of state, General Conway, warned that enforcement of the Stamp Act would not only bring a war with America, but be followed by war with Europe; the Bourbon league would seize its advantage. Britain, said Conway, was entirely without forts or troops in America. "Would you raise this temper while you are unable to resist it?" Burke, perhaps with his native Ireland in mind,

* New England has two towns named for Barré, Pennsylvania has one — Wilkes-Barre.

remarked that it was very improper to consider only the *disturbances* of America and entirely neglect their *grievances.* He took issue with all five resolutions — and was chided by Grenville, who "wondered," he said, "to hear so young a member object to the whole proceedings of the Committee."

Benjamin Franklin was in the House during many of these debates. On February third he had been summoned, and sat waiting his turn to testify concerning the American situation. The other witnesses were prominent merchants, the first of whom was not called to the bar until February eleventh. Barlow Trecothick had lived many years in America, was a close friend of Rockingham's, and served as colonial agent for New York. It was he who had incited the petitions from twenty-six mercantile British towns. Now he testified that British trade was almost entirely stopped by notices received from American merchants to ship no goods until the Stamp Act should be repealed. If the act were enforced, he for one would send out no further consignments; he would only risk losing them. His views, he said, "echoed those of the other London merchants."

Next day William Kelly of New York testified that the Sugar Act and the late molasses duty had ruined the rum trade with the "foreign islands. . . . By my Lord!" exclaimed Kelly, "all the people to a man are against the Stamp Act and think it unjust." James Balfour of Virginia said the militia of his colony amounted to about fifty-two thousand men. Virginia exported sixty thousand hogsheads of tobacco annually. This traffic would be halted, nor would any distress drive his countrymen to submit to the Stamp Act. . . . The next witness, Colonel Mercer, stamp master for Virginia, agreed concerning the number of militia — who had, he added, "behaved very brave in action."

There was a fixed idea in England that colonial militia always ran away from the enemy. "Colonel" Franklin of the late Philadelphia City Regiment must surely have smiled; likely enough he had told Mercer what to say. Grenville asked Mercer if he would be in trouble on his return to America, supposing he gave evidence in favor of the Stamp Act. No, said Mercer; he knew the people very well. He would not be in trouble for speaking the truth.

Franklin was last to be called. When he stepped forward, the Commons saw a man just turned sixty, plainly but carefully dressed, wearing a powdered short wig, his manner easy, his face composed, his hands quiet at his sides. Most members knew Franklin's reputation, many were his personal frends. Here was an American famous in his own right. Even his enemies must have felt curiosity. Like the other witnesses, Franklin stood at the bar, facing the Speaker's chair down the length of St. Stephen's Chapel. As always in a committee of the whole House, the Speaker had left his place, giving way to a temporary presiding officer, at whose feet the mace — a huge gilt scepter — lay under the table, put aside as symbol that the House met unofficially; debate would not be recorded in their journals. Behind the chair three high, roundheaded windows, dark now with winter, gave onto Old Palace Yard.

Between the bar and the Speaker's chair the Commons crowded onto what had once been choir benches, raised in four tiers against the north and south walls, with members facing each other as if they were going to sing.* The House was apt to be noisy; members moved about as they chose, wearing their hats if they so desired, sometimes their greatcoats and spurs.

The clerk of the Commons addressed Franklin, asking

---

* Bombed out by the Germans in 1941, the chamber was rebuilt after the Second World War. At Winston Churchill's suggestion the old chapel's dimensions were preserved, in order, it was said, to retain "the sense of intimacy and almost conversational form of debate, firmly established in the affection of the nation."

the question, *pro forma:* "What is your name and place of abode?"

"Franklin, of Philadelphia."

James Hewitt, a lawyer (later chief justice of Ireland) began Franklin's examination. "Do the Americans pay any considerable taxes among themselves?" Hewitt asked.

"Certainly," Franklin said. "Many, and very heavy taxes." He described them as levied in Pennsylvania: taxes on estates both real and personal; a poll tax; a tax on all offices and professions, trades and businesses according to their profits; an excise on wine, rum, and other spirits. . . . These taxes, Franklin explained, were laid for the support of the country's civil and military establishments, "and to discharge the heavy debt contracted in the last war." When peace came [1763] it was expected the debt would be discharged. "But a fresh war broke out with the Indians."

Franklin's friends in London had told him that prior to the Stamp Act affair it had been all but impossible to rouse Parliament to even a momentary interest in America; the legislature had a thousand more immediate matters to think about and dispose of. Impossible to explain the whole condition of the colonies to men so little informed. But today Franklin had at least the chance to attempt it, and he came well prepared.

"Are not the people very able to pay those taxes?" Hewitt continued.

"No," Franklin said. "The frontier counties, all along the continent, having frequently been ravaged by the enemy, and greatly impoverished, are able to pay very little tax."

For ten years, Franklin had known and had said in the Pennsylvania Assembly that persons three thousand miles distant could not know how to graduate taxes to suit conditions over so large a territory. Now at last he could say so directly, face to face with the men who devised these taxes.

To George Grenville and his adherents, it must have been already plain that the questions, so far, had been concocted beforehand by the witness and his parliamentary friends. And indeed this is borne out by Franklin's notes on his copy of the testimony, where he scribbled marginally the names of his questioners. "A friend . . . an adversary . . . Huske . . . Grenville . . . queries 8 to 13 by friends . . . 14, 15 and 16 by one of the late Administration." In all there were to be a hundred and seventy-four questions. Historians have said the whole affair was brilliantly stage-managed. No doubt. Yet every successful drama calls not only for good stage-managing but for good actors and good lines. Franklin was past master at shifting his style to meet the occasion. Had he not deliberately practiced the art since the age of sixteen? In the Commons he spoke plainly, with great simplicity. Questions 8 to 13 were asked, Franklin noted, "by Mr. Huske, another Friend, to shew the Impracticability of distributing the Stamps in America."

Q. Are not you concerned in the management of the Post Office in America?
A. Yes. I am Deputy Post-Master General of North-America.
Q. Don't you think the distribution of stamps, by post, to all the inhabitants, very practicable, if there was no opposition?
A. The posts only go along the sea coasts; they do not, except in a few instances, go back into the country; and if they did, sending for stamps by post would occasion an expense amounting, in many cases, to much more than that of the stamps themselves.
Q. Are you acquainted with Newfoundland?
A. I never was there.

Whenever Franklin saw a trap opening, he said he did not know . . . he was not familiar . . . he had never been there. . . . It was disarming, and gave an impression of simple honesty. On Huske's inquiring if the stamped paper could be distributed in Canada, Franklin replied that there was only one post office between Montreal and Quebec. "The inhabitants live so scattered and remote from each other, in that vast country, that posts cannot be supported among them, and therefore they cannot get stamped paper per post. The English colonies too, along the frontier, are very thinly settled."

Q. From the thinness of the back settlements, would not the Stamp Act be extremely inconvenient to the inhabitants, if executed?

A. To be sure it would; as many of the inhabitants could not get stamps when they had occasion for them, without taking long journies, and spending perhaps three or four pounds, that the Crown might get sixpence.

George Grenville himself now put a key question concerning a matter that rankled sorely in the British mind:

Q. Do you think it right that America should be protected by this country, and pay no part of the expense?

A. That is not the case. The Colonies raised, clothed and paid, during the last war, near 25,000 men, and spent many millions.

Q. Were you not reimbursed by Parliament?

A. We were only reimbursed what, in your opinion, we had advanced beyond our proportion, or beyond what might reasonably be expected from us; and it was a very small part of what we spent. Pennsylvania, in particular, disbursed about 500,000 pounds, and the reimbursements, in the whole, did not exceed 60,000 pounds.

Up to this point, things had gone smoothly for Franklin. Too smoothly, Grenville must have thought. The next three questions Franklin marked as "from an Adversary."

Q. Are not the Colonies, from their circumstances, very able to pay the stamp duty?

A. In my opinion there is not gold and silver enough in the Colonies to pay the stamp duty for one year.

Pennsylvania in particular had protested the Proprietary government's prohibition against printing paper money. Franklin did not say so now. Asked about the population of Pennsylvania, Franklin said he believed there might be a hundred and sixty thousand — a third of them Quakers, another third, Germans. . . . Had the Germans seen military service in Europe? Franklin was asked. . . . Yes, he replied. Altogether, America contained perhaps three hundred thousand white men, from sixteen to sixty years of age.

However shaky his figures, Franklin was answering questions designed by friends (as he later confirmed) "to make opposition to the Stamp Act appear more formidable." Again and again, Parliament returned to this vital matter.

Q. 82. Can anything less than a military force carry the Stamp Act into execution?
A. I do not see how a military force can be applied to that purpose.
Q. 83. [By one of Grenville's late ministers] Why may it not?
A. Suppose a military force sent into America, they will find nobody in arms. What are they then to do? They cannot force a man to take stamps who chooses to do without them. They will not find a rebellion; they may indeed make one.

It was a fine Franklinian answer, twisting the adversary's intent, and showing the colonists not as rebels but as loyal and much wronged British subjects.

Q. 108. What is the number of men in America able to bear arms, or of disciplined militia?
A. There are, I suppose, at least . . .

Question objected to, says the clerk's record. *He withdrew. Called in again.*

For Grenville and his friends this was dangerous territory; the late ministry had no wish to confess that Parliament feared America's strength of arms. Even Pitt in his speech at the opening of Parliament had said it was a topic to be cautiously meddled with, though "in a good cause, on a sound bottom," Britain's forces could "crush America to atoms."

One of Franklin's parliamentary friends was Grey Cooper, M.P. for Rochester and secretary to the Treasury. Cooper's questions, Franklin said later, were intended "to bring out such answers as they desired and expected from me."

Q. What was the temper of America towards Great Britain before the year 1763?

A. The best in the world. They submitted willingly to the government of the Crown, and paid, in all their courts, obedience to acts of parliament. . . . They were led by a thread.* They had not only a respect, but an affection, for Great Britain, for its laws, its customs and manners, and even a fondness for its fashions, that greatly increased the commerce. Natives of Great Britain were always treated with particular regard; to be an Old Englandman was, of itself, a character of some respect, and gave a kind of rank among us.

Q. And what is their temper now?

A. O, very much altered.

Cooper asked further concerning the temper of America toward Parliament. Again Franklin replied that previous to the Stamp Act, Americans thought of Parliament as the great bulwark of their liberties and privileges.

The member from Stockbridge, labeled by Franklin as "Mr. Prescot, an Adversary," now inquired if the witness had not heard the resolutions of this House and the

---

* Thomas Paine borrowed this phrase, in 1778, writing that when he came to America (1774) he "found the disposition of the people such that they might have been led by a thread and governed by a reed." It is to be recalled that Franklin first met Paine in London, was impressed with him and responsible for Paine's coming to America.

House of Lords, asserting the right of Parliament relating to America, including a power to tax the people there? . . . Yes, Franklin said, he had heard of such resolutions.

Q. What will be the opinion of the Americans on those Resolutions?
A. They will think them unconstitutional and unjust.

Grenville's adherents continued this line of questioning. If an American assembly should refuse to vote supplies for defense in time of war, ought not Great Britain to assert her right in the matter? And who was to judge of that right, Britain or the colony concerned?

Franklin: "Those that feel can best judge."

("Democratic states must always *feel* before they can *see*. It is this that makes their governments slow. But the people will be right at last." So General Washington would write to Lafayette in 1785.)

Resolutions concerning Parliamentary *rights,* Franklin continued, would give America very little concern, so long as they were never carried into practice. "The Colonies know you claim the same right with Ireland, but you never exercise it."

Supporters of the Stamp Act now put a series of questions concerning commerce. Could the colonies find wool enough in America to clothe themselves? Could they learn to manufacture cloth, and if so, how quickly — in one or two years? Northern winters in America (the questioner informed Franklin) were too severe for growing fine wool. And did not the witness know that in the southern colonies, as Virginia, "the wool is coarse, and only a kind of hair?" Franklin answered meticulously. Virginians, he said, clothed themselves largely in linen and cotton of their own raising. But he must have felt despair or a helpless laughter rising in him. It was like the whales leaping up Niagara after codfish. How could one man educate this people concerning America? . . .

Why was not the post office a tax? Grenville asked suddenly. Because, said Franklin, money paid for the postage of a letter was merely a quantum merit for a service done. "A man might still, if he chose, send his letter by private messenger."

The distinction between internal and external taxes was perhaps the hardest knot Franklin had to untie. (Years later he confessed he had never quite understood it himself.) Grenville put the question plainly enough. What was the difference, he demanded, "between a duty on the importation of goods [an external tax], and an excise on their consumption [an internal tax]?"

A very material difference, Franklin replied. The colonies claimed that Britain had no right to lay an excise within their country. "But the sea is yours; you maintain it by your fleets and keep it safe of pirates. You may therefore have a natural and quite equitable right to some toll or duty on merchandise carried — toward defraying the expense you are at in ships to maintain the safety of that carriage."

The tobacco trade was brought up, and trade with the West Indies. How many ships were laden annually with flaxseed for Ireland? What did America do with the flax that was left over? Were there any slitting mills in America? Any fulling mills? What was the annual amount of taxes paid in Pennsylvania, and how much poll tax did unmarried men pay? What was the reason Americans increased faster than people in England? Had the witness never heard that a great quantity of stockings for the army were manufactured in Philadelphia during the late war?

Franklin answered with facts and figures. No one challenged them. "An Adversary" asked whether Americans, if protected from the abuse of neighbors, would use the stamped paper rather than run into debt.

"It is hard to say what they would do," Franklin replied. "I can only judge what other people will think, and how they will act, by what I feel within myself. I have a great many debts due to me in America, and I had rather they would remain unrecoverable by any law, than submit to the Stamp Act. They will be debts of honor."

A member of Grenville's ministry inquired what Franklin meant by the stamp tax being "inexpedient." If the act were repealed, and Parliament showed its resentment, what would the colonies do?

It was now that Franklin, for perhaps the only time in his life, made what amounted to a speech. In public meetings he was notably taciturn.* Proceedings in America, he said, had been considered too much together — no difference made between peaceable resolves of colonial assemblies and the riots made by mobs. The assemblies had passed resolutions as to their rights, but they had taken no measures for opposition by force. "They have not built a fort, raised a man, or provided a grain of ammunition . . . But as to any internal tax, how small soever, laid by the legislature here on the people there, while they have no representatives in this legislature, I think it will never be submitted to."

The colonies raised, paid and clothed nearly twenty-five thousand men during the last war, Franklin said again — a number equal to those sent from Britain, and far beyond their proportion. They went deeply into debt doing this. "They consider themselves a part of the British empire, and as having one common interest with it. They may be looked on here as foreigners, but they do not consider themselves as such. They are zealous for the honor and prosperity of this nation, and, while they are well used, will always be ready to support it."

---

* Thomas Jefferson said he had served with Washington in the Virginia legislature and with Franklin in Congress, and that he "never heard either of them speak ten minutes at a time, nor to any but the main point that was to decide the question. They laid their shoulders to the great points, knowing that the little ones would follow of themselves."

Franklin spoke without interruption. At the end, in response to a question from "an adversary," he gave what was surely, to most members of Parliament, a new definition of the Empire. "The colonies," Franklin said, "are not supposed to be within the realm. They have assemblies of their own, which are their parliaments." Great Britain's Petition of Right (1628) had stated that common consent was required for the raising of supply. "And the people of America have no representatives in Parliament to make a part of that common consent."

After this the questions were brief and fast. Once, to a question about the post office, Franklin replied simply, "I have answered that." Another question he said he could not answer (whether the colonies would submit if Parliament ordered them to indemnify the victims of the late riots.) Still another he called "a deep question," and said his reply must be taken as his own personal opinion; he could not speak for America.

Q. 166. [By an adversary] If the Stamp Act should be repealed, would it induce the assemblies of America to acknowledge the right of Parliament to tax them, and would they erase their resolutions?

A. No, never.

Q. Is there no means of obliging them to erase those resolutions?

A. None that I know of; they will never do it unless compelled by force of arms.

Q. 168. [By a friend] Is there a power on earth that can force them to erase the resolutions?

A. No power, how great soever, can force men to change their opinions.

The ordeal was nearly over — if it can be called an ordeal. Franklin had been four hours on his feet. His answers were sure, with no hint of fluster or hesitation. No man objects to challenge when he knows he is equal to it.

SCENE FIVE

THE MAKING OF A
REVOLUTIONARY

CHAPTER THIRTEEN

1774: The Cockpit.
Franklin's humiliation.
The Grand Incendiary.

Thomas Hutchinson to William Whately, Boston, October 20, 1769: "They deserve punishment, you will say, but laying or continuing taxes upon all cannot be thought equal, seeing many will be punished who are not offenders. *Penalties of another kind seem better adopted. . . .*"

In the seven years since Franklin's triumphant appearance before the House of Commons, his reputation, as well as his influence, had grown and spread. He was famous throughout Europe for his scientific achievements. In America he held the position of postmaster general, an office he coveted. Also, he acted as agent in London for Massachusetts, Pennsylvania, New Jersey and Georgia. By all odds he was the best known American in England. He had, as he wrote Lord Kames, spent the greater part of his life in Britain. There were his friends, Joseph Priestley, Jeremy Bentham, William Strahan and a host of others, all Britishers. But even with the ties of friendship, circumstances, the violence of events in the colonies, the harsh and punitive reaction of Parliament, constantly challenged

Franklin's loyalty to England, narrowing his hope of reconciliation.

After he had testified before the Commons in 1766, the Stamp Act had been almost immediately repealed, followed, however, by an abrupt change of the parliamentary heart. Apparently chagrined by its own leniency, Parliament passed a declaratory act, asserting their right to tax the colonies at any time. Charles Townshend, chancellor of the Exchequer, sought a revenue by regulating American trade, setting duties on articles such as glass, lead, painters' colors, tea and paper. The New York Assembly had already been dissolved for refusing to comply with a quartering act; the Massachusetts legislature suffered a like fate when Samuel Adams persuaded members to send out a circular letter to Massachusetts towns, calling for united resistance and urging the defense of colonial rights. The Virginia House of Burgesses was dissolved when it endorsed the letter.

Conditions worsened with the landing of two regiments of British soldiers in Boston. At once trouble flared up; the soldiers behaved insolently toward the New Englanders and were bitterly resented. The result was foreseeable and culminated in violence — the so-called Boston Massacre of 1770. British soldiers, on sentry duty, finding themselves attacked at night by a Boston mob hurling ice, oystershells and clubs, fired into the crowd killing five people. Parliament repealed the Townshend duties except the tax on tea. To the colonists this was only a further outrage, and in December of 1773, when the East India Company's ships arrived in Boston laden with a cargo of tea, Boston refused to let it be unloaded. All the world knows the result. Citizens disguised as Mohawks boarded the vessels at night and dumped six hundred pounds of tea into the harbor. For days tea lined the high-water mark on beaches as far south as Nantasket. Hearing of it, Horace Walpole wrote, "An ostrich egg has been laid in America, where the Bostonians have canted three hundred chests of tea into the harbor." Later Walpole declared, "The Americans have at least acted like men. Our conduct has been that of pert children; we have thrown a pebble at a mastiff and are surprised that he was not frightened."

Meanwhile in England the ministry changed hands so often that Franklin said following it was like following a rope of sand. Not only were British politics at low ebb during this period, but about America politicians seemed deliberately misinformed and uninterested. Merchants as well as ministers and courtiers still persisted in looking upon the colony as ripe for speculation. Manufacturers in Nottingham and Leicester, as well as bankers in London, viewed the colony solely as a market for British goods . . . a vast "forest" to be "planted" and regulated for the enrichment of England, a "dumping ground for the unwanted or the incompetent." Horace Walpole said that in 1763 the English ruling class, "born with Roman insolence," was acting with "more haughtiness than an Asiatic monarch." America had brilliant support from William Pitt, who spoke before Parliament in defense of the colonies. "I rejoice," he said, "that America has resisted. Three millions of people so dead to all the feelings of liberty as voluntarily to submit to be slaves would have been fit instruments to make slaves of all the rest." But no eloquence or foresight seemed to affect Parliament, which continued to demand not only humiliating subservience from the colonies, but quite evidently intended to establish a "system of real British control." They appeared deliberately blind to the colonies' pride in their increasing political maturity and entirely failed to realize how deeply the colonists resented Parliament's continued insistence upon supremacy. This attitude was not only irremissible but showed a stubbornness incomprehensible to Parliament. The issue of taxes was all-embracing, and threatened the very fabric of colonial policy. Insubordination would not be tolerated. The tax levied on America was regarded by Parliament as fair and reasonable. British troops had defended the colonists against the French and the Indians, an extremely costly war. Benjamin Franklin himself admitted as much before the Commons. Now the colonists were refusing to repay their government for the war, firing on British soldiers and throwing tea into the harbor. America's behavior, the evidence of growing discontent, made members of Parliament suspect that dangerous fomenters, rebellious spirits, moved abroad and must be searched out and exposed.

That a new concept of government confronted Great Britain did not seem to penetrate those in Parliament. "There are some great eras," said James Wilson, "when important and very perceptible alterations take place in the situations of men and things." There could be no doubt that "America was in the midst of one of those great eras." Thomas Paine foresaw the consequences. "The independence of America," he said, "considered merely as a separation from England, would have been a matter of but little importance had it not been accompanied by a revolution in the principles and practices of governments."

As revolution became ever more apparent, such good Whigs as John Dickinson "agonizingly hesitated," fearing that America would cut herself off from the "source of its own life-blood of liberty. . . ." John Randolph said, "If the Ligament between Britain and America be burst asunder our Strength will be weakened and our Security at an End."

On January 11, 1774, Benjamin Franklin received a summons from Privy Council. As agent for Massachusetts he quite naturally supposed the summons concerned a petition from the Massachusetts legislature to the King. The petition had already been five months before the Council and no notice or action taken. The Massachusetts

Assembly had so couched the document as to give no cause for offense. It was humble, respectful, propitiatory and good-natured. The petition stated that Massachusetts was loyal and wished to do what England wanted, but "with all due submission . . . beg leave to represent that Thomas Hutchinson and Andrew Oliver . . . have not only been greatly instrumental in disturbing the peace and harmony of government and causing hateful discords but are justly chargeable with causing misery and bloodshed . . . wherefore we humbly pray that your Majesty will remove them from their posts." The petition added that the Assembly had derived their new information concerning Oliver and Hutchinson from "certain papers" they had "very lately before them."

The "certain papers" referred to were the famous ten letters written between June 18, 1768, and December 12, 1768, by Governor Thomas Hutchinson and his brother-in-law, Andrew Oliver (lieutenant governor of Massachusetts), to one Thomas Whately, known as a busy London gossip-collector and go-between. Whately held such offices as "Director of Progresses," and undersecretary of state. He was a member of Parliament. More importantly, he had the ear of Lord North and maintained an extensive correspondence with persons in distant parts of the Empire. An excellent, no doubt a calculated choice of correspondent, said to have been selected with particular care by the governor and his lieutenant.

Hutchinson and Oliver wrote freely, describing the meetings of the Massachusetts Assembly, for which they had little or no respect. Their views were biased and autocratic; they had easy access to information; Thomas Hutchinson had served the colony in a public capacity for some forty years. He was a native of Massachusetts and had been educated at Harvard. A further political advantage lay in his not being Church of England. Hutchinson was a puritan, supposedly a Sabbatarian, a group known to be "promoters of all those irksome restraints upon citizens . . . which produce a species of oppression that is hateful. . . ."

In consequence, Thomas Hutchinson was respected by half the inhabitants of Massachusetts and despised by the rest. At the time of the Stamp Act, his house had been attacked by a senseless mob and destroyed, his life threatened.

Corresponding with Thomas Whately, the object, quite evidently, was to report secretly upon the evidence of insurrection which was everywhere apparent, but also to show that Americans were not only inept at governing, but totally unfit. Speaking of the Massachusetts Assembly, Hutchinson wrote, "Ignorant though they be, yet the heads of Boston passed a number of weak but very criminal votes." Later Hutchinson tells Whately that the two regiments of troops have landed in Boston and ends by saying, "The government of the province has been so long in the hands of the populace that it will be a work of time to bring the people to just notions of the nature of government." The letters continued to deplore mob action (understandably bitter to both Hutchinson and Oliver because of their own experience), spoke of "the licentiousness of such as call themselves sons of liberty . . ."; "our incendiaries . . . our scandalous newspapers . . ."; "It is not possible that this anarchy should last." In one letter Andrew Oliver proposes the formation of a colonial aristocracy to be exempt from service in the lower offices and "monopolists of those higher. . . ." The legislative council, he says, should be "composed of men possessing landed estate of one hundred pounds a year and be called the Order of Patricians. . . ." Plainly Oliver, as well as Hutchinson, aimed to render the colonists powerless.

Most offensive of all was Hutchinson's statement that "there must be an abridgement of what are called English liberties. I doubt whether it is possible to project a system of government in which a colony 3,000 miles distant shall enjoy all the liberty of the parent state."

More followed in the same vein. The whole packet of letters fell into Franklin's hands; to this day nobody knows how, and he refused to tell. What he did was to send the entire correspondence to his old friend in Boston, Thomas Cushing, Speaker of the Massachusetts House of Representatives. The letters were not to be copied, only shown to a few trusted friends. It was Franklin's hope that these letters, which apparently so misinformed the British ministry, would reveal that Englishmen in the colonies and at home differed in their point of view about the same events. If this were established to the proper governing bodies then surely the difference could be met reasonably and in peace.

The moment Sam Adams laid eyes on the letters, they were doomed to be public property. Published in the *Boston Gazette,* they went under the heading "Born and Educated Among Us." John Adams, reading, could hardly believe his eyes. "Cool, thinking, deliberate villain," he wrote in his diary. "Bone of our Bone," he said, "born and educated among us! . . . Vile serpent." It was, of course, this correspondence that caused the Massachusetts legislature to compose its petition to the King for the removal of Hutchinson and Oliver.

In England the letters made a great stir. *Who had revealed them?* The original recipient, Thomas Whately, was dead, but his brother William swore he had nothing to do with the letters and accused John Temple, an American living in England, onetime governor of New Hampshire, now an officer of customs. The matter came to such a pass that Temple challenged Whately to a duel, which like duels on stage, was fought with pistol and sword, only Whately the worse for it with two minor wounds. Nevertheless, they both threatened to take up the duel at some later date.

Franklin, alarmed, at once sent a letter to the newspapers, saying that he alone was responsible. He had exposed the letters in hopes of effecting closer understanding with America, he said. If the Americans knew that the hateful taxes, the regiments of soldiers, originated from the urging of one of their own number, a Massachusetts man who for a generation had served his country in a public capacity, the general dissatisfaction would turn from Parliament to the two governors. This reasoning, although differing from that given to Thomas Cushing, had little impact.

London did not agree, nor was Privy Council impressed by this argument. Franklin was summoned before the Council and told by Solicitor General Wedderburn to secure a lawyer for his defense. Franklin, surprised, said he had thought only political matters were to be discussed, meaning the Massachusetts petition for the removal of Hutchinson and Oliver. But Wedderburn, who had actually been engaged to defend the two men, indicated otherwise. The hearing was delayed until Franklin could obtain the services of barristers Charles Dunning and John Lee — one on the day of the trial had such a cold he could barely be heard, the other proved ineffectual. Possibly they both feared that Franklin's defense would hamper their own careers at the British bar.

On January 29, 1774, Franklin appeared before Privy Council at Whitehall in The Cockpit. Henry VIII, that sporting monarch, had built a cockpit on the spot, a tennis court next door. Long ago the pit had been destroyed and a two-story building erected on its site, but the chamber on the ground floor continued to be called by its old name. The English cling to their traditions, and up until the nineteenth century letters from the Council chamber were formally headed "The Cockpit."

Today the room was crowded, perhaps thirty-five Councillors were present, more than had attended any previous meeting. The president, Lord Gower, presided in his robes. Solicitor General Alexander Wedderburn stood directly behind a long table at which the Councillors were seated. Spectators pushed into every corner, overflowing the hallway and the rooms beyond. Many peers were present, and seven or eight of Franklin's friends, among them Joseph Priestley, Richard Price, Jeremy Bentham, Edmund Burke. Franklin was prepared for unpleasantness — but not for the torrent of personal invective that came from Wedderburn, the derision, the laughter and applause of the spectators.

Franklin stood for an hour and a half, this being the custom for anyone being interrogated. The proceedings began with the petition from the Massachusetts Assembly requesting the dismissal of Oliver and Hutchinson. Next, Mr. Dunning, Franklin's lawyer, spoke in a voice "very feeble and husky. . . . No cause had been instituted, no prosecution intended," he said. "The Assembly did not come before the throne demanding justice; they appealed to the wisdom and goodness of their sovereign, which the King could grant or refuse. As the Assembly had no impeachment to make so they had no evidence to offer." Mr. John Lee followed in much the same strain.

Solicitor Alexander Wedderburn then addressed the Council. He posed the question whether the Crown should ever have in its power to employ a faithful and steady servant in the administration of a colony, a question, he said, "well worthy the attendance and attention of so great a number of lords and so large an audience." He went on to declare that Governor Hutchinson had shown himself eminently faithful and steady, and proceeded to outline Hutchinson's background, his administration, saying that "his conduct was praiseworthy to a high degree, he had been moderate, patient, and patriotic." According to Wedderburn the petition from the Massachusetts Assembly simply stated that "they *disliked* the governor and lieutenant governor." Such being the case, would the colony henceforward pay respect to any authority derived from this country?

Wedderburn then turned his attention to Franklin, saying that this whole misunderstanding between the Assembly and Hutchinson "was caused by Dr. Franklin's interference; that the letters were, in the fullest sense of the word, private letters; that they must have been stolen by Dr. Franklin whose . . . motive was to become governor of Massachusetts."

Franklin, standing in The Cockpit, found himself faced with a rancor and resentment among the lords present he had not foreseen. In this gathering of Councillors and spectators were many who desired his ruin, wanted him branded traitor, disgraced.

Falsely accused, with little or inadequate defense, Franklin tolerated the ordeal before Privy Council by standing in silence, making no answer or defense. On that day Franklin wore a suit of brown-figured Manchester velvet. His gray locks, as usual, fell below his ears. His face remained impassive and his body never moved.

Solicitor Wedderburn was relentless, his accusations lasted a full three-quarters of an hour. Franklin had stolen the correspondence, he kept insisting. "No gentleman's papers would now be safe unless locked into his escritoire. . . . Gentlemen will hide their papers . . . Franklin will henceforth esteem it a libel to be called a man of letters. This was a man of three letters." *

Wedderburn stood facing Franklin across the room. On the Council table before him was a cushion. This Wedderburn pounded from time to time to bring out his points. Wedderburn was an extraordinary man, rather small, elegant, hawk-nosed. He was a master of invective. Born and

---

* In the Roman republic a thief could be branded on the forehead with the word for thief, FVR, and thus "a man of three letters."

educated in Scotland he had always longed for the flesh-pots of England, where barristers made fortunes and acquired a reputation. He left Scotland, took his examinations in London, and became a barrister. He could not fail, however, to notice that when he spoke with his Scottish accent Englishmen smiled. Wedderburn determined the dialect was a great drawback to his advancement and went to the elder Sheridan and took lessons in elocution. Having conquered his brogue, an extremely difficult accomplishment, Wedderburn became so rabid on the disadvantages of Scottish dialect that he instigated a movement to rid all Scotland of the accent.

By now he had trained himself until his manner was polished and worldly. "The wary Wedderburn," he was called: "elegant, subtle, and insinuating." When reason or statement of the law did not accomplish his purpose, Wedderburn became ironical and bitterly sarcastic.

"Nothing," he insisted again, "will acquit Franklin of the charge of obtaining the letters by fraudulent or corrupt means for the most malignant purposes, unless he stole them from the person that stole them. I hope, my lords, that you will mark and brand the man for the honor of this country, of Europe, and of mankind."

There is no doubt that Wedderburn's invective was bolstered by recent events. The previous summer, Franklin had published two satires in *Gentleman's Magazine*, both of them widely read in England and extremely clever. The first, purporting to come from Danzig, was entitled "An Edict by the King of Prussia": "FREDERIC," it said, "by the grace of God, &c.&c.&c., to all present and to come, Health." All the world knows, it went on, that Britain was first settled by our "ducal ancestors . . . under the conduct of Hengist, Horsa, Hella, Uff, Cerdicus, Ida, and others . . . and that the said colonies . . . under the protection of our august house for ages past . . . have hitherto yielded little profit to the same." Therefore duties should be laid "on all goods of whatever kind imported into the same. . . ."

The edict continued, enumerating exactly the duties that had been laid on America by Britain: ". . . no mill or slitting engine could be erected for the making of steel, no wool transported thence, even to the mother country, Prussia . . . no hats or felts whatsoever be put upon any vessel, cart, carriage, or house to be conveyed into another country . . . and lastly . . . all the *thieves,* highway and street robbers, housebreakers, forgerers, murderers, s-d-tes . . . shall be emptied out of our gaols into the said island of Great Britain, for the better peopling of that country. . . . Given at Potsdam, this twenty-fifth day of the month of August, one thousand seven hundred and seventy-three, and in the thirty-third year of our reign. By the king, in his council. RECHTMAESSIG, *Sec.*"

The whole was so plausibly composed that many people believed it to be true. Franklin, staying in the country with Lord Le Despencer, was hugely amused when a gentleman ran into the room, magazine in hand, and in a state of excitement read it to the company as truth. The hoax was widely reprinted in England, America, and even in France, infuriating the English court party and highly amusing the friends of America.

The second article, *Rules by Which a Great Empire May Be Reduced to a Small One,* is also plausible and highly entertaining, setting out everything that Britain was doing to her colonies, under guise that Britain wished to be rid of them: "An ancient Sage boasted, that, tho' he could not fiddle, he knew how to make a *great city* of a *little one.* The science that I . . . am about to communicate is the very reverse. I address myself to all ministers who have the management of extensive dominions, which from their very greatness are becoming troublesome to govern. . . . Quarter troops among them,

THE MAKING OF A REVOLUTIONARY

who by their insolence may *provoke* the rising of mobs, and by their bullets and bayonets *suppress* them. By this means, like the husband who uses his wife ill *from suspicion,* you may in time convert your *suspicions* into *realities.* . . . Let the Parliaments flout their claims, reject their petitions, refuse even to suffer the reading of them, and treat the petitioners with the utmost contempt. Nothing can have a better effect in producing the alienation proposed; for though many can forgive injuries, *none ever forgave contempt.* . . ."

There was much more, all of it reasonable and plausible. The world loves a good laugh; the satire was reprinted many times. Although unsigned, it soon became known that Franklin had written both articles.

Franklin's very renown seemed to irritate Wedderburn and went beyond the indiscreet distribution of letters or the publication of a satire. He was incensed by Franklin's role as agent. Thomas Cushing had already warned Franklin in a letter. "Agents," Cushing said, "were looked on with an evil eye, as obstructors of ministerial measures, and the secretary [Hillsborough] would be well pleased to get rid of them . . . being of the opinion that agents are unnecessary and that whatever is to be transacted . . . may be done through and by the governor's letters, and more properly than any agent whatever. . . ."

American agents, said the solicitor general, had developed into figures far more significant than the mere agents for England's subjects in America. In the newspapers their comings and goings were recorded as if they were ambassadors or ministers of free states. "A foreign ambassador," said Wedderburn, "when residing here, just before the breaking out of a war, or upon particular occasions, may bribe a villain to steal or betray any state papers; he is under the command of another state, and is not amenable to the laws of the country where he resides;

and the secure exemption from punishment may induce a laxer morality. But Dr. Franklin, whatever he may teach the people at Boston, while he is *here,* at least, is a subject; and if a subject injure a subject, he is answerable to the law. And the Court of Chancery will not much attend to his new self-created importance." Wedderburn added that he had instituted a suit in Chancery against Franklin. Then Wedderburn said, "I hope, my Lords, you will mark and brand this man. . . . He has forfeited all the respect of societies of men. Into what companies will he hereafter go with an unembarrassed face of the honest intrepidity of virtue?"

Jeremy Bentham, in the audience, said he was "not more astonished at the brilliancy of Wedderburn's lightning than astounded by the thunder that accompanied it." As Wedderburn made his points and pounded the cushion on the Council table, "the ear was stunned at every blow . . . the table groaned under the assault. . . . Alone in the recess, on the left hand of the president, stood Benjamin Franklin, remaining the whole time like a rock in the same posture, his head resting on his left hand; and in that attitude abiding the pelting of the pitiless storm." Joseph Priestley also has told of the affair. "At the sallies of Wedderburn's sarcastic wit," said Priestley, "all members of Council, the president himself not excepted, frequently laughed outright. No person belonging to the Council behaved with decent gravity, except Lord North, who, coming late, took his stand behind the chair opposite me."

The newspapers did not print Wedderburn's speech in full, but Benjamin Vaughan, one of Franklin's old friends, published it.

When the hearing came to an end, Franklin walked out calmly, his countenance still unruffled. The following day, as he expected, Franklin received a letter telling him that he had been dismissed from his office of postmaster general in America. This he resented extremely, more even than the false accusations made about him in The Cockpit. He wrote to his son William:

February 2, 1774

Dear Son:

This Line is just to acquaint you that I am well, and that my Office of Deputy-Postmaster is taken from me. As there is no Prospect of your being ever promoted to a better Government, and that you hold has never defray'd its Expenses, I wish you were well settled in your farm. 'Tis an honester and a more honourable, because a more independent Employment. You will hear from others the Treatment I have receiv'd. I leave you to your own Reflections and Determinations upon it, and remain ever your affectionate Father,

B. Franklin

From now on, Franklin's enemies, being those who were unalterably opposed to an independent America, came out virulently against him. Lord Sandwich, in the House of Lords, called him "one of the bitterest and most mischievous Enemies this Country ever had known." Franklin was present at the time, leaning on the bar at the House of Lords. He kept his face calm and immovable. The British press called him, "the old veteran of Mischief" . . . "this old snake." They spoke of his "vindictive subtlety, watchfulness, and politician tricks." He was the *"grand incendiary, this living emblem of iniquity in Grey Hairs"* . . . *"Old Traitor, Old Doubleface. . . ."* His apartment in Mrs. Stevenson's house became "Judas's office in Craven Street." Remarkable expletives for a man of sixty-eight to receive.

Franklin did not seem to mind what was said about him, though he was deeply hurt at being deprived of his postmaster generalship. When he took the office over in 1754, Britain had never received a penny of revenue from the post office, but under his management, and at the time of his dismissal, postal revenue came to three thousand pounds a year. On February 17, 1774, some two weeks after the hearing at The Cockpit, Franklin wrote to his sister, Jane Mecom, a sturdy, humorous and faithful woman: "You will hear before this comes to hand, that I am depriv'd of my Office. Don't let this give you any Uneasiness. You and I have almost finished this Journey of Life; we are now but a little way from home, and have enough in our Pockets to pay the Post Chaises. Intending to disgrace me, they have rather done me Honour. No Failure of Duty of my Office is alleg'd against me; such a Fault I should have been asham'd of. But I am too much attached to the Interests of America, and an Opposer of the Measures of Administration. . . . The Displacing me therefore is a Testimony of my being uncorrupted. . . ." Franklin said also that for many years in America he had been considered as too much an Englishman, trying openly to preserve "that fine and noble China vase, the British Empire." Now in England he was considered too much an American.

Writing Thomas Cushing only a few weeks before his experience in The Cockpit, Franklin said, "Grievances cannot be redressed unless they are known, and they cannot be known but through complaints and petition. But where complaining is a crime, hope becomes despair." It has been said that on January 29, 1774, Benjamin Franklin, man of peace, instigator of the Albany Plan for Colonial Union, beloved by many Englishmen, whose bond with England was as much a part of him as bone and sinew, relinquished his final hope of reconciliation with the King and Parliament, and turned reluctantly toward Revolution.

Benjamin Rush gave the final interpretation as to the effect of Franklin's so-called trial in The Cockpit: "As a result of this humiliation," Rush said, "Franklin is a very popular character in every part of America. He will be received and carried in triumph to his house when he arrives amongst us. It is to be hoped that he will not consent to hold any more [British] offices under government. No step but this can prevent his being handed down to posterity among the first and greatest characters in the world."

AFTERWORD

*O*n October 14, 1973, Catherine Drinker Bowen was at work on the final pages of Chapter 13. The notes she had made and quotations to be used were in order, the necessary reference books — Parton, Smyth, Labaree — arranged within easy distance of her bed. She knew she was gravely ill. She had been operated on twice for cancer. Her long training, discipline, the correct ordering of her mind, the drive to finish — traits uppermost in all her works — stood to her now. When it was no longer possible to write, she dictated into a tape recorder an analysis of Franklin's character drawn from all her research. In this dictation there is a new quality; it is intimate and brilliant as she ranges back and forth in the material she has collected, speaking her thoughts. She outlines what must be written in her plan for the final pages and how it should end. She speaks of people and events which either she intends to use or who come to mind. She plans to write an afterword where she will tell "some of Frank-

lin's traits that I could not put in the book," then most
fortunately gives her own interpretation of his character.
She died on November 1, 1973.

How did this happen, this Cockpit — this terrible Cockpit which turned Franklin from a British American to
an American? There has never, in my knowledge, except
for the McCarthy hearings, been so public a disgrace of a
good man more magnificently received and taken than
when Franklin, nearly seventy years old, stood silent. . . .
Every patriot has something personal in his life which
makes him a rebel; you are not just born one. It was the
mezzotint engraving of Benjamin Franklin appearing before Privy Council, which I have downstairs in my house,
that first started me on this Franklin book.

When Benjamin Franklin writes the letter to his son
William, governor of New Jersey, telling him of the incident (The Cockpit) and saying that he supposes William
will not wish to continue as governor of Jersey, he still
hopes, I think, that William will not — in fact I doubt
Franklin even dreams William is going to turn Tory.
William keeps his place; Franklin loses his. However, he
does not go right home, but stays in London, visiting
friends. The account of his "hearing" before Privy Council is carefully cut out from the printed account and sent
to America that it may be distributed in proper places.

Meanwhile, his wife Debbie dies in December of 1774,
without Franklin's being there or even knowing she is ill.
She must have had a premonition, for she is known to
have said that if her husband did not come back that
winter she doubted she would ever see him again. Deborah
Franklin suffered a stroke on December 14 and died
"without a sound" on December 19. Her son William,
riding through "wind and storm," arrived immediately
before the funeral. In 1774 Franklin had written her: "It

seems but t'other day since you and I were ranked among the boys and girls, so swiftly does time fly. We have, however, great reason to be thankful that so much of our lives has passed so happily."

No matter how often Franklin laid plans to have Debbie join him abroad, or wrote friends that he hoped she would come, Deborah Franklin never was willing to cross the Atlantic. That Franklin wanted her in England, there can be no doubt.

In March of 1775 Franklin boards ship — an extraordinarily calm passage. "None of his voyages," writes James Parton, "was richer in results than this one. His first labor was to write, in the form of a letter to his son, a full account of his late interviews and negotiations. . . . The material parts of this narrative must have filled about two hundred fifty pages of foolscap; a severe strain for a man of sixty-nine, in the cabin of a small ship."

Besides the account of his last years in England, Franklin also takes the temperature of the Gulf Stream by thermometer, experiments which turned out to be of value and were used later.

When Franklin arrives home he is greeted with the news of the Battle of Lexington. Even then, however, many who were afterward firebrands still hoped for peace with England. Franklin's letter to Lord Kames some years earlier had said that he loved England. "I wish it prosperity and therefore wish to see that union on which alone I think it can be secured and established. As to America, the advantage of such a union to her are not so apparent. . . ."

In 1774 Franklin had written *A Tract Relative to the Affair of Hutchinson's Letters*. "But, I trust," he said, "the general Prudence of our Countrymen will see, that by our growing Strength we advance fast to a Situation in which our Claims must be allow'd; that by a premature Struggle we may be crippled and kept down another Age; that as between Friends every Affront is not worth a Duel, between Nations every Injury not worth a War, so between the Governed and the Governing, every Mistake in Government, every Encroachment on Rights, is not worth a Rebellion."

If I stop the book in 1774, then I want to have an entirely new section. Here I wish to tell some of Franklin's traits that I have not put in the book. I shall dictate them here so as to remember them.

"This," I wrote once, when I was thinking about my preface, "is the best integrated man I ever studied." He accepted what came, never agonized in the Romantic manner of Jonathan Edwards, who wrote, "My soul breaketh for the longing it hath." Franklin never would have said anything like this, nor would he have given Thomas Jefferson's reply when made commissioner to France: "I would go to Hell for my country." On September 26, 1776, as Congress voted unanimously for Franklin to be commissioner to France, he turned to Benjamin Rush, who was sitting beside him, and said: "I am old and good for nothing; but, as the storekeepers say of their remnants of cloth, 'I am but a fag end, and you may have me for what you please,' just so my country may command my services in any way they choose."

Then I want to say something about Franklin not having, as Herbert Butterfield says, "the tragic sense of life" that many great men have had, such as you might say of Lincoln, or Jonathan Edwards, or many others. . . . Franklin was apparently one of those men who was born with a cheerful disposition. This is a tremendous gift. He had a talent for happiness, just as George Washington had a talent for character, integrity. Franklin said when he was old and suffering terribly, so that he had to lie in

bed and use opium, that if he had the chance he would
live his life over again. You do not find many men who
would say this. To me it is very admirable. He suffered in
his life a great deal of sickness, sore throats, gout, stone,
all kinds of very difficult and painful illnesses. He never
seemed to worry whether he would get well, he just got
well. Sainte-Beuve called him "this most graceful of all
utilitarians. . . ." And it has been said that "Benjamin
Franklin is enigmatic, always held something back." Carl
Becker in the *Dictionary of American Biography* says,
"Benjamin Franklin is nevertheless not wholly committed. Some thought remains uncommunicated, some pene-
trating observation is held in reserve." I'm not sure that
I agree with this. I would rather believe that Franklin
simply said what he thought as far as he had thought at
the moment. Later he may change his mind.

Dr. Holmes, O. W. Holmes's father, said that sanctimo-
nious people made him sneeze and go home with a cold.
I think Franklin was like that. He hated solemn, pompous
people. He simply never replied to them. He talked very
little in company, but talked freely with a friend or two,
especially over a few drinks.

As I said, it is true that Benjamin Franklin lacked that
tragic sense of life that makes heroes, but I love him for
it; he simply accepted. Though I doubt if he ever accepted the Wedderburn scene, and why should he? What
a brute that man was! I think the English can be more
insulting than any nation on earth, perhaps because they
do it politely.

Benjamin Franklin simply wrested a happy life from
circumstances that would have dulled or embittered a
lesser man. His wife could have bored him, he could
easily have abandoned her. He never did. His son William

was imprisoned for two or three years as a Tory, his grandson became a social climber or a fop. . . . Franklin's autobiography gives only his years as a tradesman, but at seventy he had been declared a leader of a revolution, and signed the Declaration of Independence.

John Adams, for instance, was very concerned with himself, very apt to be jealous, at times pompous. He was a more intellectual man than Franklin, with a real knowledge of history that enabled him to compare systems of governments, ancient and modern. Yet Benjamin Franklin was a philosopher, he absolutely knew himself, never had feared to face himself, and without self-guilt or self-righteousness set about improving himself. What young revolutionary today wants to improve himself? He only wants to improve other people. To seek self-improvement a man has to believe in life, which means believing in himself. Montaigne said, "Of all the infirmities we have, the most savage is to despise our being."

Franklin lived his life in cities, not on the land like Thomas Jefferson and Washington. He gave away much of his money, maintained many of his family. He sent cordwood to his sister Jane, gave loans to nephews and grandchildren. When poor he much desired money, it set him free.

Of course the eighteenth century was a great believer in Reason. Benjamin Franklin says to Jane, ". . . our Reason would still be of more use to us if it could enable us to prevent the evils it can hardly enable us to bear, but in that it is so deficient and in other things so often misleads us that I have sometimes been almost tempted to wish we have been furnished with a good sensible *instinct* instead of it."

Benjamin Franklin loved to sing. He tells us that a certain song, "The Old Man's Wish," he had sung at least a thousand times. The chorus says:

> May I govern my passions with absolute sway
> Grow wiser and better as my strength wears away,
> Without gout or stone by gentle decay.

Of course he had both gout and stone, but he governed his passions, that we know. In many ways it is easier to write about somebody who did not govern his passions, somebody like John Adams, who thumped with his cane on the floor at the Continental Congress. Even George Washington could become terribly angry and burst out. It is true that every now and then Franklin lost his temper, but not often.

I want to say something about the ease with which Benjamin Franklin moved to his tasks, the lack of pretentiousness. Francis Bacon has a wonderful phrase in his essays about "the slide and ease with which one should learn to move." Carl Van Doren says "Franklin must have been what he was because nobody could have invented such a figure." I wish I'd thought of that.

Franklin used to talk about "happy mediocrity" and he used to be proud that America — American citizens — were in a state of "happy mediocrity." Nobody could have said this except someone who was himself immensely superior, and yet, is not this a revolutionary saying?

From Tyler's *Literary History of the American Revolution:* "It is only by continuous reading of the entire body of Franklin's Revolutionary writings, from grave to gay, from lively to severe, that anyone can know how brilliant was his wisdom, or how wise was his brilliance, or how humane and gentle and helpful were both. . . ."

Franklin said: "Methinks life should have a dramatic ending like a stage piece. . . ." And he said, "Live as if you are to live forever."

And he had that quality that I call "grace."

BIBLIOGRAPHY

General Note

The title *The Most Dangerous Man in America* was suggested by the following excerpt from a letter written by Lord Stormont, the British ambassador in Paris, to his friend, Lord Weymouth, when Franklin landed in France in 1776: "In a word, my lord, I look upon him as a dangerous engine, and am very sorry that some English frigate did not meet with him by the way."

F. L. Lucas, *The Art of Living*, p. 243

Bibliographical Note

In compiling the following bibliography we have been guided by the author's own alphabetical file and the notes she made. Catherine Drinker Bowen considered her bibliography a most important aid to her readers and was meticulous in recording her sources and commenting on them.

Historians have spent a lifetime examining Benjamin Franklin; the available material is monumental. Mrs. Bowen made no claim to original research but used the recognized authorities and sources in the field. First were the Franklin papers, available in two editions. Albert Henry Smyth edited *The Writings of Benjamin Franklin* in 1905–1907, and these ten volumes were reprinted in 1970. Currently, a team of scholars under the direction of Leonard W. Labaree and his successor, William B. Willcox, of Yale University, is compiling a new edition of the Franklin works, including not only his own writings but letters to him. To date, seventeen volumes covering the period January, 1706, to December, 1770, have been published. More volumes from the Yale University Press are expected shortly.

Mrs. Bowen made frequent use of James Parton's *Life and Times of Benjamin Franklin* (2 vols. New York, 1864) and Carl Van Doren's definitive biography, *Benjamin Franklin* (New York, 1938). Various collections of Franklin's works, such as Van Doren's edition of *Franklin's Autobiographical Writings* (New York, 1945) and the Yale University Press edition of the Franklin *Autobiography* edited by Labaree (New Haven, 1964) were also helpful.

As Mrs. Bowen planned Franklin's life in scenes, we accordingly have followed her plan, omitting titles only where duplication occurs.

Scene I: The Dogood Papers
Chapters 1 and 2

Adams, Charles F. *Massachusetts: Its Historians and Its History.* Boston and New York, 1893.

Aldridge, Alfred Owen. *Benjamin Franklin, Philosopher and Man.* Philadelphia, 1965.

Beall, Otto T., Jr., and Shryock, Richard H. *Cotton Mather: First Significant Figure in American Medicine.* Baltimore, 1954.

Boas, Ralph and Louise. *Cotton Mather: Keeper of the Puritan Conscience.* New York, 1928.

Bonner, John. *Map of Boston.* Boston, 1722.

Bridenbaugh, Carl. *Cities in the Wilderness, 1625–1742.* New York, 1938.

Chamberlain, Allen. *Beacon Hill.* Boston, 1925.

City of Boston. *Report of the Record Commissioners.* December 17, 1885.

Drake, Samuel G. *The History and Antiquities of Boston.* 2 vols. Boston, 1857.

Duniway, Clyde Augustus. *The Development of Freedom of the Press in Massachusetts.* Cambridge, Mass., 1906.

Forty of Boston's Historic Homes. Boston, 1912.

Holmes, Abiel. *The Annals of America, 1492–1826.* 2 vols. Cambridge, Mass., 1829.

Hornberger, Theodore. "Benjamin Franklin." University of Minnesota *Pamphlets on American Writers,* no. 19. Minneapolis, 1962.

Howe, M. A. DeWolfe. *Boston.* New York, 1903.

Lingelbach, William E. "Franklin's American Instructor: Early Americanism in the Art of Writing." American Philosophical Society *Proceedings* 96 (1952): 367–387.

Mather, Cotton. *Bonifacius: An Essay Upon the Good.* David Levin, ed. Cambridge, Mass., 1966.

Miller, C. William. "Franklin's Type: Its Study Past and Present." American Philosophical Society *Proceedings* 99 (1955): 418–432.

Miller, Perry, ed. *The New England Courant: A Selection of Certain Issues Containing Writings of Benjamin Franklin*. Boston, 1956.

Morison, Samuel Eliot. *The Intellectual Life of Colonial New England*. New York, 1956.

Murdock, Kenneth Ballard. *Increase Mather, the Foremost American Puritan*. Boston, 1925.

Records of Boston Selectmen, 1716–1736. Boston Atheneum, n.d.

Ross, Marjorie Drake. *The Book of Boston: The Colonial Period*. New York, 1960.

Shaw, Charles. *Topographical and Historical Description of Boston*. Boston, 1817.

Sirkis, Nancy. *Boston*. New York, 1965.

Snow, Caleb H., M.D. *History of Boston*. Boston, 1825.

Stark, James H. *Antique Views of Ye Town of Boston*. Boston, 1882.

Thomas, Isaiah. *The History of Printing in America*. 2 vols. Albany, 1874.

Thwing, Annie Haven. *The Crooked and Narrow Streets of the Town of Boston*. Boston, 1920.

Van Doren, Carl. *Benjamin Franklin and Jonathan Edwards*. New York, c. 1920.

——, ed. *The Letters of Benjamin Franklin and Jane Mecom*. Princeton, 1950.

Wendell, Barrett. *Cotton Mather: The Puritan Priest*. New York, 1891.

Whitehill, Walter M. *Boston in the Age of John Fitzgerald Kennedy*. Norman, Oklahoma, 1966.

——. *Boston: A Topographical History*. 2nd ed. Cambridge, Mass., 1968.

Wroth, Lawrence C. *The Colonial Printer*. New York, 1931.

Scene II: Franklin and Electricity
Chapters 3, 4 and 5

Asimov, Isaac. "Light, Magnetism and Electricity." *Understanding Physics*. Vol. II. New York, 1966.

Bridenbaugh, Carl and Jessica. *Rebels and Gentlemen: Philadelphia in the Age of Franklin*. New York, 1942.

Brinton, Crane. *The Shaping of the Modern Mind*. New York, 1956.

Bronowski, Jacob. *Science and Human Values*. New York, 1956.

Browne, Dr. Thomas. *Pseudodoxia Epidemica: Or, Enquiries into very many received Tenents and commonly Presumed Truths*. 3rd ed. London, 1658.

Butterfield, Herbert. *The Origins of Modern Science, 1300–1800*. New York, 1950.

Cohen, I. Bernard, ed. *Benjamin Franklin's Experiments*. Cambridge, Mass., 1941.

——. "Benjamin Franklin and the Mysterious 'Dr. Spence.'" *Journal of the Franklin Institute* 235 (1943): 1–25.

——. *Benjamin Franklin: His Contribution to the American Tradition*. Indianapolis, 1953.

——. "How Practical Was Benjamin Franklin's Science?" *Pennsylvania Magazine of History and Biography* 69 (1954): 284–293.

——. *Franklin and Newton: An Inquiry into Speculative Newtonian Experimental Science and Franklin's Work in Electricity as an Example Thereof*. Philadelphia, 1956.

Colden, Cadwallader. *Letter Books*. 2 vols. New York, 1876–1877.

——. *Letters and Papers.* 9 vols. New York, 1917–1923, 1934–1935.

Faÿ, Bernard. *Franklin: The Apostle of Modern Times.* Boston, 1929.

Fleming, Thomas J. *The Man Who Dared the Lightning.* New York, 1971.

Heathcote, N. H. deV. "Franklin's Introduction to Electricity." *Isis* 46 (1955): 29–35.

Hindle, Brooke. *The Pursuit of Science in Revolutionary America, 1735–1789.* Chapel Hill, 1956.

Holton, Gerald; Roller, Duane H. D.; and Roller, Duane. *Foundations of Modern Physical Science.* Reading, Mass., 1956.

Lucas, F. L. *The Art of Living: Four Eighteenth-Century Minds.* New York, 1959.

MacLaurin, Lois Margaret. *Franklin's Vocabulary.* Garden City, 1928.

Mather, Cotton. *The Christian Philosopher: A Collection of the Best Discoveries in Nature with Religious Improvements* (1721). A facsimile reproduction. Josephine Piercy, ed. Gainesville, 1968.

Meet Dr. Franklin. Philadelphia, 1943.

Pepper, William. *The Medical Side of Dr. Franklin.* Philadelphia, 1911.

Priestley, Joseph. *The History and Present State of Electricity with Original Experiments.* Reprint from 3rd ed. London, 1775. 2 vols. Introduction by Robert E. Schofield. New York, 1966.

Roller, Duane, and Roller, Duane H. D. *The Development of the Concept of Electric Charge.* Cambridge, Mass., 1954.

Royal Society of London. *Philosophical Transactions* I–VI (1665–1671); XXII (1700–1701).

Taylor, F. Sherwood. *A Short History of Science and Scientific Thought.* New York, 1949.

Weisskopf, Victor Frederick. *Knowledge and Wonder: The Natural World as Man Knows It.* Garden City, 1963.

Wolf, A. *A History of Science, Technology and Philosophy in the Eighteenth Century.* New York, 1939.

Scene III: The Albany Congress of 1754, and Franklin's Plan of Union
Chapters 6, 7 and 8

Albany's Historic Streets. National Savings Bank, Albany, 1918.

Bailey, Edith Anna. "Influences toward Radicalism in Connecticut, 1754–1775." *Smith College Studies in History* V, no. 4 (1920).

Bancroft, George. *History of the Formation of the Constitution of the United States of America.* 2 vols. New York, 1882.

Becker, Carl. *The Declaration of Independence: A Study in the History of Political Ideas.* New York, 1922.

Bonomi, Patricia U. *A Factious People.* New York, 1971.

Boyd, Julian P., ed. *The Susquehanna Company Papers.* 4 vols. Wilkes-Barre, 1930–1933.

——. *Indian Treaties, Printed by Benjamin Franklin, 1736–1762.* Philadelphia, 1938.

——. *Anglo-American Union.* Philadelphia, 1941.

Calendar of the Papers of Benjamin Franklin. 5 vols. Philadelphia, 1908.

Carmer, Carl. *The Susquehanna.* New York, 1955.

Carson, Hampton L., ed. *History of the Celebration of the One Hun-*

dredth Anniversary of the Promulgation of the Constitution of the United States. 2 vols. Philadelphia, 1889.

Chinard, Gilbert. "Eighteenth Century Theories on America as a Human Habitat." American Philosophical Society Proceedings 91 (1947): 27–57.

Colden, Cadwallader. The History of the Five Nations of Canada. 3rd ed. 2 vols. London, 1755.

Collections on the History of Albany from Its Discovery to the Present Time. 4 vols. Joel Munsell, ed. Albany, 1865–1871.

Cummings, Hubertis. Richard Peters: Provincial Secretary and Cleric, 1704–1776. Philadelphia, 1944.

De Voto, Bernard. The Course of Empire. Boston, 1952.

Documents Relative to the Colonial History of the State of New York. Vols. IV, VI. Albany, 1854, 1855.

Edmonds, Walter D. The Musket and the Cross. Boston, 1968.

Flexner, J. T. Mohawk Baronet: Sir William Johnson of New York. New York, 1959.

Gipson, Lawrence Henry. The British Empire Before the American Revolution. 15 vols. New York, 1936–1970.

Grant, Mrs. Anne. Memoirs of an American Lady. Albany, 1876.

Halsey, Francis Whiting. The Old New York Frontier, 1614–1800. New York, 1901.

Hislop, Codman. Albany: Dutch, English and American. Albany, 1936.

Hutchinson, Thomas. The History of the Colony and Province of Massachusetts Bay. 3 vols. Cambridge, Mass., 1936.

Hutson, James H. Pennsylvania Politics, 1746–1770. Princeton, 1972.

Jenkins, Howard M. The Family of William Penn. Philadelphia, 1899.

Jennings, Francis Paul. "The Indian Trade of the Susquehanna Valley." American Philosophical Society Proceedings 110 (1966): 406–424.

Johnson, Sir William. Papers. 14 vols. James Sullivan et al., eds. Albany, 1921–1965.

Kalm, Peter. Travels into North America, 1748–1750. 2 vols. New York, 1937.

Katz, Stanley N. Newcastle's New York: Anglo-American Politics, 1732–1753. Cambridge, Mass., 1968.

Lucas, Paul. "A Note on the Comparative Study of the Structure of Politics in Mid-Eighteenth Century Britain and Its American Colonies." William and Mary Quarterly 28, 3rd Series (1971): 301–309.

McAnear, Beverly, ed. "Personal Accounts of the Albany Congress." Mississippi Valley Historical Review 39. (1952–1953): 727–746.

Mariboe, William Herbert. "The Life of William Franklin." Unpublished Ph.D. thesis. University of Pennsylvania, 1962.

Minutes of the Court of Albany, Rensslaerswyck and Schenectady. 3 vols. Albany, 1926–1932.

Morgan, Edmund S. "The American Indian: Incorrigible Individualist." An Address to the John Carter Brown Library. Providence, 1958.

Morgan, Lewis H. The League of the Iroquois. 2 vols. New Haven, 1954.

Newbold, R. C. The Albany Congress and the Plan of Union of 1754. New York, 1955.

Olson, A. G., and Brown, Richard M. Anglo-American Political Relations, 1675–1775. New Brunswick, N.J., 1970.

Parkman, Francis. Montcalm and Wolfe. 2 vols. Boston, 1884.

——. A Half-Century of Conflict: France and England in North America. 2 vols. Boston, 1892.

Penn, John, and Peters, Richard. "Report of Proceedings at Albany." Pennsylvania Archives, Series IV, II: 697–713.

Pennsylvania Colonial Records. 16 vols. Philadelphia, 1838–1853.

Pound, Arthur. *The Penns of Pennsylvania and England.* New York, 1932.

Robbins, Caroline. "When Is It That Colonies May Turn Independent?" *William and Mary Quarterly,* 3rd Series, 11 (1954): 214–251.

Schuyler, George W. *Colonial New York.* 2 vols. New York, 1885.

Sharpless, Isaac. *Political Leaders of Provincial Pennsylvania.* New York, 1919.

Shirley, William. *Correspondence 1731–1760.* 2 vols. Charles H. Lincoln, ed. New York, 1912.

Smith, William. *History of New York, from the First Discovery to the Year, 1733.* Albany, 1814.

Story, D. A. *The deLanceys.* London, 1931.

Tebbel, John. *The Compact History of the Indian Wars.* New York, 1966.

Thayer, Theodore. *Israel Pemberton: King of the Quakers.* Philadelphia, 1943.

Tolles, Frederick B. *Meeting House and Counting House: The Merchants of Colonial Philadelphia, 1682–1763.* Chapel Hill, 1948.

Trelease, Allen W. *Indian Affairs in Colonial New York.* Ithaca, 1960.

Varga, Nicholas. "Robert Charles, New York Agent 1748." *William and Mary Quarterly,* 3rd Series, 18 (1961): 211–235.

Volwiler, Albert T. *George Croghan and the Westward Movement.* Cleveland, 1926.

Wallace, Paul A. W. *Conrad Weiser, Friend to Colonist and Mohawk, 1696–1760.* Philadelphia, 1945.

——. *Indians in Pennsylvania.* Harrisburg, 1961.

Walton, Joseph S. *Conrad Weiser and the Indian Policy of Colonial Pennsylvania.* Philadelphia, c. 1900.

Weiser, Conrad. "Journal." Vol. I in *Early Western Travels.* 32 vols. Reuben G. Thwaites, ed. Cleveland, 1904–1907.

Wellenreuther, Hermann. "The Political Dilemma of the Quakers in Pennsylvania, 1681–1748." *Pennsylvania Magazine of History and Biography* 94 (1970): 135–172.

Wright, Louis B. *The Atlantic Frontier.* New York, 1947.

Chapter Note, Chapter 8, page 139

In the light of Franklin's statements to Colden and Collinson, it is surprising to find historians arguing over what they call the "primary authorship" of the Albany Plan. Lawrence H. Gipson, in his monumental *British Empire Before the American Revolution,* maintains that Hutchinson, like Franklin, came to Albany with a plan in hand. Professor Verner Crane disagrees. Yet in Volume XIII (*Summary of the Series*) Gipson speaks of "the famous Albany Plan of Union" — very properly known as "the Franklin Plan of Union." The entire argument is set out in Volume V of *The Papers of Benjamin Franklin* (Labaree and Bell, eds.). The decisive facts seem to be Franklin's letters as quoted in this chapter, and Hutchinson's own statement in Volume III of his history of Massachusetts, written in England in the 1780's: "The plan for a general union was projected by Benjamin Franklin, Esq., one of the commissioners from the province of Pennsylvania, the heads whereof he brought with him."

Interlude: Franklin Is Fifty
Chapter 9

Bell, Whitfield J., Jr. "Some Aspects of the Social History of Pennsylvania, 1760–1790." *Pennsylvania Magazine of History and Biography.* 1938: 281–308.

——. "Benjamin Franklin and the German Charity Schools." American Philosophical Society *Proceedings* 101 (1957): 551–558.

Conner, Paul W. *Poor Richard's Politicks.* New York, 1965.

Dunn, Mary Maples. *William Penn, Politics and Conscience.* Princeton, 1967.

Echeverria, Durand. *Mirage in the West.* Princeton, 1957.

Fiala, Peter D. "Quakers and the British Monarchy: A Study in Anglo-American Attitudes and Practices in the Early 1760s." *Pennsylvania History* 37 (1970): 151–168.

Hanna, W. S. *Benjamin Franklin and Pennsylvania Politics.* Stanford, 1964.

Hunter, William A. *Forts on the Pennsylvania Frontier, 1753–1758.* Harrisburg, 1960.

Hutson, James H. "Benjamin Franklin and the Parliamentary Grant for 1758." *William and Mary Quarterly,* 3rd Series, 23 (1966): 575–595.

Lincoln, Charles H. *The Revolutionary Movement in Pennsylvania, 1760–1776.* Philadelphia, 1901.

Martin, James Kirby. "The Return of the Paxton Boys and the Historical State of the Pennsylvania Frontier, 1764–1774." *Pennsylvania History* 38 (1971): 117–133.

Parkman, Francis. *The Conspiracy of Pontiac.* 2 vols. Boston, 1870.

Thayer, Theodore. *Pennsylvania Politics and the Growth of Democracy, 1740–1776.* Harrisburg, 1953.

Young, Chester Raymond. "The Evolution of the Pennsylvania Assembly, 1682–1748." *Pennsylvania History* 35 (1968): 147–168.

Zimmerman, John J. "Governor Denny and the Quartering Act of 1756." *Pennsylvania Magazine of History and Biography* 91 (1967): 266–281.

Scene IV: Franklin in London, 1757–1766
Chapters 10, 11 and 12

Bancroft, George. *History of the United States of America.* 6 vols. New York, 1883–1885.

Becker, Carl. "The History of Political Parties in the Province of New York, 1760–1776." *Bulletin of the University of Wisconsin, History Series* II, no. 1 (1909).

Bell, Whitfield J., Jr. " 'All Clear Sunshine': New Letters of Franklin and Mary Stevenson Hewson." American Philosophical Society *Proceedings* 100 (1956): 521–536.

Bemis, Samuel Flagg. *The Diplomacy of the American Revolution.* New York, 1935.

Brooke, John. *The Chatham Administration, 1766–1768.* London, 1956.

Butterfield, Herbert. *George III and the Historians.* London, 1957.

Butterfield, L. H., ed. *Letters of Benjamin Rush.* 2 vols. Princeton, 1951.

Crane, Verner W. *Benjamin Franklin's Letters to the Press, 1758–75.* Chapel Hill, 1950.

Currey, Cecil B. *Road to Revolution: Benjamin Franklin in England, 1765–1775*. Garden City, 1968.

Davidson, Philip. *Propaganda and the American Revolution*. Chapel Hill, 1941.

Davis, H. W. Carless. *The Age of Grey and Peel*. Oxford, 1929.

Fennelly, Catharine. "William Franklin of New Jersey." *William and Mary Quarterly*, 3rd Series, VI (1949): 361–382.

Fisher, Sydney George. *The True Benjamin Franklin*. Philadelphia, 1899.

Ford, Paul Leicester. *The Many-Sided Franklin*. New York, 1899.

Fox, Dixon Ryan. *Yankees and Yorkers*. New York, 1940.

Gleason, J. F. "A Scurrilous Colonial Election and Franklin's Reputation." *William and Mary Quarterly*, 3rd Series, XVIII (1961): 68–84.

Granger, Bruce I. *Benjamin Franklin: An American Man of Letters*. Ithaca, 1964.

Guttmacher, Manfred S. *America's Last King*. New York, 1941.

Hawke, David. *In the Midst of a Revolution*. Philadelphia, 1961.

Henretta, James A. *Salutary Neglect*. Princeton, 1972.

Hutson, James H. "The Campaign to Make Pennsylvania a Royal Province, 1764–1770." Part I. *Pennsylvania Magazine of History and Biography* 94 (1970): 427–463; Part II. *Pennsylvania Magazine of History and Biography* 95 (1971): 28–49.

Jordon, Helen and Clarence. *Benjamin Franklin's Unfinished Business*. Philadelphia, 1957.

Kallich, Martin, and MacLeish, Andrew, eds. *The American Revolution through British Eyes*. Evanston, 1962.

Kammen, Michael G. *A Rope of Sand*. Ithaca, 1968.

Knollenberg, Bernhard. "Three Letters of William Franklin." *Yale Library Gazette* 21 (1946): 18–27.

Lillywhite, Bryant. *London Coffee Houses*. London, 1963.

London Topographical Record. Vol. VIII. London, 1913.

Lopez, Claude-Anne. *Mon Cher Papa: Franklin and the Ladies of Paris*. New Haven, 1966.

Margetson, Stella. *Journey by Stages, 1660–1840*. London, 1967.

Mee, Arthur. *London*. London, 1937.

Morris, Richard B. *The Peacemakers*. New York, 1965.

Newcomb, Benjamin H. "Effects of the Stamp Act on Colonial Pennsylvania Politics." *William and Mary Quarterly*, 3rd Series, 23 (1966): 257–272.

Nicolson, Harold. *The Age of Reason*. Garden City, 1961.

Nolan, J. Bennett. *Benjamin Franklin in Scotland and Ireland, 1759 and 1771*. Philadelphia, 1938.

Palmer, R. R. *The Age of Democratic Revolution*. 2 vols. Princeton, 1959–1964.

Phillips, Hugh. *Mid-Georgian London*. London, 1964.

Robbins, Caroline. "Discordant Parties: A Study of the Acceptance of Party by Englishmen." *Political Science Quarterly* 73 (1958): 505–529.

——. *The Eighteenth-Century Commonwealthman*. Cambridge, Mass., 1959.

——. "Edmund Burke's Rationale of Cabinet Government." *The Burke Newsletter*. VII (1965).

Sainte-Beuve, C. A. *English Portraits*. London, 1875.

Smith, John Thomas. *Antiquities of Westminster*. London, 1807.

Stifler, James Madison. *"My Dear Girl."* New York, 1927.

Stow, John. *A Survey of London*. 2 vols. Charles Kingsford, ed. Oxford, 1908.

Tawney, R. H. *Religion and the Rise of Capitalism*. London, 1938.

Thomson, Mark A. *A Constitutional History of England, 1642 to 1801.* London, 1938.

Trevelyan, Sir George Otto. *The American Revolution.* 4 vols. New York, 1912.

Van Alstyne, R. W. *The Rising of the American Empire.* Oxford, 1960.

Van Doren, Carl, ed. *Letters and Papers of Benjamin Franklin and Richard Jackson, 1753–1785.* Philadelphia, 1947.

Watson, John Steven. *The Reign of George III, 1760–1815.* Oxford, 1960.

Wheatley, Henry B. *London Past and Present.* London, 1967.

Williams, E. Neville, ed. *The Eighteenth-Century Constitution, 1688–1815.* Cambridge, England, 1960.

Wolf, Edwin II. "Benjamin Franklin's Stamp Act Cartoon." American Philosophical Society *Proceedings* 99 (1955): 381–387.

Chapter Note, Chapter 10, page 179

Franklin's part in the investment of Pennsylvania's fund is a complex story, which rightfully should include discussion of the current political turmoil in Britain, the struggle for power between Pitt and Bute, and the ramifications of Bourbon ambitions in Europe. Any reader wishing to pursue the subject can find it in L. H. Gipson's *The Triumphant Empire* (Vol. IX), and, more succinctly, in James Hutson's article, "Benjamin Franklin and the Parliamentary Grant of 1758," *William and Mary Quarterly,* 1966.

Scene V: The Making of a Revolutionary
Chapter 13

Amacher, Richard E. *Benjamin Franklin.* New York, 1962.

Bentham, Jeremy. *Works.* 11 vols. Reprinted. John Bowring, ed. New York, 1962.

Binger, Carl. *Revolutionary Doctor, Benjamin Rush, 1746–1813.* New York, 1966.

Campbell, John Baron. *Lives of the Lord Chancellors and Keepers of the Great Seal of England.* 10 vols. London, 1857.

Corner, George W., ed. *The Autobiography of Benjamin Rush.* Princeton, 1948.

Crane, Verner W. *Benjamin Franklin, Englishman and American.* Providence, 1936.

——. *Benjamin Franklin and a Rising People.* Boston, 1954.

——. "The Club of Honest Whigs, Friends of Science and Liberty." *William and Mary Quarterly,* 3rd Series, 23 (1966): 210–233.

Donovan, Frank R. *The Many Worlds of Benjamin Franklin.* New York, 1963.

Franklin Before the Privy Council, Whitehall Chapel, London, 1774. Philadelphia, 1860.

Keyes, Nelson Beecher. *Benjamin Franklin: An Affectionate Portrait.* Garden City, 1956.

Knollenberg, Bernhard. *Origin of the American Revolution, 1759–1766.* New York, 1960.

Labaree, Leonard W. "Benjamin Franklin's British Friendships." American Philosophical Society *Proceedings* 108 (1964): 423–428.

Liebert, Herman W. "British Look at America During the Age of

Samuel Johnson." Address to the John Carter Brown Library, Providence, 1971.

Miles, Richard D. "The American Image of Benjamin Franklin." *American Quarterly* IX (1957): 117–143.

Price, Richard. *Observations on the Nature of Civil Liberty*. London, 1776.

Sabine, Lorenzo. *Biographical Sketches of Loyalists of the American Revolution*. 2 vols. Boston, 1864.

Sellers, Charles C. *Benjamin Franklin in Portraiture*. New Haven, 1962.

Stourzh, Gerald. *Benjamin Franklin and American Foreign Policy*. Chicago, 1954.

Thomas, P. D. G. *The House of Commons in the Eighteenth Century*. Oxford, 1971.

Tyler, Moses Coit. *The Literary History of the American Revolution*. 2 vols. New York, 1897.

Van Alstyne, Richard W. *Empire and Independence*. New York, 1965.

Vaughan, Benjamin, ed. *Political, Miscellaneous and Philosophical Pieces, Written by Benjamin Franklin*. London, 1779.

INDEX